Born in 1912, David Daiches was brought up and educated in Edinburgh. By profession a literary critic and literary and cultural historian, he has taught in universities in England and the USA and was Professor of English at the University of Sussex from its foundation in 1961 until his retirement in 1977. A biographer of Burns, Boswell, Scott and Stevenson, he is the author of *A Critical History of English Literature* (2 vols.) and *The Novel and the Modern World*. He has written two autobiographical books, *Two Worlds* and *Was*. His most recent books have concentrated more particularly on Scottish history and culture: they include *Scotch Whisky, Glasgow and Scotland and the Union*. He is also General Editor of an encyclopaedic *Companion to Scottish Culture*.

David Daiches
Edinburgh

A PANTHER BOOK

GRANADA
London Toronto Sydney New York

Published by Granada Publishing Limited in 1980

ISBN 0 586 05237 2

First published in Great Britain by
Hamish Hamilton Limited 1978
Copyright © David Daiches 1978

Granada Publishing Limited
Frogmore, St Albans, Herts AL2 2NF
and
3 Upper James Street, London W1R 4BP
866 United Nations Plaza, New York, NY 10017, USA
117 York Street, Sydney, NSW 2000, Australia
100 Skyway Avenue, Rexdale, Ontario, M9W 3A6, Canada
PO Box 84165, Greenside, 2034 Johannesburg, South Africa
61 Beach Road, Auckland, New Zealand

Made and printed in Great Britain by
Richard Clay (The Chaucer Press) Ltd,
Bungay, Suffolk
Set in Linotype Times

Granada ®
Granada Publishing ®

I dedicate this book to my wife Billie,
who died on 5th August 1977,
remembering that March day in Edinburgh in 1933
when we first discovered our love for each other
and all the happy years that followed.

Contents

Illustrations

Prologue

One afternoon in December 1944 two of us were sitting at an upstairs window of a Princes Street tea-room as the winter dusk was falling and the Castle grew dark and mysterious on its high rock. 'Mine own romantic town,' murmured my companion, quoting Scott's famous phrase about his native city. It was wartime, and when darkness fell on the street below it was unrelieved. Years later they took to flood-lighting the Castle and visitors to the Edinburgh Festival looked up in admiration at the impossible fairy-tale building floating in white light above the city. Dark or shining, that Edinburgh scene can always be counted on to arouse emotion. But for me the most moving Edinburgh illuminations were those I used to see at Christmas time in my childhood and youth in the little shops near the Meadows. They were not illuminations at all really, but decorations, bravely attempted to challenge the long dark winter afternoons. Net Christmas stockings full of cheap little toys; tinsel strung across the window shining in gas-light; varieties of 'fancy goods' on special Christmas display. R. L. Stevenson knew shops like that, and described one in Antigua Street, Leith Walk, in his essay 'A Penny Plain and Two Pence Coloured'. They preserved Victorian Edinburgh well into the twentieth century. There are very few left now.

The north side of Princes Street is a jumble of confused architecture, but the street's splendour is ensured by its open south side dominated by the Castle. Behind Princes Street lie the ordered streets of the New Town, and behind them the roads to Granton and Leith and the Firth of Forth which today marks the northern boundary of the city. Each area has its own flavour, its own social atmosphere, its own colourful history. The Old Town, that looks down on the New from the South, is redolent of the violence and passion of Edinburgh's early history. South of the Old Town, between the High Street and the Meadows, old and new mingle in unexpected ways – that is, where the blank imagination of 'developers' has allowed the old to remain. And south of the Meadows lies another Edinburgh, largely Victorian, speaking neither of the neo-classic elegance of the New Town nor of the violence and passion of the Old, but of gen-tility, decency, middle-class respectability. The further south towards

Blackford Hill you go the bigger the houses, the leafier the streets, the more quietly prosperous the atmosphere. Blackford Hill itself is the most genteel (and gentle) of Edinburgh hills, lacking the ruggedness of Arthur's Seat to the east and the spaciousness of the Braid Hills behind it to the south. And behind the Braids are the Pentlands where, within the present city limits, you can find yourself in wild open country.

The judges and advocates and solicitors who live in the New Town and by their presence signify the importance of the law in the social and professional life of the city represent a different kind of middle-class respectability than that represented by ministers, teachers, bank employees, small publishers and reasonably successful grocers (to pick out only a few categories) who live on the South Side. But where the western corner of the New Town moves north into Comely Bank you get a similar kind of social atmosphere to that of the South Side. The windows tell much of the story: the small windows of the tall old buildings in the Lawnmarket, at the heart of the Old Town, the elegantly proportioned Georgian windows of the New Town, the later bow windows, and then the bay windows of Victorian Edinburgh.

A city of contrasts; a city where social and economic differences are not only visible area by area and street by street (drop down from India Street to N.W. Circus Place then go round the corner to St Stephen's Street or walk south from Marchmont Road to Blackford Avenue and you will see this at once) but also produce their own atmosphere that seems to appeal to all the senses simultaneously. As the Festival visitors throng the city in late August and early September and explore historic buildings and tartan shops they may not always be aware of the atmospheric subtleties of the different parts, but anyone who has lived long in the city – certainly anyone who has grown up in it – is aware of them immediately. What we are aware of is the top layer of history, as it were. Edinburgh is what its history has made it. And the story of its past is the clue to the appeal of its present.

CHAPTER 1

Fortress and Burgh

If you cross the Scottish Border at Carter Bar and proceed north by Jedburgh through Lauderdale to Soutra Hill, at the west of the Lammermuir Hills, you will, on a reasonably clear day, be able to look down on Edinburgh. This was the route taken by many a raiding force from England throughout Scotland's history. It is not a long route from the Border to the city which became Scotland's capital about the beginning of the sixteenth century, and its relative easiness and shortness made the city vulnerable to English attack. Yet Edinburgh owes its existence to its assumed invulnerability: it began as a fortress on a rock.

Edinburgh Castle, the modern descendant of that fortress, is still a prominent feature of the Edinburgh townscape. The rock on which it stands is volcanic, as are the other two prominent features of the scene, Arthur's Seat and Calton Hill. Ages after the volcanic activity ceased, slow glacier movement over the volcanic rock carved out the shapes we now know, with the ridge extending eastward from the Castle on its protecting eminence. On this ridge the old city was built, but first there was the fortress, with perhaps some primitive dwellings clustering around it.

The Romans, who came to Scotland with Agricola in A.D. 80 and established a variety of relationships with the original inhabitants before their legions melted away from about 400 in the face of Germanic attacks on their armies in Europe, established a port at Cramond, on the Firth of Forth just to the north-west of Edinburgh, but Edinburgh itself was never a Roman town. The early second century Alexandrian astronomer and geographer Ptolemy gives the names of various tribes who inhabited what we now call Scotland, and among these are the Votadini who inhabited the region between the Tyne and the Forth, comprising modern Northumberland, Berwickshire and East Lothian. These tribes spoke that form of the Celtic language we call P-Celtic: they were what history knows as Britons, of the same stock as the Britons whom the Romans encountered and conquered in England. The equivalent in their language of what Ptolemy called Votadini was *Gododdin*, and their territory was one of a group of British kingdoms – others were

Strathclyde and Rheged – that are found stretched across southern Scotland after the departure of the Romans. The Gododdin capital is called Dineidin, 'fortress of the hill-slope', in the poem *Y Gododdin* by the sixth century Welsh poet Aneirin, and it appears in other early sources as Dineiddyn, Mynyd (=Mount) Eidden, Mons Agned, and Dunedene. Welsh (P-Celtic) *din* is Gaelic (Q-Celtic) *dun* (fortress, castle), which is the equivalent of Old English *burh*. Hence Dunedin, and Edinburgh.

But why should a Celtic place-name exchange a Celtic ending for an Old English one? The answer lies with the consequences of the Anglo-Saxon invasions of and settlements in England after the departure of the Romans. The Angles had established themselves in Yorkshire by the fifth century in a kingdom called Deira and in the mid-sixth century were also established in the kingdom of Bernicia to the north and east of this. The two kingdoms eventually united as Northumbria, and under a succession of powerful kings Northumbria succeeded in conquering the British kingdoms in Scotland, with the exception of Strathclyde. In 638 they captured Edinburgh, and though the powerful Northumbrian King Edwin had died in 632 (five years after accepting Christianity) his name was long remembered and became associated with the name of the fortress that the Northumbrians now possessed. Hence we find in the twelfth century the spellings Edwinesburg and Edwinesburch, forms that developed in the erroneous belief that Edwin had actually founded the fortress.

So the Gododdin strong hold of Dineidin became Edinburgh, now under the influence of Northumbrian culture with its Anglican speech, that northern form of English that was to develop into what we call Scots: Edinburgh can thus be said to have been an English-speaking centre (using English as the general term to include all the forms that developed from the speech of the Angles and Saxons) from the seventh century. North of the Forth-Clyde line were the Picts, largely a Celtic people who spoke their own variety of P-Celtic. And from the beginning of the sixth century there were the Scots, whom Fergus Mór had brought from Ireland to found the kingdom of Dalriada in what later became Argyllshire. The Scots spoke the variety of Celtic known as Q-Celtic which became Gaelic (whereas P-Celtic produced Welsh, Cornish and Breton). About 843 Kenneth MacAlpin, King of Scots, gained the throne of Pictland either through marriage alliance or conquest or both, uniting the kingdom of the Picts with his own kingdom of Dalriada to form the kingdom of Scotland, *Alba* in Gaelic, *Scotia* in Latin. The Picts, who left no literature, disappear from history together with their language. The MacAlpin kings pushed east and south into the Lowlands and in the reign of Indulf (954–62) captured Edinburgh (Dunedin they called it, *Oppidum Eden* in the Latin chronicle; but the Anglian form of Edinburgh stuck). Edinburgh was now in Scotland. In 1018 Malcolm II gained Lothian for Scotland from the English at the battle of Carham and in 1032 his grandson Duncan, who had already succeeded to the throne of the British kingdom of Strathclyde, succeeded his father as King of a Scotland whose boundaries now became roughly what they are today.

Between Indulf's capture of Edinburgh, replacing Northumbrian by Scottish rule, and the reign of Malcolm III (1058–93) we hear nothing of Edinburgh. About 1070 Malcolm married, as his second wife, Margaret, sister of Edward Atheling, of the royal house of Wessex that had been dispossessed by the Norman Conquest in 1066. Malcolm kept his Court and residence at Dunfermline, on the other side of the Forth, and it was apparently the influence of Margaret that caused him to pay more attention to Edinburgh. He built a hunting lodge on the castle rock, using it as his base for hunting expeditions in the great forest of Drumselch which then stretched widely to the south and east. Queen Margaret, who was deeply devout, preferred more meditative pursuits and it was for her that Malcolm built the chapel by his hunting lodge that survives today (considerably restored) as by far the oldest building on the castle rock. Malcolm, who was known by the Gaelic appellation Ceann-Mor, 'big head', was himself a Gaelic-speaking Scot, while his Saxon wife (who, incidentally, had been brought up in Hungary) saw civilization in the Anglo-Norman south rather than in the Celtic north and encouraged her husband to reform the manners and procedures of the Court in the light of Norman standards. Saxon though she was, Margaret admired Norman civilization and in particular Norman ecclesiastical organization, and with her strong-minded religious character succeeded in introducing a similar organization into the rather differently organized Celtic Church in Scotland. She brought the use of English into the Church and into the Court, and in general was largely responsible for bringing the organization of the kingdom of Scotland nearer the Anglo-Norman pattern. She was canonized about a century and a half after her death, and her chapel, still standing on the highest pinnacle of the castle rock, is known as St Margaret's Chapel. Her frequent journeying across the Forth between Edinburgh and the royal palace at Dunfermline gave the name Queensferry to the present South Queensferry just north of Edinburgh, where a ferry must have operated for at least nine hundred years until the opening of the Forth Road Bridge in 1964.

It is possible that St Margaret's Chapel was built not by Malcolm for his wife but by their son David I in his mother's memory. Certainly King David was responsible for the founding of the Abbey of Holyrood in 1128. David inherited his mother's piety, his lavish ecclesiastical endowments impoverishing the Scottish Crown so that James VI later described him as 'ane sair sanct for the Crown'. The Abbey of the Holy Rood was occupied and controlled by the canons of the Order of St Augustine, who had been established at Scone in 1114 by David's elder brother and predecessor on the Scottish throne, Alexander I. The Abbey was built about a mile from the Castle, at the eastern end of the sloping ridge that later became known as the Royal Mile, in the shadow of Arthur's Seat. There are two stories about its founding. One is that David founded it in honour of a marvellous cross owned by his mother, covered in gold and containing within it a part of the true cross. The other is that once when out hunting he was attacked by a stag, 'the farest hart that ever was sene afore with levand creatour'. When, endeavouring to save himself, he seized hold of the stag's 'auful and braid' antlers, he found a cross suddenly left in his hands and the stag disappeared. Either story explains why the abbey was called the Abbey of the Holy Rood. The road eastward from it to the Nether Bow, which was Edinburgh's eastern entrance, later became known as the Canongate, i.e. the Canons' Way or Road.

The Abbey of Holyrood may first have had a brief existence at the foot of the castle rock (on the top of which were now both fortress and palace), but if so the canons soon persuaded the religious David to provide a more ample site. His charter to the Abbey, issued some time between 1128 and 1136, provided ample endowments. To it, and 'to the canons regular serving God therein' (as the Latin charter stated), he granted 'the Church of the Castle with all its appendages and rights' together with a great deal of land in Crostorfin (Corstorphine), Libertun and elsewhere, and also 'forty shillings from my burgh of Edinburgh yearly'. The charter also granted to the canons 'leave to establish a burgh between that church and my burgh; and I grant that their burgesses have common right of selling their wares, and of buying, in my market freely and quit of claim and custom in like manner as my own burgesses'. This makes clear that by now Edinburgh (which the charter spells 'Edwinesburg') was established as a market town with its own merchants and tradesmen and it also explains why the Canongate remained a separate burgh until 1856 and why Edinburgh Castle, in spite of its physical separation from it, still remains within the parish of Canongate.

The Church of St Giles, which became the High Kirk of Edinburgh, was also founded about this time, or it may be that a new Norman building now replaced an even older structure dating from the ninth century. This church lasted until 1385, when Richard II brought an army into the Lowlands which burned it (and much else) as a reprisal for the arrival of French troops in Scotland : the present Gothic building dates from the fifteenth century. Among other churches built by David was St Mary's Church, on the castle rock where the Scottish National War Memorial now stands. This is 'the Church of the Castle' mentioned in the Holyrood charter. That charter was renewed by David's grandson William the Lyon in 1171 (where Edinburgh is spelt 'Edenesburch') and by Robert I (Bruce) in 1327 (where it is 'Edinburgh'), while the latter's son David II granted the Abbey still further privileges. Holyrood Abbey, with its Abbey Church (of which the ruined nave survives), grew to be one of the great ecclesiastical buildings in the British Isles. Royalty sometimes resided there; James II (1437–60) was born, married and buried there; James IV (1488–1513) had a lodging built beside it; and James V (1513–42) built there 'hes fayre Pallais with three towers', the Palace of Holyroodhouse, which was enlarged and modernized in the seventeenth century in the reigns of Charles I and II.

If the activities of Margaret and her son David I helped to bring the Scottish church into the main current of European Catholicism, David's reign saw a very different and for Edinburgh an even more important development, the formal organization of town life in burghs. The royal burgh, granted rights and privileges by the King, began as a place of defence chosen for its geographical suitability for that function; its protective presence encouraged settlement and the development of trade in its immediate vicinity, and the more trade flourished the more new immigrants were attracted to settle. Monopolistic trading rights granted by royal charter to a burgh encouraged the traders to develop a form of self-government under laws and procedures which were carefully elaborated. We first see such laws and procedures in Scotland in the 'Laws of the Four Burghs' (of Edinburgh, Roxburgh, Berwick and Stirling) compiled in David's reign and adapted from those of Newcastle upon Tyne. To become a burgess one had to purchase a 'burrowage' (burgage, tenure of property) and reside in it for a minimum of a year and a day without challenge; then 'he sall be evirmare fre as a burges wythin that kyngis burgh and joyse the fredome of that burgh'. There could be non-resident burgesses who, like those who sold goods at stalls, were known as 'stallengers', and had to attend the three annual 'head courts' of the burgh on penalty of a fine of 8s. (while a resident burgess was only fined 4d. for non-attendance).

In addition to attending the three head courts of the burgh, a burgess had a number of duties and obligations: he had to defend his burrowage, maintain a house upon it, provide himself with weights and measures sealed with the burgh seal, and take his turn as a night watchman. In return, he enjoyed a number of important privileges, the chief among which was protection against competition in trade from non-burgesses. Merchants from abroad were not allowed to sell their merchandise elsewhere than in the burgh and there only to burgesses. Other privileges enjoyed by burgesses included carefully defined rights of transmitting and selling their property and the right of electing their own magistrates who administered their laws in the burgh courts. David I's grandson, William the Lyon, also legislated in favour of burghs and burgesses and by the end of the twelfth century there is a recognizable pattern of town life in Edinburgh and other towns in Southern and Eastern Scotland, with a considerable international element (largely English and Flemish) who eventually assimilated with the local population with whom, as the Gaelic language was pushed back to the north and west, they shared the northern English speech that in Scotland had by now developed into the phase we call Middle Scots. These commercial centres were of course tiny by modern standards and still depended largely on agriculture: every burgh had its own burgh lands and grazings on which it grew a considerable proportion of it own food and grazed its cattle.

We can perhaps get some idea of the town scene in these early days from those of the Laws of the Four Burghs that regulate the display of goods. For example, 'wha that takis brede to sell aw nocht for to hyde it bot sett it in thair window or in the mercat that it may be opynly sauld.' A butcher, too, 'sal sett his flesche opynly in his wyndow that it be sene communly till al men that will tharof', and the same goes for brewers. Buying and selling on a larger scale was done in the open at the town market, as one of William the Lyon's laws makes clear: 'And it is commandit be the King that the merchandises for said and all other merchandises salbe presentit at the

mercat and mercat cross of burghis and thar at the lest salbe prof-
ferait to the merchandis of the burgh effectuously wythout fraude or
gyle. And the custom tharof salbe payit to the King.' This last sentence reminds us that in return for their privileges the burghs had to
pay taxes : they made in fact a significant contribution to royal funds,
providing an eighth of the king's revenue by the end of the thirteenth
century.

We have no records of the election of magistrates in Edinburgh
before the fifteenth century, but it is clear from the Laws of the Four
Burghs and the accounts of such elections in Aberdeen records of the
late fourteenth century, that a provost and baillies (aldermen and
magistrates) were elected at the first court after Michaelmas 'with
the consent and assent of the whole community of the ... burgh'. The
Laws of the Four Burghs refer to the consent to such an election
required from *probi homines fideles et bone fame*, 'the gudemen of
the toune, lele and of gud fame', and it seems clear that this must
refer to properly recognized and admitted burgesses. The Laws of
the Four Burghs also refer to twelve 'of the lelest burges and of the
wysast of the burgh' who should be sworn to do their utmost lawfully
to maintain the customs of the burgh, and this must be the germ of
the body later known as the town council.

The organization of the merchants into guilds must already have
begun by the time of the passing of the Laws of the Four Burghs, for
one law specifies that dyers, fleshers (butchers), shoemakers and
fishers should not enjoy membership of the merchant guild unless
they abjured the practice of their trade with their own hands and
conducted it exclusively by servants. This emphasizes the element of
social snobbery involved in the organization of merchant guilds.
Craftsmen, as distinct from those engaged in buying and selling, were
excluded, and formed their own craft guilds, which continually struggled to improve the conditions and prestige of craftsmen.

The earliest surviving royal charter (in Latin) granted to the burgh
of Edinburgh is that of Robert I in 1329 :

Robert, by the grace of God King of Scots, to all good men of his
whole land, greeting. Know ye that we have given, granted and set
in feu-ferm and by this our present charter confirmed to the burgesses of our burgh of Edinburgh our foresaid burgh of Edinburgh
with the harbour of Leith ('*Burgum nostrum de Edenburgh, una
cum Portu de Lethe*'), its mills and the rest of its pertinents : to be
held and had by the same burgesses and their successors of us and

our heirs freely, quietly, fully and honourably, by all its right
bounds and marches, with all the commodities, liberties and ease-
ments which were wont rightly to pertain to the said burgh in the
time of King Alexander of good memory, our predecessor last
deceased: rendering therefor yearly, the said burgesses and their
successors to us and our heirs, fifty-two merks sterling [equivalent
to £34 3s. 4d.] at Whitsunday and Martinmas by equal portions. In
witness whereof we have ordered our seal to this our present
charter.... At Cardross, the 29th day of May in the 24th year of
our reign.

It is interesting that this charter grants to the burgh of Edinburgh
'the harbour of Leith, its mills and the rest of its pertinents'. Leith is
first mentioned (as 'Inverlet', i.e., Inverleith, 'Mouth of the Water of
Leith') in David I's charter to the Abbey of Holyrood, which granted
to the canons 'Inverlet, that which is nearest the harbour, with its
right marches, and with that harbour, and with the half of the fishing,
and with a tithe of the whole fishing which belongs to the Church of
Saint Cuthbert'. The Water of Leith must then have been a much
broader and deeper stream than it is now, navigable some distance
up, as the name 'Inverleith', still applied to the area immediately
north of Stockbridge and Canonmills, suggests. And the name
'Canonmills', originally a village on the Water of Leith nearly two
miles upstream and now a district of Edinburgh at the southern end
of Inverleith Row, reminds us of where the mills granted to the
canons of Holyrood were originally sited. In granting the port of
Leith to the burgh of Edinburgh, Robert started a quarrel between
the two that went on until the City Agreement Act of 1838 made
Leith a separate municipality. But Leith was finally merged in
Edinburgh by the Edinburgh Boundaries Extension Act of 1920.

English claims to the overlordship of Scotland erupted intermit-
tently throughout the Middle Ages, with English military expeditions
into Scotland and Scottish expeditions into England carrying out
blows and counter-blows on either side of the argument. Edinburgh,
because of its relative nearness to the Border, was much more vulnerable to English attack than any major English town was to attack by
the Scots. In 1174 William the Lyon was taken prisoner on a raid
into England and by the Treaty of Falaise forced to deliver Edinburgh Castle (among others) to Henry II: it was restored in 1186
when William married a cousin of King Henry. In 1291 the English
King Edward I, adopting the title of Lord Paramount of Scotland in

virtue of his having been asked to arbitrate the disputed succession
to the Scottish throne on the death of Alexander III, took possession
of Edinburgh Castle and removed from it all public muniments and
records stored there. In 1296, with Scotland now in open revolt
against him, Edward spent two nights in Edinburgh on his way to
Elgin : all the plate and jewellery found in the Castle were looted and
sent off to England, and some years later Edward carried off to
London the Stone of Destiny, on which generations of Kings of
Scots had been crowned at Scone and which seems to have been
either temporarily or permanently deposited in the Castle. The Castle
was recaptured by the Scots under King Robert's nephew, Thomas
Randolph, Earl of Moray, in 1314 by a brilliantly daring manoeuvre
and then destroyed so that it could never again be of service to an
enemy. Only St Margaret's Chapel was spared. In 1322 Edward II
came up to Scotland and sacked Holyrood Abbey and in 1335 Edward III wrought havoc in the city with an army, and at the same
time rebuilt the Castle as one of a series designed to keep the south
of Scotland in subjection. But the Scots recaptured it, with other
Scottish castles, in 1341, and again destroyed it.

The Scottish King was now David II (1329–71), who spent five
years in captivity in England after his unsuccessful invasion of
England and defeat at Neville's Cross in 1346. He returned to Scotland in 1357, and built on the castle rock the massive keep, sixty feet
high, known as King David's Tower. He lived there and administered
his kingdom from there during the last years of his life, although it
was still unfinished at his death, not being completed until about
1367. Defended by rows of cannon, it successfully withstood an attack in 1385 when Richard II of England invaded Scotland with a
large army that wrought havoc in Edinburgh, and it also survived a
siege by Henry IV in 1400. In 1573, in the troubled reign of Mary
Queen of Scots, during the regency of the Earl of Morton (who had
the support of England in his struggle against Queen Mary's party),
Sir William Drury and his English artillery battered King David's
Tower to pieces in spite of its gallant defence by Kirkaldy of Grange.
Its ruins were absorbed in the Half-Moon Battery that was built soon
afterwards, but parts of the original tower building were discovered
during excavations below the Half-Moon Battery in 1912.

The Stewart kings of the fifteenth century tended more and more
to look on Edinburgh as their country's principal town, and they
made Edinburgh Castle their main residence. The Exchequer Rolls
for 1433–34 record the spending of a large amount on building a

great hall for the King: this later became the meeting place for the
Scottish Parliament (before it moved to the new Parliament Hall,
behind St Giles, in 1640). The fifteenth century Parliament Hall was
a building of conspicuous splendour for its time and was the scene of
some memorable feasting, including a banquet after Charles I's
coronation at Holyrood in 1633 and another when the Earl of Leven
entertained Cromwell and other Commonwealth leaders in 1648.

Although a charter of 1385 had granted 'the Burgesses of the
Community of the Burgh of Edinburgh' the right to build their houses
'in the Castle of Edinburgh', the real life of Edinburgh went on
beneath the Castle, in the houses that clustered in the narrow streets
that went off at right angles from the High Street. The High Street
ran eastwards along the ridge from the Castle to the Nether Bow,
where the Netherbow Port (gate) was built as the eastern entrance
through the wall erected after the disastrous battle of Flodden in
1513. Beyond that lay the Canongate and the sloping road to Holyrood. The herring-bone pattern – narrow 'wynds' and 'closes' going
off from the wide main street that ran along the ridge from the
Castle – remained the shape of the city for centuries. We get a vivid
if not very flattering picture of late fourteenth and early fifteenth
century Edinburgh in the poems of William Dunbar. He reproached
the merchants of Edinburgh for their greed, quarrelsomeness and
lack of hygiene:

> Quhy will ye, merchantis of renoun,
> Lat Edinburgh, your nobill toun,
> For laik of reformatioun
> The common proffeitt tyine and fame?   [lose the common
>   Think ye not schame,   profit and fame]
> That onie uther regioun
> Sall with dishonour hurt your name!
>
> May nane pas throw your principall gaittis
> For stink of Haddockis and of scattis,
> For cryis of carlingis and debaittis,
> For fensum flyttingis of defame: [fensum flyttingis =
>   Think ye not schame,   filthy abuse]
> Befoir strangeris of all estaititis
> That sic dishonour hurt your name!

In another stanza Dunbar reproaches them for blocking the light
from their 'parroche kirk' (St Giles) and for the fact that their 'foir-

stairs' (stairs projecting into the street, giving access to the upper tenements) made their house dark in a manner unknown in any other country. He goes on to say that at their 'hie Croce' (the cross that stood in the High Street) there were but curds and milk where there should be gold and silk, while at the Tron, the public weighing beam, they sold only cockles. whelks and tripe. He complained that tailors, soutteris (soutars, i.e. shoe-makers) and other 'craftis vyll' defiled the streets, while merchants at the 'Stinkand Styll' (a passage that led through the Luckenbooths – i.e., locked booths – small generally timber-fronted shops on the ground floor of tenements on the north side of St Giles) were squeezed together as though in a honey-comb. He also complained of the numbers of beggars, for which fifteenth century Edinburgh was notorious, as we know from the several Acts passed to repress them. In another poem Dunbar described the jostling crowd of petitioners and litigants that came to Edinburgh for the Session, the court of justice established by James I in 1425 (to be distinguished from the Court of Session established as the supreme civil tribunal of Scotland in 1532).

We get a more flattering picture of Edinburgh some years after Dunbar wrote from Alexander Alesius, who had to leave Scotland as a Lutheran heretic in 1529 and later wrote an account of his native city, the first in prose that exists, for Sebastian Munster's *Cosmographia*, published in Basle in 1550. Here is what he wrote (in Hume Brown's translation):

Edinburgh is situated in the province of Lothian, a Roman mile to the south of an arm of the sea, into which the river Forth empties itself from the west. To the east of the town itself are two mountains, the one called Arthur's Seat, the other, which faces the north, the hill of the Wild Boar. The surrounding country is extremely fertile, with pleasant meadows, little woods, lakes, streamlets, and more than a hundred castles, all within the radius of a German mile. To the north, as has been said, at the distance of a Roman mile, is an arm of the sea, and near it the town of Leith, in the heart of which a harbour has been constructed where at one time may be seen a hundred large ships of burden. At this point the arm of the sea to the north is seven miles in breadth. On its north border there is also a town and a new harbour. Edinburgh, like Prague, is situated on a hill, and is a Roman mile in length, and half a mile in breadth. It is longest from east to west. At the western extremity of the city rises a hill and a steep rock, and on

the rock a fortress, with a deep valley on all sides except towards
the city. Except from the east side, therefore, the fortress is im-
pregnable. It cannot even be scaled with ladders, so steep and hard
is the rock, in which vultures are in the habit of building. Enter-
prising youths are let down from the castle in baskets to rob their
nests. This fortress is known as the 'Maidens' Castle,' and forms
the western limit of the city. At the eastern extremity is the splendid monastery of the Holy Rood, adjoining the royal palace, and
delightful gardens, enclosed by a lake at the base of Arthur's Seat.
In this mountain are found precious stones (specially diamonds)
which glitter in the sunlight. Two great ways lead from the
Maidens' Castle to the monastery and the royal palace, paved with
square stones, King's Street (Regia Via) being the more notable.
There is a suburb to the East [he means west], half a mile long,
known as the street of St Cuthbert. The city possesses many
monasteries and churches, specially those of the Franciscans, the
Dominicans, the Church of St Mary in the Fields, the College of
Priests, another College of the Trinity, and the Hospital of St
Thomas. The city itself is not built of brick, but of natural stones
squared, so that even the private houses may bear a comparison
with great palaces. In the centre of the city are the town-house
(capitolium) and the Collegiate Church of St Giles. The bishops,
dukes, earls, barons, and the chief men of the whole kingdom all
live in palaces of their own, when they are summoned to the meetings of Parliament. The King's Palace, a spacious and magnificent
building, and one broad way, known as King's Street, connect it
with the Maidens' Castle. This street, it should be said, is wider
near the castle and narrower near the monastery, and on each side
of it are noteworthy houses, the more ambitious being built of
polished stone. Another oblong street (reckoned as a suburb), the
Canongate (Vicus Canonicorum), is somewhat narrower, and is
separated from King's Street by a wall, a gate, and towers. From
King's Street to north and south extend numberless lesser streets,
all adorned with imposing buildings, such, for example, as the
Cowgate (Via Vaccarum) where the nobility and the chief men of
the city reside, and in which are the palaces of the officers of state,
and where is nothing mean or tasteless, but all is magnificent.
Among the greater churches of Edinburgh, after the surpassing
basilica of the monastery, that of St Giles in the centre of King's
Street holds the first place. In the street that separates Edinburgh
from the Cowgate and suburb is a magnificent church called the

Queen's College within the Walls. Also, between the monasteries of the Franciscans and the Preaching Friars is the Church of St Mary in the Fields, where is likewise a college of priests. Under the rock of the Maidens' Castle is the new parish church of St Cuthbert.

It is interesting that Alesius calls Edinburgh Castle the 'Maidens' Castle' (it appears on old maps and in the Treaty of Falaise as *Castrum Puellarum*). This reflects the influence of Norman and Anglo-Norman settlers in Lowland Scotland. It was they with their love of Norman-French romances, especially the Arthurian stories, who gave Arthurian romantic names to various castles, calling Edinburgh Castle 'Le Chastel des Pucelles' and Roxburgh Castle 'le Marche Mont' (Marchmont). The 'Regia Via', the king's highway, is the High Street (the first suggestion of the later designation, the 'Royal Mile'). The Church of St Mary in the Fields is better known as Kirk o' Field, where Queen Mary's husband Darnley was murdered in 1567. The Hospital of St Thomas was in the Canongate; it was founded by the Bishop of Dunkeld in the reign of James V. In 1747 the building was converted into a coach-house, and it was pulled down in 1778.

CHAPTER 2

The Sixteenth Century

On 10 September 1513 the Town Council of Edinburgh issued a proclamation. It began: 'We do yow to witt, Foresamekill as thair is ane greit rumour now laitlie rysin within this toun tuiching our Souerane Lord and his army, of the quilk we understand thair is cumin na veritie as yit, thairfore we charge straitlie and commandis in our said Souerane Lord the Kingis name, and the presidentis for the provest and baillies within this burgh, that all maner of personis nychtbouris within the samyn haue reddye their fensabill geir and wapponis for weir, and compeir thairwith to the said presidentis at jowyng of the commoun bell, for the keiping and defens of the toun againis thame that wald invaid the samyn.'

The great rumour touching the King and his army proved only too true. The day before, the fatal day of 9 September 1513, James IV and the flower of his army had fallen in the battle of Flodden. The English army under the Earl of Surrey had won a decisive victory over a proud Scottish force which James had rashly led into England at the instigation of his ally and England's enemy, the King of France. The death of James and – according to English sources – some 12,000 Scots with the loss of only a few hundred English lives produced a *frisson* of grief and horror throughout Scotland, and especially Edinburgh. Flodden was on the English side of the Tweed, barely four miles from the Border, and Edinburgh was vulnerable to attack by the victorious English army. Her own Provost, Sir Alexander Lauder, was among those slain in battle, but the Council even without their Provost were shocked into taking prompt and efficient action as soon as the first hint of the disaster reached them.

A new Provost, Archibald Douglas, Earl of Angus, was elected, and plans were made to build a defensive wall round the city. An earlier wall had been erected for a similar defensive purpose about 1450, in the reign of James II, running eastward from below the south-east corner of the castle rock, south of and parallel to the High Street, and then turning north to come to an end just east of the North Loch. The North Loch had been created some ten years earlier by the damming of the Craig Burn, that ran through the hollow on the north side of the castle rock (where Princes Street Gardens now are): it gave protection from the north. But by 1513 the town had overflowed these limits. The Cowgate, running east and west south of and parallel to the High Street, with the Grassmarket at its western end, was now established as a fashionable quarter of the town, with some handsome houses. It was south of the old wall. The Flodden Wall, as the new wall came to be called, ran irregularly well to the south of the Cowgate. It ran from the foot of the south-eastern corner of the Castle across the western end of the Grassmarket, where there was a gate called the West Port; then it went up the steep Vennel before turning east north of the site of the future Heriot's Hospital. It turned south again to enclose the new Grey Friars' monastery, near which was the Bristo Port; then eastward by the south of the present Old College of Edinburgh University, where there was the Potterrow Port, to go along what is now Drummond Street to the Pleasance, where it turned north to cross the eastern end of the Cowgate at the Cowgate Port and the eastern end of the High Street at the Netherbow Port. It turned west just to the east of the present Waverley Station, and ended at the New Port at the Eastern end of the North Loch.

The anticipated attack on Edinburgh by the English army immediately after Flodden did not materialize, and the building of the Flodden Wall proceeded with less urgency than was originally expected. It was not in fact finished until 1560, and it defined the Ancient Royalty or official burgh limits of Edinburgh for more than two centuries. During this period Edinburgh more than tripled its population, from an estimated 10,000 to over 30,000, while (except for the occasional building beyond the limits) retaining its sixteenth century area of something under 140 acres. The expanding population had nowhere to go but up, and 'lands' of up to ten or eleven storeys high became a characteristic feature of the city, accommodating a great variety of classes living, as it were, in a vertical street, with the most distinguished near the top.

On 4 October 1514, because of one of the frequent outbreaks of pestilence, the provost, bailies and council 'statute and ordainit' (this was the general formula in promulgating burgh statutes) that 'the towne sall be diuidit in four quarteris to be assignit to four baillis' and that it should be 'fermly closit' so that entry could be only by the town ports or gates. The fifteenth century Tolbooth in the High Street at the north-west corner of St Giles, was still the centre of the town. It served a variety of purposes: here tolls were collected, the Town Council sat, the law courts and periodically even Parliament met, and there was accommodation too for a prison. Eventually it came to be used solely as a prison, in which capacity it was given world-wide notoriety in Scott's *Heart of Midlothian*. As early as 1480 we find records of the letting of small booths within the Tolbooth to individual tradesmen and craftsmen for use as shops and workshops, and this practice continued after all other uses of the Tolbooth except as a prison had been given up. This was the old Tolbooth, and although it survived until its demolition in 1817, there are records of its bad state of repair and of the need for a new Tolbooth from the middle of the sixteenth century. On 24 December 1554 the provost, bailies and council ordered the Burgh Treasurer to begin at once to formulate plans 'anent the biggin [building] of the Tolbuith'. On 19 June 1560 the Town Council noted 'laik of Rowme' in the Tolbooth 'to minister justice and to do thair other effaris at all sic tymes quhen the sessioun did sit' and ordered the Dean of Guild to start a new building that would provide for a school, tolbooth, prison house, clerk's chamber 'and all vtheris necessaris'. But in February 1562 we find a reference to the bad state of the Tolbooth ('ruinous and abill haistelie to dekay and fall doun, qhuilk wilbe werray dampnabill and skaithfull to the pepill duelland thairaboutt') and a charge from the Queen to the Provost, Bailies and Town Council 'to caus put warkmen to the taking doun of the said tolbuth'. In the meantime, they were ordered to provide 'sufficient hous and rowmes ... for the ministering of justice to the lieges of the realm'. In June 1563 a thousand merks was borrowed by the town, on the security of its mills, to pay for the completing of a new Tolbooth and the Burgh Treasurer was ordered 'with all deligence, to mend the rufe of the toure of the auld tolbuth and mak the samyn watertycht'. So now there was both a repaired old Tolbooth and, at the south-west corner of St Giles, a new Tolbooth, which survived until 1811.

St Giles' itself had been promoted in status by James III in 1466 from an ordinary parish church to a collegiate church (i.e. a church served by joint pastors), with a provost, curate, sixteen prebendaries, sacristan, beadle, minister of the choir, and four choristers. As Edinburgh grew in population and wealth new altars and chapels were founded and endowed in the church. Different crafts maintained their own altars. One of the earliest surviving records of a craft-maintained altar in St Giles' is a Latin document of January 1451 binding the Craft of Skinners to maintain the altar of St Christopher.

There was an earlier collegiate church than St Giles' in Edinburgh: this was the Church of the Holy Trinity founded in 1462 by

Mary of Gelders, widow of James II, and dedicated 'to the Holy
Trinity, to the ever blessed and glorious Virgin Mary, to St Ninian
the Confessor, and to all the saints and elect people of God'. The
foundation provided for a provost, eight prebendaries, and two
singing boys, and there was also attached to it a hospital for thirteen
poor bedesmen. It was situated at the foot of Leith Wynd, at the
east end of the North Loch, and survived until 1848 when it was
demolished to allow the building of Waverley Station.

A third collegiate church in Edinburgh was St Mary-in-the-Fields,
or Kirk o' Field, founded perhaps as early as the thirteenth century
and deriving its name from the fact that it was beyond the city wall
of 1450, in open country. It was situated where the Old College of the
University now is, just inside the Flodden Wall. It became a collegiate church in the early sixteenth century and acquired substantial
prebendal buildings and a hospital which, with the church itself,
were severely damaged in 1547 when the Duke of Somerset's army,
after defeating the Scots at Pinkie near Musselburgh, sacked the city.
The church was further damaged by zealous reformers in 1558.

Edinburgh was used to sacking, and the 1540s were a particularly
bad time. James V died in 1542, broken hearted after the defeat of
his army by the English at Solway Moss, leaving his infant daughter
Mary to be fought over by pro-French and pro-English factions in
Scotland. Henry VIII was anxious to arrange for the marriage of
Mary to his son Edward (which would have united England and
Scotland under English rule) and in fact treaties for such a marriage
were drawn up when the pro-French faction took control and gave
Henry to understand that Scotland looked to her old ally France
rather than to her old enemy England for a husband for her young
queen. The enraged Henry sent the Earl of Hertford to Scotland to
persuade the Scots to change their minds by plundering and destroying throughout the southern part of the country. This 'rough wooing',
as it was called, produced immense destruction. In 1544 the Earl of
Hertford's army burned much of Edinburgh including the abbey and
palace of Holyrood. Leith too was burned and its pier destroyed. A
drawing made by one of Hertford's men shows the burned roofs
of houses flanking the High Street. But, as the drawing suggests, behind the wooden fronts were buildings of stone, and these survived,
to have their timber fronts replaced. For the next few years Edinburgh and indeed much of southern Scotland were liable to be terror-
ized by English troops, and it was only the arrival in Scotland of a
French army in 1548 and the defeat of English forces in France in

1550 that led to the withdrawal of the English army from Scotland and gave Edinburgh relief.

Edinburgh in the sixteenth century could be violent enough without marauding English troops. Feuding families often resorted to violence in the streets. A notorious fight in the High Street in 1520 between the Hamiltons and the Douglases, in which many on both sides were killed, was known as 'Cleanse the Causeway'. Brawls on a lesser scale were common. On 3 October 1567 the Town Council, taking note of the 'manifest wrangis and oppressionis' committed daily by 'nichtbouris of this burgh' who used a variety of weapons including 'sweirdis, quhingaris, battonis and vtheris instrumentis bellical, sumtyme committing slaughter mutilatioun or lamying ather of other', ordained that anyone convicted of using a weapon and drawing blood should pay a fine of five pounds to the common works of the burgh 'without preiudice of the panis of imprisonment, satisfactioun of the pairtie, or other actis maid anent trublence of befoir'. But sporadic violence continued through the century and into the next. On 9 March 1580 four surgeons reported that they could as yet 'geve na resolute ansuer' about the extent of the injury suffered by one Robert Asbowane at the hands of James Douglas and his accomplices, 'bot that he is in danger qhuill forther tyrell'. Two days later another surgeon gave evidence concerning the state of Nicoll Haistie, cordiner (i.e., cordwainer, shoemaker), after his wounding by Thomas Crawfurd. But perhaps the most extraordinary eruption of violence in Edinburgh's history took place on 15 September 1595, when the boys of the High School, on being refused their request for a week's holiday, armed themselves and occupied the school building (erected in 1578 in the gardens of the Monastery and Church of the Blackfriars, on the same ridge where Kork o' Field was built). When Bailie John McMorran was despatched to the school with a posse of city officers to enforce the peace one of the schoolboys shot him dead from a window. This does not seem to have been deliberate murder, and the schoolboys panicked and surrendered when they realized what had happened. Surprisingly, this killing in a schoolboy revolt of one of the wealthiest and most influential of Edinburgh merchants resulted in no drastic punishment of the culprit. Lord Sinclair, to whose family the culprit belonged, used his influence with the King and the magistrates to have all the boys set free; they were after all, as one report emphasized, both scholars and, for the most part, gentlemen's sons.

Evidence of the Town Council's continuous concern with violence in the streets is found in the repeated attempts, testified to by innumerable resolutions and statutes, to improve the efficiency of the watch. On 12 May 1568 the Council ordained 'ane wache to be made nychtlie of ane hundreth men', and the following November they granted the bailies' request that they should be attended by eighteen 'men of the maist abill within this burgh, with culvering [guns]' at all needful times: these men were also 'to keip wache within the toun for saiftie of the nychtbouris houssis and guddis'. After the murder of the Regent Moray in January 1570, 'the baillies and counsale, efter lang ressonyng vpoun the apperant danger and troublis like to be now', made further provision for a morning watch, an evening watch and a night watch. They kept experimenting with different ways of organizing the watch. In November 1580 the Provost, Bailies and Council, 'for keping of better ordour in tyme cuming anent the nycht watche of this burghe, fynds that the baillies in thair quarteris sall nychtlie sett the watche thame selfis'. One can gauge the rise of political and religious conflict and see the unsettled state of the country by the frequency and urgency of the Town Council's resolutions about the watch in the turbulent 1570s and 1580s.

Then there were the 'wappinschawings', exhibitions of arms by parading men, often held on the Burgh Muir outside the southern boundary of the Royalty adjoining the Burgh Loch (which was later drained to become eventually the Meadows). These too are an indication of troubled times, and the Town Council orders for them to be held become more frequent as dangers increased. Citizens had to provide their own arms. On 2 November 1554 both Provost and Bailies made it clear that at the wappinschawing ordered for the following 2 December 'na personis be resauit and admittit in wappinschawing without tha haif lang wappinnis, sic as speiris, pikis, and culueringis'. The wappinschawings were sometimes held as a result of a direction of the Provost and Bailies from the Privy Council (as in February 1556, for example). But generally they were ordered by the Town Council, in a formula identical with or similar to that of 17 May 1570: 'The baillies and counsale ordanis proclamatioun to be maid throuch Edinburgh and Leith chargeing all the inhabitanttis of the samyn to gif thair generale mustouris and wappinschewing, in best array with armour and wappinis, throuch this toun vpoun Friday nixst, ilk persoun vnder the pain of x li.'

Merchants and craftsmen managed to keep going somehow even through periods of political unrest and violence and in spite of frequent visitations of 'pest'. In an important 'decreit arbitrall betuix the merchants and craftismen' of April 1583, defining the rights of each group, fourteen crafts are listed, each of which had its own guild presided over by a deacon. They are 'chirurgeanis (surgeons), goldsmyths, skynners, furrours, hammermen (metal workers), wrichts (wrights), masons, tailyeouris, baxteris (bakers), flescheouris, (butchers), cordinaris, wobsteris (websters, weavers), walkers (fullers), bonetmakeris'. Twenty-three years earlier the Provost, Bailies and Town Council had convened a special meeting in order to spell out 'the obligatioun of the crafts' and named smiths, tailors, masons, wrights, barbers (these were barber-surgeons, barbers and surgeons belonging to a single craft), shoemakers ('cordineris'), bakers, butchers, goldsmiths, furriers, bonnet-makers, websters, fullers ('walkeris'), cutlers and candle-makers. The 'decreit arbitrall' of 1583 resolved some long standing differences between merchants and craftsmen and resulted in agreement by the Provost, Bailies, Dean of Guild (head of the merchants' guild) and Burgh Treasurer ('thesaurer') that the Town Council should consist of 'ten merchantis and aucht (eight) craftismen, thairof sex deykins and two vther craftismen'.

By a law made under James III and re-affirmed several times later, the old Town Council annually chose the new at Michaelmas. The Council met in the Tolbooth, and at least in the 1570s and 1580s met twice a week on Wednesdays and Fridays at 10 a.m. In accordance with a statute of 4 November 1581, members absent when ten o'clock finished striking had to pay a fine of 18d., and 5s. for a whole day's absence. In November 1579 it was specifically stated that no civil office could be held for life.

There was frequent royal interference with the Council's election of its Provost, which was resented though rarely actively resisted. There was also interference from the various regents who governed Scotland between the forced abdication of Mary Queen of Scots in 1567 and the forced resignation of the Regent Morton in March 1578. In October 1568 Moray wrote to the Town Council pretty much ordering them to re-elect their existing Provost and two of the existing Bailies. On 25 September 1583 young King James VI sent 'to baillies, counsale, and deykins of crafts' a letter giving 'the speciall names quhome we can best lyke to be chosin of the new counsall, and in baillies, thesaurer, and dean of gild for the yeir to come'. On 6 October 1584 James wrote again insisting on the election of James Earl of Arran 'our chancellare, and burges of our said burgh' as Provost and also naming the deputies who should serve in his stead

during any time when he was absent. On one occasion – on 12 April
1578 – the Privy Council ordered the Town Council to change their
Provost on the grounds that the existing Provost, George Douglas,
'capitane of the castell of Edinburgh', had aroused the 'gruge and
myslyking' of some inhabitants of Edinburgh in the course of his
duties as 'capitane of the said Castell'. The Bailies and Council gave
'all humbil obedience' to this order, and elected Archibald Stewart to
serve for the remainder of Douglas's term.

Though the Town Council were sometimes forced to succumb to
royal interference, they stood up when they could to attempted
bullying by neighbouring lairds. Sir Robert Logan of Restalrig (an
estate, later a village, about a mile east-north-east of Holyrood) sent
a curt letter to the Bailies of Edinburgh on 11 September 1560
ordering them to release 'ane puir fallow of myne' they had imprisoned in the Tolbooth, and threatening dire consequences if this
was not done. The Bailies, Council and Deacons met and agreed
that the Laird of Restalrig and his 'wikit companye' were a danger
to the common people of the burgh and ordered that he be imprisoned until sufficient caution be found, 'vnder the pane of ten
thousand pundis', that he and his men would do them no harm. A
fortnight later we find him secretly imprisoned in the Tolbooth, with
the Council complaining that he was receiving too many visitors.
They decided that only men of honour and judgment who were
known to fear God and carried no weapons, and were of a mind to
give him good counsel, should be allowed to visit him.

Edinburgh's burgesses were very jealous of their privileges and
proud of their status: the Town Council, which was composed of
burgesses, frequently passed statutes defining the method of achieving the status of burgess and limiting the entry to burgess-ship. In
May 1555, 'the prouest baillies and counsale sittand in jugement'
complained of the abuse involved in receiving as burgesses 'outlandis
men nocht beand maryit nor haiffand famele nor sufficient substance
and vsand thame self aus vnhonestlie that the haill towne hes bene
eschamyit thairby', and ordered that only 'honest habil qualyfyit
men' that were married and dwelt within the burgh, and had sufficient substance 'with stob and staik' (i.e., having a permanent residence there) should be eligible to be made burgesses, and that
burgesses should be made only on council days in the presence of
the Provost, Bailies and Town Council. In January 1580 it was
decided that burgesses should only be made at one of the four Head
Courts. In November 1557 the Town Council answered a request by

the Earl of Glencairn and other 'gentillmen of court' that a particular person whom they patronized should be made a burgess by pointing out that they would not grant any burgess-ship 'except to men of fame honestie and sufficiente substance quhilkis had or shortle sud hawe stob and staik within this towne'. On 18 June 1567 the Provost, Bailies and Council repeated their complaint of May 1555 and promulgated once again the same regulations. They seem to have been constantly in fear of infiltration into their ranks of unworthy men lacking respectability and substance.

They also regularly re-drafted the burgess oath. The form of the oath was set out in February 1585 as follows: 'I sall be leill and trew to our Souerane Lord and to his Hienes successoures, to the provest and bailyeis of this burgh. I sall vnderly and keip the lawis and statutes of this burgh. I sall obey the officers of the burgh, fortefie, and menteyne thame in executioun of thair offices with my bodie and my guids. I sall nocht collour vnfriemenis guids vnder collour of my awin. I sall nocht purches lordschips nor authoriteis contrare the fredome of the burgh. In all taxatiouns, watcheing, wairding, and all vther chairges to be layet vpoun the burgh, I sall willinglie beir my pairt of the Commoun burding thairof ... and sall nocht purches exemptiouns privilegeis, nor immuniteis to be frie of the sam, ... Fynally, I sall attempt or do nathing hurtfull or preiudiciall to the libertie and common weill of this burgh.' In July 1587 a religious clause was added: 'Heir I protest before God and your lordschips that I profes and allow with my hairt the trew relligioun quhilk at this present is publictly preachet within this realme and authorizitt be the lawes thairof, and sall abyde thairatt and defend the sam to my lives end, detesting the Romayne relligioun callit papistry.' It was clear enough that Edinburgh by now was a passionately Protestant city. This had been made clear, at least as far as the Town Council was concerned, as early as October 1561, when they issued a proclamation ordering 'preistis, monkis, freris, and vtheris of the wikit rable of the antechrist the paip', including 'nonnys, adulteraris, fornicatouris, and all sic filthy personis' to remove themselves from the town within twenty-four hours. This brought them into conflict with the Catholic Queen Mary, recently returned from her long stay in France and trying to establish a policy amid the conflicting religious and political currents now running fiercely in Scotland. She at once sent a letter to the Town Council brusquely setting forth her displeasure and ordering the Council to convene immediately in the Tolbooth and elect a new Provost and Bailies. At her bidding the

Council discharged Archibald Douglas from his provostship and also discharged two bailies of their offices and elected Thomas Makcalyeane as the new Provost. Several members protested vehemently at the Queen's affront 'to the fredome and libertie of this burgh'. The Council's pride was saved by the production of a note from the Queen to William Maitland of Lethington which contained a list of three names from which the Provost should be chosen, the list not including Thomas Makcalyeane.

The pride saved by this device was very real. In a judgement against an incompetent master of the High School, delivered on 2 October 1562, the Council gave as one reason for replacing him that since 'this burgh is the maist nobill and famous burgh and mirrour of gude maneris and ciuillitie within this realme, sua the same aucht to haue the maist famois and literat pedagogis for instructing the yowtheid of the samin'. They were careful of the physical appearance of the town, too, and took frequent measures to mend 'the tounis calsayis' (causeways, paved streets). They also took regular measures for cleaning the town, especially during and immediately after a visitation of 'pest'. 'It is statut and ordanit be the provost and counsale and community of this burch of Edinburgh,' ran a 'statut for clengeing the calsay' of 1505, 'for the guid rewle and honour and policy of the saymn, and for the haldin of it clene bayth in somer and wynter on the hie streitt' that the town bellman (an official of the Tolbooth, which was originally called the Bellhouse) should, with a horse and cart and two servants, daily remove from the High Street between the 'Castlehil, and Sanct Mary Wynd and Leith Wynd heids, ... all manner of mwk, filth and fulzie (filth).' They were particularly zealous in legislating for the removal of refuse from butchers and skinners. In October 1556 they decreed that all butchers of the burgh should have their 'feilth' carried to the North Loch 'or outwith the porttis to secrete partis, and erd (bury) the samyn vnder the eird'. The frequency of legislation for removing filth suggests that it was not wholly effective.

The threat of plague regularly stirred the Town Council to great activity. On 2 August 1530 one David Duly, tailor, was convicted of having concealed the fact that his wife had contracted 'the contagius seiknes of pestilens' and had actually gone to the kirk of St Giles on a Sunday when she was '*in extremis* in the said seiknes' so that he was likely 'till haif infekkit all the toune'. He was sentenced to be hanged on a gibbet before his own door, but the rope broke while the hanging was taking place, and this was regarded as a sign

that God willed that he should live. Therefore, since after all he was
'ane pure man with small barnis', he was simply banished from the
town for life. Another offender, who put a plague-stricken woman
out of his house while concealing the fact that she had plague, was
sentenced to be burnt on the cheek. Throughout the whole of that
month of August statute after statute was promulgated by the Council about cleaning infected houses and goods. There were severe
visitations of plague in 1568–9, 1574, 1585–6 and 1587.

Sometimes the Council ordered particular individuals to remove
filth from before their houses (Adam Yule at the West Port was so
distinguished in December 1581). On other occasions they issued
general prohibitions, a frequent one being directed against letting
pigs and dogs roam freely in the streets. In October 1512 they ordained that 'na doggis nor swyne be haldin in this towne furth of
band vnder payne of slawchter of thame', and similar regulations
were re-issued throughout the century.

Attacks from England, rival families feuding in the streets, schoolboy revolts (there were sit-ins by pupils of the High School in 1580
and 1587 as well as the more serious revolt in 1595), visitations of the
plague, filth in the streets – these were some of the hazards of life in
Edinburgh in the sixteenth century. There was also the problem of
unruly apprentices. A particularly serious insurrection of apprentices
took place on 9 May 1561, in spite of that day 'being the Saboth of
the Lord'. That afternoon 'the craftismennis seruandis and prentis-
ses enterit at the Nether Bow with displayit baner in armour and
wappinis and passit throuch the toun to the Castill Hill, nochtwith-
standing they war chargit ... in our Souerainis name and in the
name and behalf of the prouest and baillies of this burgh'. They
returned in the same manner between eight and nine at night and
stayed around the Nether Bow Port 'in manifest contempt of oure
Soueranis authorite and magistratis of this burgh'. Whether the
apprentices were voicing grievances or simply indulging in high
spirits is not made clear from contemporary records. It seems to
have been something of a generation war, for the Council minutes
refer to them more than once as 'the craftis childer', the children of
craftsmen. They spent some time in irons in the Tolbooth until
they were able to find guarantors that they would not again disturb
the peace.

The Town Council regularly manifested concern for the town's
poor, sometimes by making general regulations for the collecting of
alms, sometimes by assisting in particular cases as when in March

1555 they arranged to raise money to assist the widow and 'sex small bairnis' of the recently deceased Doctour Smyth. An ordinance of 31 May 1575 provided for the collection of alms every Saturday after-noon in St Giles and their delivery to the deacons appointed by the kirk for distribution to the poor. Schemes 'for the ordour and sustentatioun of the pure' were not always entirely charitable in intent: one professed aim was to keep the poor off the streets and from 'begging at mennis duris'. We have already noticed William Dunbar's complaints about Edinburgh's beggars. Right through the sixteenth century we find repeated attempts by the Town Council to control them by legislation. In September 1557 it was ordained that only beggars born in the burgh would be allowed in it, and the only ones allowed to beg would be 'ald cruikit lame or debilitat be greit seiknes' so that they were wholly incapable of work. A statute of 4 August 1559 complains of 'the gret multitude and dailie confluance of maisterfull strang beggeris to this burgh' and repeats the limita-tion of allowed beggars to the native born. But only a fortnight later there were complaints that masterful and strong beggars from other parts were terrorizing the native beggars, and provision was made for expelling them. The statute in favour of native born beggars was frequently repeated. Legitimate beggars were distinguished not only from those born outside the town but also from 'vagaboundis fydlaris pyparis minstrallis and otheris without maisteris, nocht haifing houssis within this toun nor sum honest shift to vphald thame self with', who were periodically ordered to remove themselves from the burgh 'vnder the pane of byrning of the cheik'. Again, the frequency of this issue of the regulations makes one doubt of their effective-ness.

The scourge of leprosy required more practical provision. Lepers had to be isolated outside the town. A Carmelite friary founded at Greenside (at the foot of the Calton Hill by the road to Leith) in 1520 was later converted into a leper hospital, conveniently situated just outside the city wall. This appears to be the 'awld fundation of the lipper hous besyde Dingwall' referred to in a Council minute of 30 September 1584, for an ancient stronghold known as Dingwall Castle stood just north of Greenside beside the road to Leith. (Greenside was an open space given to the burgesses in 1456 by James II for their recreation.) In March 1585 the Council authorized the Town Treasurer and others to inspect St Paul's Work and report on its suitability for a leper hospital. St Paul's Work, also known as Our Lady Hospital, was a hospital in the same area, situated near the site of the present General Post Office. It appears in fact not to have been used as a leper hospital. The disease diminished as the century progressed.

Edinburgh was still a small town and a fairly close-knit community that was soon aware of strangers in its midst. A Town Council proclamation of 15 January 1585 ordered all persons who had any strangers lodging with them to give their names in writing to the bailie of the quarter every night at 6 o'clock, under penalty of £5. Yet they were used to foreigners – French, Flemish, and others – and though angered by English pillagers and sometimes exasperated by French swaggerers (when the French were in Scotland supporting the Catholic faction against the pro-English Protestant faction) the citizens of Edinburgh were not xenophobic. The Reformation drove a new wedge between groups of people. In May 1588 two Flemish weavers dwelling within the burgh were, 'be ressoun of the difference in materis of religion betuix the kirk' and them, ordered to leave the town. But the following November they were still there, and it was 'fund expedient' to put them to work 'that thai be helpit in their present necessitie'. On 21 February 1589 we learn that they have gone to St Andrews.

The Reformation Parliament of 1560 and the civil strife that followed the return of Mary Queen of Scots from France the following year, with Protestant and Catholic, pro-English and pro-French, factions warring with each other, brought disturbance and violence to Edinburgh: we have already noticed the frequency of proclamations about the watch and the holding of wappenschawings. The Protestant Lords – the 'Lords of the Congregation', who effected the Protestant revolution in Scotland – sent a message to the Town Council in July 1659 explaining their objectives in language characteristic of the reformed faith. 'Beluffit brethering,' it began, 'we think ye ar nocht ignorant quhat hes movit my lordis of this present congregation to convene within this burgh at this tyme ...' They protested that they were meeting in the town 'onlie for the awanciement and furthsetting of Godis glore acording to the trew and pure ewangell'. Later the same month the Lords of the Congregation announced that the town of Edinburgh could choose its own form of religion 'without compulsion' by the 10th of January following, until which date every man could have freedom of his conscience. Bailie Adam Fullertoun, on behalf of 'the haill brether of the congregatioun within thus toun', presented a declaration stating that they knew that the religion they now professed was in conformity to the word of God while 'the mes and the papis haill religioun' was without the word of God and 'altogither superstitious damnable idolatrie and of the devill'. They were not willing to have God's truth decided by popular vote, for from the beginning of the world to the present time the majority had always been against God. They welcomed the guarantee that the preachers of the reformed faith would not be molested and would remain free to preach, but insisted yet again on their objection to submitting religious faith to the vote, which was plain wrong and injury and an opposing to God's word. To all this the Lords of the Congregation replied that 'thai wald compell na men to do by his conscience'.

From this time on we find an increasing number of Council edicts against a class of people often loosely lumped together as whore-masters, harlots, fornicators, vicious persons and idolators; one cannot avoid the impression – indeed, sometimes it is explicitly stated – that these were considered likely to be supporters of the unreformed church. Such people, said a proclamation of June 1560, provoked the indignation of God. An order of 22 May 1562 made special arrangements for the ducking of fornicators in the North Loch. This seemed to have had little deterrent effect, for the following November the Council was lamenting 'that the abhominabill viceis of adulterie and fornicatioun daylie increscit within this burgh for laik of pvnisment': they ordered that fornicators and adulterers, whether male or female, should be put in irons and fed only bread and water for one month before being banished from the town for ever. In September 1566 Queen Mary herself wrote to the Council from Stirling complaining that adultery, fornication, open harlotry and other such filthy lusts of the flesh were committed and suffered in Edinburgh to the great dishonour of God and the slander of the whole realm, though it seems that the letter was drafted for her by a minister called John Craig. On this occasion at least there was no association between such vices and Roman Catholicism. In October 1566 the Council once more legislated against 'the filthie vyce and cryme of adultrie and fornicatioun'; and so it went on year after year.

The reformers, in their zeal against what one edict described as 'the vyces of nicht walking, drinking, harletry and dissolut living', tended to associate them with festivals, ballad singing, and other popular forms of entertainment that had come down from earliest times. May Day ceremonies, the Robin Hood procession and plays, the antics of the Abbot of Unreason – these and other seasonal popular amusements were frowned on by the reformers, and periodic attempts by

Edinburgh

some craftsmen and apprentices to revive them were suppressed. On 1 May 1579 the Provost, Bailies, Council and Deacons ordered a proclamation to be made throughout the burgh 'be sound of tabouryne that na inhabitant within this burgh presume to accompany any sic as ar of mynde to renew the players of Robene Hude'. Edinburgh had put on a more puritan face, and it was to last a long time.

On 17 November 1587 the Town Council issued a proclamation expelling from the burgh 'all menstrallis, pyperis, fidleris, common sangsteris, and specially of badrie and filthy sangs, and siclyke all vagabounds and maisterless persouns quha hes na seruice nor honest industrie to leif be (live by)' and the same day one Martelmo Bell was apprehended 'for ane vicious and sclanderous persoun and for singing oppinly of filthie and baldrie sangs'; he was ordered to leave the burgh immediately. A few weeks later the spouse of James Ramsay was set 'in the jogs' with a paper on her head for two hours as a punishment for backbiting, slandering and injuring the minister William Aird and for blaspheming God 'quhen he gently admonist hir'. A proclamation of 5 April 1588 ordered the removal of all persons, not burgesses or freemen, suspected of 'papistry, blasphemeris of God and his word, or leding ane euill lyfe in tyme past'. The Reformation also brought in a stream of regulations concerning the proper observance of the sabbath. The first of these was issued in October 1560, and forbade the holding of markets, selling of merchandise, opening of booths or the exercise of any worldly occupation on 'the Sabbaothe day or day of rest commonlie callit be Sounday'. Among the many subsequent proclamations about the sabbath was one in May 1587 'commanding all persouns to resorte to the preichings' and forbidding them to 'pas to the feylds or playes the tyme of the sermones afoir or afternone on the Sondayes' under penalty of a 40s. fine.

The Reformation also produced a zeal for education. There was an early Grammar School attached to Holyrood Abbey. In 1554 the High School occupied temporarily the building in Blackfriars Wynd that had been built early in the century by John Bethune, Archbishop of Glasgow and was once the residence of Cardinal Beaton, but in March of the following year the Council authorized the Burgh Treasurer to provide for the building of a school on a site on the east side of the Kirk o' Field Wynd. In August 1577 it was discovered that the school building was neither water-tight, wind-tight, nor lock-fast, and repairs were authorized before the onset of winter 'sua that the bairnis sit warm and dry'. But plans were already on foot for building a new school and in January 1578 the Council authorized the appointment of the 'maist perfyte' craftsmen, masons and wrights to build a 'Hie Scole' in the Blackfriar's kirkyard, not very far to the east of where Edinburgh's new college was soon to be built. This building was the High School of Edinburgh from 1578 until 1777.

The Council took a keen interest in the new High School. On 10 April 1579 they instructed the newly appointed master, William Robertson, in his duties to keep the building wind-tight and water-tight and to provide 'all vther necessaris, as lokis, durris, braddis, stanchellis of irne, glas wyndois . . .' From every child receiving instruction at the school Robertson was authorized to collect two pennies at Whitsun and two pennies at Martinmas. Later they had difficulty in getting rid of Robertson after they found him to be aged and failing even though they offered him an annual pension of 200 merks if he would renounce his 'rycht, title, and kyndness' to the position. In August 1584, with Hercules Rollok now serving as master, they had to rule officially that Robertson should have no more pupils. He appears to have been teaching elsewhere in makeshift schools, and the Town Council ordered that all such schools be 'viseted and dischairget' and that all burgesses with children of school age should be 'dischairget' from sending them to any other school except the High School, under the penalty of having to pay Hercules Rollok quarterly 'for euery bairne vtherwaies teachet'. The Council expressed constant concern about the academic qualifications of the masters it appointed.

A Council decision to build a College for the town was made in 1581 and the royal charter for its foundation was granted by James VI on 14 April 1582. In 1583 the Council authorized a sum 'to be employet vpoun the commoun wark of the erection of ane college in the Kirk of Feild'. By the following October they were promulgating statutes for 'the College founded be the guid town in the Kirk of Feyld' which made it clear that the College was already functioning and attracting students from outside the city ('the students thairof beand strayngers and na burges bairnis of this burgh' had to occupy chambers within the College building, with 'twa in ilk bed', and to pay 40s. annually for their room). The 'maisters of the College' were appointed by the Council. In May 1585 the whole student body left temporarily 'throw the feir and bruit of the pestilence'. But the College flourished. In 1614 a formal visitation of the College took place, the Town Council appointing for the purpose sixteen of their own number and five city ministers, with three advocates as assessors. When James VI returned to Scotland in 1617, fourteen years after having left to become also James I of England he invited the Principal and Regents (professors) of the College to hold a public disputation before him at Stirling. He was pleased with the result, and on 25 July sent a letter to the Town Council expressing his satisfaction with the town's College and desiring them 'to order the said college to be callit in all times hereafter by the name of King James's College'. But it remained more generally known locally as the Tounis College. It was not officially known as the University of Edinburgh until 1858.* It was from the beginning a post-Renaissance, post-Reformation university, different in this respect from the other three older Scottish universities.

Edinburgh also had its Sang Scule for teaching religious music, and this survived the Reformation. In December 1553 we find the Town Council making provision for payment 'to Sir Eduard Henrisoun maister of thair sang scule', and a minute of August 1554 refers to provision for the building of a new Sang Scule. The part-music of the Catholic Church was succeeded by the part-music of the Reformed Kirk. An indication of the function of the Sang Scule after the Reformation is given in the appointment of three members of the Town Council in November 1579 to arrange for paying the stipend of a music teacher 'for vptaking of the psalmes in the kirk and eruditioun of the youth heid in the art of musik'. This of course was very different from the Court music – mostly Court song – that flourished in sixteenth century Scotland. 'Musik fyne' they called it, and there is evidence that James V was skilled in it (as well as in verse-writing), though none of the Court song of his reign has survived. Mary Queen of Scots, when she returned from France in 1561, brought with her music and dance; she had a group of musicians for part-singing and her Italian secretary David Riccio, with his fine singing voice, who was murdered by jealous Scots (including Mary's husband Darnley) in Holyrood in 1566. Mary's son James VI was the last Scottish king to preside over a Court culture, both music and poetry. When he went south to England in 1603 taking his Court poets and musicians with him, Edinburgh lost her place as a centre of patronage of the arts. When she regained it, in the Scottish Enlightenment of the late eighteenth and early nineteenth centuries, it was a very different kind of arts that were encouraged.

* See Appendix.

Printing came to Edinburgh in 1507, when James IV granted a patent to Walter Chepman and Andrew Myllar giving them the exclusive privilege of printing there. In 1508 Chepman and Myllar produced in Edinburgh the first printed work in Scotland, a print of six poems by the poet William Dunbar together with one poem attributed to Dunbar. James IV's death at Flodden in 1513 ended for a time the royal patronage of printing, but towards the end of the century James VI, who prided himself on being a scholar, gave renewed encouragement to learning and printing. The Reformation had its effect on printing: in December 1562 the General Assembly convened in Edinburgh granted the printer Robert Lekprevik two hundred pounds to buy equipment and pay craftsmen to print a metrical version of the Psalms, which duly appeared, together with the form of prayers as used at Geneva, in Edinburgh in 1564. Printing was late in coming to Scotland, but Edinburgh was to make up for this in a later period of her history.

Developments in Scotland's national history are reflected at every point in the history of Edinburgh. The effects of the Reformation meet us everywhere. A Town Council proclamation of 20 September 1560 denounces the corrupt sacraments 'of baptism and of the bodye and blude of Jesus Christ' as practised by 'the papisticall kirk and be their ministeris', and is only one of many similar proclamations. 'The relict callit the arme of Sanct Geill' – which had been left to the kirk of St Giles by William Preston of Goirton in 1454 and was held to be responsible for many miracles – was ordered to be handed over to the Dean of Guild in August 1560, and the silver work belonging to the kirk was ordered to be sold and the proceeds used for the common good of the town. There are many references in the Council minutes to John Knox – to payments to him in 1560, 1561 and 1565 and to money spent on repairing his house in 1568 (not, incidentally, the house popularly supposed today to be John Knox's house, which was almost certainly not his).

When Mary returned from France in August 1561 she made a ceremonial entry into Edinburgh (from Leith) to the blazing of bonfires on Calton Hill and Salisbury Crags. The Town Council arranged for 'ane honorable banquet' to celebrate the occasion. They provided funds for a 'triumph' also, and made elaborate preparations for a ceremonial welcome, with each of the town officials dressed for the occasion in 'ane goun of fyne blak weluot syde to thair fut lynit with pane weluot, ane coit of blak weluot, ane doublet of crammosyne satyne, with weluot bonet and hois efferand thairto'. Exactly a year later a troubled Town Council addressed the Queen on the question of the increase of poverty, the growth of the number of sturdy beggars, the decay of 'leirning and scienceis' and the lamentable growth of 'barbarous ignorance'. They wanted a new school, a hospital for the poor, and the yard of Grayfriars to use as a burial place. The Queen replied by appointing Grayfriar's yard as a burial place (the graveyard around St Giles' and southward towards the Cowgate was grossly congested) and promised her support for a school at Kirk o' Field and a hospital for the poor at Blackfriars.

John Knox, in his *Historie of the Reformatioun*, gives a sour description of Mary's return to Scotland, as well he might for they remained bitterly opposed. He remarked on the dolorous face of Heaven, the corruption of the air, the thick and dark mist. But, in spite of religious and political differences that were about to tear Scotland apart, there was a period of welcome and festivity, an era of good feeling, before tragedy closed in, with Riccio's murder, then Darnley's murder at Kirk o' Field on 10 February 1567 (in which Mary herself was believed by many to have been involved), Mary's hasty and fatal marriage to Bothwell, her imprisonment, escape and flight to England, where Queen Elizabeth eventually had her executed. Against all this we can set the welcome for the Queen written by the poet Alexander Scott:

> Welcum! illustrat ladye, and oure quene;
> Welcum! oure lyone with the floure de lyce;
> Welcum! oure thrissal with the lorane grene;
> Welcum! oure rubent roiss vpoun the ryce;
> Welcum! oure jem and joyfull genetryce;
> Welcum! oure beill of albion to beir;
> Welcum! oure pleasand princes, maist of pryce;
> God gif the grace aganis this guid new-yeir.

That is the courtly Edinburgh speaking, through one of the last of its Court poets. It was a kind of voice that was soon to disappear.

The infant James VI was crowned at Stirling on 29 July 1567 and spent his early days under the firm control of a succession of regents and tutors. He survived plots and conspiracies, and in May 1587, now twenty-one years of age, he endeavoured to compose the feuds of the rival magnates who had fought over him by providing them with an entertainment at the palace of Holyrood House before having them walk with him, two by two and hand in hand in token of amity, to the Mercat (Market) Cross where the Town Council had prepared a banquet of wines and sweetmeats. There they drank to friendship, and the young King beamed. The Council minutes curtly record that the banquet cost them thirty pounds ten shillings and eightpence. The Council soon learned to be wary of expenses they might incur on the King's account: he made several attempts to borrow large sums of money from them. Nevertheless, they treated him to a much more expensive entertainment in the spring of 1598 when they gave a banquet for him, Anne of Denmark his Queen, and her brother the Duke of Holstein and other visiting Danish nobles. The banquet was held in the fine mansion at Riddle's Court belonging to Ninian McMorran, who had inherited it from his brother, the unfortunate Bailie John McMorran shot by a revolting schoolboy in 1595.

In 1603 King James left to take up his English throne and henceforth ruled Scotland, as he boasted, with his pen. Though still the capital city that it had become by the early sixteenth century, the centre of Scotland's legal establishment, and soon to be the settled home of Scotland's Parliament (until 1707), Edinburgh was now no longer a royal city. It lost something of its colour and pageantry and a major source of patronage of the arts. But it was far from done with violence.

CHAPTER 3

Civil and Religious Conflicts

Edinburgh was squarely at the centre of Scottish history in the last
third of the sixteenth century. Mary of Guise, widow of James V and
mother of Mary Queen of Scots, spent her last days in the royal
apartments of Edinburgh Castle, built in the fifteenth century and
altered at various times; she died there on 10 June 1560, two months
before her young widowed daughter returned to Scotland from
France. After Mary's marriage to Darnley on 29 July 1565 the
couple frequently resided in the Castle, and it was there, on 19 June
1566, in a small room barely nine feet long at the south-east corner
of the Grand Parade, that Mary gave birth to the future James VI.
The Town Council paid ten pounds for a puncheon of wine to run at
the Mercat Cross to celebrate the birth. Darnley's murder at Kirk o'
Field the following February, Mary's scandalous marriage to Bothwell (one of Darnley's murderers) in May, her consequent loss of
popularity and her surrender to a confederacy of nobles at Carberry,
led to her last entry into Edinburgh, deserted, mocked and insulted,
dressed in borrowed clothes, on the evening of 15 June 1567. 'Burn
the whore! Kill her, drown her!' the soldiers shouted as they conveyed her to the city, and the spectators stood silent as she passed
along the Canongate, through the Netherbow Port, and up the High
Street. They would not let her stay at either of her own residences at
the Castle or Holyrood, but lodged her in the house of the Provost,
Sir Symon Prestoun of Craigmillar, opposite the Mercat Cross. Out
of her window there she saw her former counsellor and secretary
Maitland of Lethington, and called on him with tears for help, but
Maitland pretended not to hear and pulled his hat over his ears. The
next day she appealed again from her window to people in the street,
but received only mocking insults. Her captors now removed her for
safety to Holyrood. From there she was taken to imprisonment at
Lochleven Castle and forced to abdicate in favour of her infant son.

In 1579 the thirteen-year-old James VI transferred his residence
from Stirling to Edinburgh. On 20 August the Town Council ordered
that 'ane cupburde of syluer, ourgiltt, of weichtt vunderwtittin, be
paid and prepaired with diligence to the Kingis Maiestie cuming to
Edinburgh', and on 4 September gave orders to the master of the

High School for 'tragedies to be maid be the bairnis agane the Kingis heir cuming'. Excitement mounted as the day of the King's entry approached. The Council gave the most detailed instructions about the ceremonial dress to be worn by their officers: they had each to provide for themselves 'thre elnis of blak inglis stemyng to be thair hois, vj quarteris of rowane canvas to be thair doubletis ... together with ane blak hatt and ane quhyte string'. On 14 October a proclamation was made throughout the burgh to the sound of drums ordering the inhabitants to hang their stairs with tapestry and prohibiting the throwing by night or day of 'ony fyre ballis, fyre arrowis, of vther ingynes of fyre': swine and beggars had to be removed from the town. Middens and filth had to be cleared from the High Street.

When the King made his ceremonial entry a few days later, he was received by the Provost and Bailies at the West Port, under a pall of purple velvet. An allegory of 'King Solomon with the twa wemen' was presented there, signifying the young King's Solomonic wisdom. The keys of the city were delivered to him in a silver basin. At the Tolbooth three ladies representing Peace, Plenty and Justice made speeches in Greek, Latin and Scots, and as the King approached St Giles' Dame Religion appeared and bid him enter in the Hebrew tongue. After the service and the sermon the King and congregation came out of the church to find Bacchus distributing free wine at the Cross. The elaborate proceedings came to a climax with an astrological display showing the conjunction of the planets at the time of the King's happy nativity. James then proceeded to the Palace of Holyroodhouse with an escort of two hundred horsemen. Immediately afterwards Parliament met in the Tolbooth.

From this time onwards James increasingly asserted himself in Edinburgh, interfering with Town Council elections and trying a variety of devices to raise money from the city. In October 1589 he embarked at Leith for Norway, to bring home his bride Anne of Denmark to whom he had been married by proxy. He gave detailed orders to the Town Council for the reception of himself and his Queen on his return, which included the double lining with armed men of the streets between Leith and Holyrood. The Town Council was also expected to bear the cost of entertaining Anne and her retinue from the time of her arrival until the Palace of Holyroodhouse could be suitably fitted up for her reception. The Council offered James 5,000 merks to avoid this expense and, in obedience to a royal precept, fitted out a ship to bring home the royal couple. They arrived at Leith on 1 May 1590 and remained on board until the 6th while the Palace was being prepared. It had been a stormy passage, caused, as James firmly believed, by the malevolent incantations of witches, whose 'cantrips', he asserted, were only frustrated by his faith. A boat carrying wedding presents to the young Queen from Burntisland to Leith was wrecked in a storm, with the loss of all hands, testimony that this time the witches were successful in their plots, having, it was asserted, raised the storm by the remarkable agency of a christened cat.

The landing at Leith was accompanied by the booming of cannon and the recitation of a long Latin oration by James Elphinstone, later one of 'the King's Octavians' (a committee of eight advisers) and a Lord of Session. On 17 May the Queen was crowned in Holyrood Abbey, the Reverend Robert Bruce anointing her with 'a bonye quantitie of oyll' after which she was treated to an oration of two hundred Latin verses by the Presbyterian scholar and theologian Andrew Melville. On the 19th the King and Queen made a formal entry into Edinburgh by the West Port, where the Queen had to listen to another Latin speech before being conveyed 'through the haill toun, under a paill, to Holyrood-house'. The contemporary account also tells us that 'there was 42 young men all clade in white taffitie, and visors of black colour on their faces, like Moors, all full of gold cheynes, that dancit before her grace all the way'. When we consider also that the couple brought with them a train of 224 persons, together with the Admiral of Denmark and 'sundry other noblemen of the realm; and besides that 30 or 40 persons in golden cheynes', all of whom were entertained to daily banquets during the period of celebration, we can understand why the Town Council murmured at the expense. In recording these events William Maitland, who published his history of Edinburgh in 1753, burst out in indignation against James's 'intolerable impositions and exactions' in his dealings with the city.

More disturbing to many citizens of Edinburgh was James's fondness for episcopacy and his endeavour to promote a Protestantism in Scotland that rejected equally the papal authority subscribed to by the Roman Catholic Church and the form of church government – by presbytery, synod and General Assembly – insisted on by the Presbyterians. Andrew Melville had the audacity to tell the King to his face in 1596 that he was 'God's sillie (weak) vassal' and that while he was King of Scotland he was only an ordinary member in the Kingdom of Christ, which was the Kirk. Shortly afterwards the St Andrews minister David Black attacked Queen Elizabeth as an 'atheist', provoking a protest from the English ambassador. Black was tried before the King-in-Council, convicted and sentenced to imprisonment. The Presbyterians of Edinburgh were bitterly indignant at these proceedings and apprehensive about the King's assumed favouritism towards popery. The King was with members of his Council in the Tolbooth when a crowd, excited by a vehement sermon in St Giles' delivered by Mr Walter Balnacquall, broke in on the meeting. The King left the room and shut himself in the court-room of the Tolbooth, where the Lords of Session were sitting, and the crowd returned to St Giles' to report that they had not been heard. Something like a riot ensued, but the tumult was quieted by the skilful words of the Provost, Sir Alexander Hume, and the King and his Council were able to retreat quietly to Holyrood. The next day they withdrew to Linlithgow.

James was not going to tolerate mob rule in his capital city. From Linlithgow he sent a proclamation to be read out at the Mercat Cross of Edinburgh announcing that in view of what had happened he thought 'the said town an unfit place for the ministration of justice' and had therefore ordained the Lords of Session, sheriffs, commissaries, and justices, with their several members and deputies, to leave Edinburgh and 'repair unto such place as should be appointed'. This announcement produced an immediate effect on the burgesses who stood to lose massively, in material as well as in civic pride, if Edinburgh lost its status as a legal and judicial centre and as a centre for the Court. The city's most eminent burgesses publicly dissociated themselves from the tumult and pleaded abjectly for their city: they even got Queen Elizabeth to intervene in Edinburgh's favour (which she did for her own reasons). James, who had won his point, accepted the apologies and explanations and in 1597 he re-entered his capital in triumphant tranquillity.

When James left Edinburgh in April 1603 on succeeding to the throne of England, he bade farewell to its citizens at a crowded congregation in St Giles'. He listened in unusual equanimity as the Reverend Mr Hall gave a long exhortatory discourse, then himself addressed the people in language of warm friendship, which is said to have moved many of his hearers to tears. He promised to return to his capital every three years, but in fact he was to return only once – in 1617 – in the twenty-two remaining years of his reign. The month before he left he granted a charter to Edinburgh confirming all royal gifts to the town since the time of Robert I.

The departure of the Court to London brought considerable loss of trade and consequent bankruptcies among tradesmen: in 1604 the Court of Session ordered that insolvent debtors should sit each morning, in quartered brown-and-yellow coats and yellow bonnets, in a pillory beside the Mercat Cross known as the Dyvours' Stone. But some Edinburgh citizens prospered. Notable among them was George Heriot, 'Jingling Geordie,' a goldsmith who was Deacon Convenor of the Incorporated Trades of Edinburgh and who in 1595 was appointed goldsmith to the Queen and in 1601 goldsmith to the King. He more than once lent money to the royal couple, and in 1603 followed them to London. He returned to Scotland in 1608, on the death of his first wife, and there he married the daughter of James Primrose of Carrington, grandfather of the 1st Earl of Rose-berry. In 1609 he returned to London, where he continued to pros-per. In 1623, the year before his death, he executed a deed assigning his fortune to the Town Council of Edinburgh for the education of fatherless boys who were sons of freemen of the town of Edinburgh and in his will made further provision for this endowment of 'Heriot's Hospital'. The building was begun in 1628 on a site to the west of Greyfriars' Churchyard, but its completion was delayed be-cause at first the work was paid for out of interest on the capital sum, which had been invested in property that suffered in the disturbances of the Civil War. Cromwell used it as a military hospital in 1650 and it was not handed back to the trustees until General Monck removed the wounded soldiers in 1658. It was completed in 1659 and in that year admitted thirty fatherless boys. The building, one of the finest public buildings erected in seventeenth century Scotland, still houses George Heriot's School.

The thirty-four years between James's departure in 1603 and the riots over Charles I's new service book in 1637 were years of relative tranquillity in Edinburgh. The Town Council continued to expect the return of James VI in accordance with his promise and in 1606–7 went to considerable expense to repair and beautify the Netherbow Port, by which gate the King would enter the city on his way from Holyrood. On 1 May 1607, 'understanding that it is the custome of maist renownit cities to have the effigie or statue of their Prince set up upon the maist patent part of the citie', the Council ordered that there should be 'set up upon the maist patent and honorabill part of the Nether Bow the image or statue of his majesty gravin in maist prynclie and decent form in remembrance of his majesty, and of their sinecere affectioun borne unto him'. This was not in fact done until September 1616, when the Council ordered

'Johne Byris, Thesaurer, to content and pay to Banjamin Lambert the sowme of 433 merks and 6 schillingis 8 penys for the Kingis portrait and New Armis to be erected at the Nether Bow'. This was just in time for the King's return to Scotland in May 1617.

James entered Scotland on 13 May and stayed until 5 August. His main political objective in returning was to impose on Scotland the same kind of episcopalian church government and form of worship that prevailed in England: his more personal intention was to enjoy his favourite sport of hunting the red deer. He brought with him a host of English notables and, among the clergy, William Laud (later Archbishop of Canterbury), whose presence aroused the deepest suspicion among the Scottish Presbyterians. He entered Edinburgh on 16 May amid the usual elaborate ceremonies, which included, amid a great deal of fulsome Latin eulogy, a poem in English by Drummond of Hawthornden, 'The Muses' Welcome to the High and Mighty Prince James, ... at his Majesty's happie Returne to his old and native Kingdome of Scotland'. Drummond also published another poem to mark this occasion, entitled 'Forth Feasting: a Panegyricke to the Kings Most Excellent Majesty', in which he represented the Forth as rejoicing 'that my much-loved Prince is come again'. He addressed James directly in terms of high flattery.

> O *Vertues* Patterne, Glorie of our Times,
> Sent of past Dayes to expiate the Crimes,
> Great King, but better farre than thou art greate,
> Whome State not honours, but who honours State, ...
> If *Brutus* knew the Blisse Thy Rule doth give,
> Even *Brutus* joye would under Thee to live:
> For thou thy people dost so dearlie love,
> That they a Father, more than Prince Thee prove.

The reality was rather different. James gave great offence in Edinburgh by introducing the Anglican service with conspicuous ritual in Holyrood Chapel, 'with singing of quiristours, surplices, and playing on organs'. At a meeting of Parliament that began in Edinburgh on 17 July he asked for approval of a Bill that would have had the effect of making the King, in consultation with the bishops, supreme in matters of Scottish ecclesiastical policy. Fifty-five ministers joined in drawing up a protest, and James reluctantly gave way.

James visited other towns in Scotland as well as Edinburgh, including Linlithgow, St Andrews, Stirling, Glasgow and Dumfries, and enjoyed his ceremonial welcomes and his hunting. But when he left Scotland early in August, never to return, he left behind discontent with and suspicion of his ecclesiastical policy. After his return to England he forced the so-called Five Articles of Perth on a General Assembly that met at that town – measures which were regarded by committed Scottish Presbyterians as savouring of papistical ritual and superstition. When he died in 1625 he left an unsolved ecclesiastical problem in Scotland to his son Charles I, who did not know Scotland as his father had known it and was unable to see when it was expedient to refrain from pushing a desired measure to its extreme point in the face of considerable national hostility.

James I was a firm believer in witchcraft, and during his reign Scotland, and Edinburgh in particular, was disgraced by numbers of burnings, mostly of women but sometimes of men who under torture had confessed to consorting with the devil. Many who did not confess were simply judged for that reason to be wickedly obstinate and met the same fate of being burned alive, generally on the Castle Hill. This frenzy against witches persisted until late in the seventeenth century. John Nicoll, born in Glasgow but for most of his life an Edinburgh Writer to the Signet, left in his diary some grim accounts of these proceedings in the middle of the century. Writing in 1658 he noted:

> Burning of witches and warlocks were maist frequent. In Februar two women and ane man were prisoners for this crime in the Tolbooth of Edinburgh. One of the women died in the prison; the warlock was worryit at the stake on Castlehill. The other women, Jonet Anderson, who had only been married three months before, confessit that she had given hersel, bodie and soul, to the devil, and that at her wedding she saw Satan standing in the kirk ahint the pulpit ... In the August the same year four women, ane of them a maiden, were burnt on the Castlehill, all confessing the sin of witchcraft. Two months later five women belonging to Dunbar were burnt on the Castlehill together, all confessing ... Yet, despite all this, the clergy were not satisfied, and complained: 'There is much witchery up and down our land; the English be but too sparing to try it, though some they execut.'

Agnes Finnie, who sold groceries in the Potterrow, was tried as a witch and condemned to be burned alive in 1643 for what from the records of the trial seems to have been little more than bad temper.

Among the charges against her was: 'scolding with Bettie Currie about the changing of a sixpence, which she alleged to be ill, ye in great rage threatened that ye would make the devil take a bite of her'. She was also charged with abusing one Isabel Atchesone and bidding the devil ride about the town with her and hers, so that the said Isabel Atchesone fell from a horse and broke her leg the very next day. The witch fever lasted from about 1590 (the year of a notorious witchcraft scandal in North Berwick) until the early 1670s, a period when the rest of Europe was outgrowing the disease.

Charles I visited Scotland in 1633 bent on forcing the Church of Scotland into the same pattern as that of the Church of England with respect alike to church government, ritual and the form of prayers. He entered Edinburgh on 15 June amid the usual lavish ceremony that greeted the entry of a monarch. The nymph Edina received him at the West Port with complimentary verses, as did the Lady Caledonia at the Over Bow, while Fergus I received him at the Tolbooth with a long speech of solemn advice. At the Tron a mound purporting to be Mount Parnassus was erected covered with 'a great variety of vegetables, rocks, and other decorations peculiar to mountains' as well as with numerous specimens of its ancient inhabitants. John Spalding, the town-clerk of Aberdeen who was visiting Edinburgh at the time, has left a detailed account of the elaborate pageantry and speech-making that accompanied Charles's entry. There were seven welcoming speeches in all, 'which haill orations his majesty with great pleasure and delight, sitting on horseback as his company did, heard pleasantly'. The Provost and Bailies received him at the West Port clothed in scarlet and fur, with the town councillors in black velvet, and presented him with a 'propyne' (present, literally 'drink money') in the form of a golden bowl that cost 5,000 merks and contained a thousand double angels in gold (equal to £1,000 sterling). The procession to Holyrood (specially renovated and decorated for the occasion) was accompanied by an augmented City Guard in white satin doublets, black velvet breeches and silk stockings.

On the 17th Charles was crowned King of Scotland (not, interestingly enough, 'King of Scots', the style always used hitherto) with great pomp and solemnity in the Abbey Church of Holyrood. Sir James Balfour, Lord Lyon King-at-Arms, who organized the ceremony, published a full account of it. He commented: 'Because this was the most glorious and magnifique coronation that ever was seen in this kingdom, and the first King of Great Britain that ever was crowned in Scotland, to behold these triumphs and ceremonies many strangers of great quality resorted hither from divers countries.'

Spalding – who was not a Presbyterian but a moderate and conservative prelatist – noted that there was a four-cornered table standing in the church during the ceremony in the manner of an altar and that on it were 'twa books at least resembling clasped books, called blind books, with twa wax chandeliers, and twa wax candles whilk was unlighted, and ane basin wherein there was nothing.' He noted other things that bitterly offended the Presbyterians: 'At the back of this altar, covered with tapestry, there was ane rich tapestry wherein the crucifix was curiously wrought; and as these bishops who were in service passed by this crucifix they were seen to bow their knee and beck, which, with their habit, was noticed, and bred great fear of inbringing of Popery, ... The Archbishop of Glasgow and remanent of the bishops there present who was not in service changed not their habit, but wore their black gowns without rochets or white sleeves.' Charles further offended the Presbyterian burgesses of Edinburgh by having two English chaplains conduct an Anglican service in St Giles' the following Sunday, after which there was a banquet in a neighbouring house from which proceeded such a noise of singing, trumpeting and even shooting of cannon that the afternoon service had to be abandoned.

Parliament met in Edinburgh on 18 June and, managed by the King through the committee known as the Lords of the Articles, which drew up Bills desired by the King and prepared the agenda in advance, passed in the ten days of its sitting no fewer than one hundred and sixty-eight Acts, including two relating to religion (one confirming all of James VI's Acts relating to religion and one specifying the proper ceremonial apparel of bishops and inferior clergy – a minor matter that nevertheless infuriated the anti-ritualistic Presbyterians). In spite of the Lords of the Articles, and of the bishops who were now influential members of the House, Charles won only a small majority for his measures. The opposition organized a formal protest, and as they registered their votes Charles coolly took down their names. They also intended to sign a document of protest, but Parliament had risen before they could all do so. Charles left Edinburgh for England on 18 July 1633.

When he was in Edinburgh Charles erected it into an episcopal see, appointing as its diocese all the lands south of the Forth which had belonged to the Archbishopric of St Andrews: he gave the Bishop of Edinburgh precedence next to the Archbishops of St

Andrews and Glasgow, and named St Giles' as the cathedral. Thus the church which had begun simply as a parish church and had become a collegiate church in 1466 and was generally known as the High Kirk of St Giles was now St Giles' Cathedral. This was a short-lived distinction, as episcopacy in the Church of Scotland was abolished in 1639. It was re-established at the Restoration in 1660 but finally abolished at the Glorious Revolution in 1689.

The year of Charles's visit saw the founding of the Tron Kirk, designed by John Mylne, by the public weighing beam (the 'tron') about midway between St Giles' and the Netherbow Port. (It was extensively damaged in the great fire of 1824 and the present steeple was built in 1828). This was the time, too, of the building of Parliament House, just south of St Giles', to house the Scottish Paliament. It was begun in 1632 and completed in 1639.

Sir William Brereton, a Cheshire traveller, visited Edinburgh in 1636 and was much impressed by the High Street, 'the best paved street ... that I have seen ... This street is the glory and beauty of this city; it is the broadest street (except in the Low Countries, where there is a navigable channel in the middle of the street) and the longest street I have seen ... Indeed, if the houses, which are very high and substantially built of stone (some five, some six storeys high) were not lined to the outside and faced with boards, it were the most stately and graceful street that I ever saw in my life.' Brereton praised Edinburgh's 'dainty, healthful, pure air' and added that it would be a most healthful place to live in 'were not the inhabitants most sluttish, nasty and slothful people'. He complained of the smell everywhere with 'nothing neat, but very slovenly'. He added : 'Their houses of office are tubs or firkins placed on end, which they never empty until they be full, so as the scent thereof annoyeth and offendeth the whole house ... I never came to my own lodging in Edinburgh, or went out, but I was constrained to hold my nose, or to use wormwood or some such scented plant.' Edinburgh smells were to become a common subject of complaint.

Presbyterian Edinburgh's fears of Charles I's ecclesiastical policy for Scotland were more than confirmed when, without reference either to the General Assembly or the Scottish Parliament, he ordained that a new Service Book (popularly known as 'Laud's Liturgy' as it was prepared by William Laud, now Archbishop of Canterbury) be exclusively used in Scotland. The Service Book, which was widely regarded as savouring of popery, was produced at St Giles' on 23 July 1637. The Dean of Edinburgh had no sooner opened the book in preparation for reading from it than uproar broke out. Edinburgh's first bishop, David Lindsay, mounted the pulpit in the hope of quelling the tumult, but it only became worse. Somebody – there is a tradition that it was a woman called Jenny Geddes, but there is no strictly contemporary record of this – or some people apparently threw a stool or stools at the Dean or the Bishop. The church was packed for the solemn inauguration of the new ritual and the congregation included both the Scottish arch-bishops, several bishops, the lords of the Privy Council, judges, and the magistrates. The magistrates ordered the church to be cleared, and when this was done the service continued behind locked doors, the people outside seething in rage. The Dean stole out of the church by a back way, but Bishop Lindsay boldly came out at the front entrance and faced the angry crowd. He was rescued by the Earl of Roxburgh who was passing in his coach and pulled the Bishop in, and as they rode off the crowd pelted the coach with stones taken from the Tron Church.

A weak and divided Scottish Privy Council received simultan-eously stern messages from the King ordering them to punish the rioters and impose the Service Book and masses of petitions or 'supplications' against it coming from a wide range of classes – nobility, lairds, ministers and burgesses. Charles's continued insis-tence on the acceptance of the Service Book produced another riot in Edinburgh on 18 October 1637, to which Charles responded by ordering the Privy Council to move to Linlithgow. Each of the four groups just mentioned then chose four representatives, known as the 'Tables', to put their case before the Privy Council, and on 21 December they presented a collective 'supplication' demanding the removal of the bishops from the Council on the grounds that they were interested parties in the matter to be decided. Charles replied with a proclamation at Stirling on 19 February 1638 announcing that the Service Book would be maintained and declaring the sup-plications against it to be illegal. To this the Supplicants, as they were called, replied by asking two of the most distinguished Scots lawyers of the day, Sir Thomas Hope and Archibald Johnston of Warriston, to prepare a document known as the National Covenant. This lengthy document begins by citing the various Scottish Acts relative to religion drawn up since 1581 (a year in which there was considerable anxiety about the activity of Papists). Chief among these was the so-called 'Negative Confession' of 1581 proclaiming as 'the onely true Christiane fayth and religion pleasing God and bringing salvation to man' that which was professed 'by manie and sundrie notable kyrkis and realmes, but chiefly by the kyrk of Scotland, the kingis majestie, and three estatis of this realme, as Godis eternall trueth' and repudiating 'the usurped authorities of that Romane Antichrist upon the scriptures of God, upon the kyrk, the civill magistrate and conscience of men'. This was ingeniously done, because the Negative Confession had been approved by Charles's father James VI, even though he later developed ideas for the Church of Scotland more like those of his son. After quoting this Confession the National Covenant goes on to list the successive Acts of Parliament by which it was confirmed, all of them in the reign of JamesVI. 'And that notwithstanding of the King's Majesty's licences on the contrary, which are discharged & declared to be of no force in so farre as they tend in any wayes, to the prejudice & hinder of the execution of the Acts of Parliament against Papists & adversaries of true Religion . . .' The Covenant repudiated any desire to do anything to the dishonour of God 'or to the dimunition of the Kings greatness and authority : But on the contrary, we promise and sweare, that we shall, to the uttermost of our power, with our meanes and lives, stand to the defence of our dread Soveraigne, the Kings Majesty, his Person, and Authority, in the defence and preservation of the foresaid true Religion, Liberties and Lawes of the Kingdom',

In spite of the Covenant's protestation of loyalty to the King, its tenor was flatly and uncompromisingly against his ecclesiastical policy for Scotland. The document was ready by 28 February, and on that day the signing of it by masses of people began in Greyfriars Church in Edinburgh (built in 1620) amid scenes of remarkable enthusiasm.

Charles sent the Marquis of Hamilton to Scotland as his Royal Commissioner to treat with the Covenanters, but his indecision and deviousness produced only further distrust and by the end of August 1638, after two visits by Hamilton, the Covenanters remained adamant and Edinburgh unsettled. Indeed, the Covenanters now made further demands, adding to their insistence on the recall of the Service Book and the removal of bishops from the Privy Council a call for a free Parliament and a free General Assembly to decide all disputed matters. On 20 September Hamilton appeared in Edinburgh for the third time, bringing Charles's assent to a free Assembly and a free Parliament but also proposing to substitute for the National Covenant Charles's own 'King's Covenant' that involved the repudiation of the former. The King's Covenant received little support in any Scottish city except Aberdeen.

On 21 November 1638 the General Assembly met in Glasgow Cathedral, carefully packed with Covenanters. Hamilton, as Lord High Commissioner, attacked its constitution and denied its validity, and tried to terminate the meeting on the 29th, himself leaving abruptly and ordering all members to go home. But the members ignored him and continued the Assembly in his absence. They repealed or annulled various acts of preceding Assemblies from 1606, repudiated the new Service Book, and charged the Scottish bishops with having acted against the laws of the Church of Scotland: six of the fourteen Scottish prelates were deposed and eight were both deposed and excommunicated. Episcopacy in Scotland was abolished. The powerful Earl of Argyll, with his strong private army, was welcomed as a supporter of the cause. Civil war seemed inevitable.

In March 1639 the Covenanters elected a committee of twenty-six charged with the duty of defending Scotland against English invasion and their forces were placed under the command of Alexander Leslie who had served with distinction in the campaigns of Gustavus Adolphus in the Thirty Years War and had joined the Covenanters on returning to Scotland in 1638. His first exploit was to capture Edinburgh Castle, which had been fortified by the King, and held for him by Patrick Ruthven, the Governor; this was achieved without the loss of a single life. On 1 May a royalist fleet commanded by Hamilton entered the Firth of Forth, and Leith was fortified. But Hamilton's fleet, many of the men sick with smallpox, proved impotent. Leslie assembled his army – which included a contingent of five hundred men raised by Edinburgh Town Council – southwards after mustering them on the Links of Leith. On 5 June he encamped on Duns Law, some twelve miles north of the Border. Charles and his army took up their position on the south Bank of the Tweed some three miles from Berwick.

The Covenanting army, for all their enthusiasm, hesitated to proceed to actual fighting against their lawful sovereign, while Charles, already in difficulties with his English subjects, was even less anxious to fight. Charles agreed to negotiate and the result was the Pacification of Berwick of 18 June 1639. The King agreed to the summoning of the General Assembly and of Parliament. Thus ended the so-called First Bishops' War.

Charles was playing for time, and the Covenanters remained distrustful. A riot in the streets of Edinburgh, in which the Lord

Treasurer Traquair was roughly handled, provided an excuse for Charles not to be present at the coming General Assembly and Parliament, and he left Berwick for London on 29 June. On 12 August the General Assembly met at Edinburgh and took an even more extreme line than that of the previous year's Assembly in Glasgow, going so far as to recommend making subscription to the Covenant compulsory. Parliament met on 31 August and, in the absence of bishops and other spokesmen for the King's view, proceeded to ratify all the Acts of the General Assembly. An incensed Charles prorogued Parliament against its will until the following June. Though he later postponed the June date, Parliament met on 2 June 1640 without royal approval or a royal representative, declared itself a valid Parliament, and proceeded to pass a number of revolutionary Acts, including making the Covenant compulsory.

After the Pacification of Berwick the royalist Sir Patrick Ruthven was restored to his position as Governor of Edinburgh Castle, to the consternation of the majority of its inhabitants, who prepared to protect their homes against attack. Ruthven made defiant remarks about the Covenanters and the Marquis of Montrose (then with the Covenanters, though in 1641 he became disgusted with their extremism and joined the royalist side as a moderating force) was sent by Leslie under a flag of truce to demand the surrender of the Castle. Ruthven refused, and the Scottish Parliament passed an Act removing him from the governorship. Ruthven remained defiant, and the Covenanters began a siege. Finally, with over two hundred of his garrison dead from wounds or starvation, Ruthven surrendered on 18 September. He was allowed to march out of the Castle with flag flying and drums beating, and he and the seventy survivors of the garrison, under an escort of six hundred Covenanting soldiers to protect them from the fury of the Edinburgh mob, marched to Leith whence they took ship for London.

Further conflict between the Covenanting and royalist forces was inevitable, and on 20 August 1640 the veteran General Alexander Leslie crossed the Tweed with an army of some 20,000 men. After a ridiculously short campaign Leslie defeated a royalist army under Viscount Conway near Newcastle, which the Scots then occupied, as they did soon afterwards all of Northumberland and Durham. The victorious Covenanting army agreed at Ripon to advance no further on condition of receiving subsistence from the territory occupied at the rate of £850 daily. After the English Long Parliament had ratified the terms the following year, they returned to Scotland, pockets bulging. This was the Second Bishops' War.

Charles, who was now in dangerous confrontation with his English Parliament, came to Edinburgh on 14 August 1641 where he presided over his Scottish Parliament at which he had no option but to concede the Covenanters' demands. He had formerly refused to ratify the Acts of the Glasgow Assembly, but now he did so. He continued to resist the demand that officers of State, Privy Councillors and Lords of Session should be chosen by the King 'with the advice and approbation' of Parliament, but after a tough struggle he eventually had to yield on this point as well. On 17 November Charles gave a banquet to the Scottish peers in the Palace of Holyroodhouse and left for England next morning to confront the increasingly recalcitrant Long Parliament. His concessions to the Covenanters, he felt, had at least made sure that the Scots would be on his side. There was already one Scottish group, headed by Montrose, ready if necessary to fight for him.

Scotland was not at first involved when civil war broke out in England between Charles and his opponents in August 1642. But in 1643 the English Parliamentary forces sought help from the Scots in their struggle against the King, and the result was the treaty called the Solemn League and Covenant. On Scottish insistence, this treaty was cast in an uncompromisingly religious form. 'We Noblemen, Barons, Knights, Gentlemen, Citizens, Burgesses, Ministers of the Gospel, and Commons of all sorts in the Kingdoms of Scotland, England and Ireland' solemnly swore to 'endeavour in our several places and callings the preservation of the Reformed Religion in the Church of Scotland, in Doctrine, Worship, Discipline and Government against our common Enemies; The Reformation of Religion in the Kingdoms of England and Ireland, in Doctrine, Worship, Discipline and Government, according to the Word of God, and the example of the best Reformed Churches; And we shall endeavour to bring the Churches of God in the three Kingdoms to the nearest conjunction and uniformity in Religion, Confession of Faith, Form of Church-government, Directory for Worship and Catechezing; . . .' They swore to extirpate 'Popery, Prelacy, Superstition, Heresy, Schism, Prophaneness, and whatsoever shall be found to be contrary to sound Doctrine' and 'to preserve the Rights and Privileges of the Parliaments, and the Liberties of the Kingdoms; And to preserve and defend the Kings Majesty's Person and Authority, in the preservation and defence of the true Religion and Liberties of the Kingdoms'. They also agreed to seek out and bring to public trial 'all such as have been, or shall be Incendiaries, Malignants, or evil instruments, by hindering the Reformation of Religion, dividing the King from his people, or one of the Kingdoms from another, or making any faction, or parties amongst the people contrary to this League and Covenant'. In the eyes of the Scottish General Assembly (largely responsible for its drafting), this was the promise of a joint crusade to establish their own presbyterian system in England and Ireland as well as in Scotland. To the English Parliament it was simply a treaty of alliance between them and the Scots in their struggle against Charles. On 19 January 1644 Leslie, now Earl of Leven, led his army across the Tweed in aid of the English Parliamentary forces. This arm played a significant part in the victory of the Parliamentary over the Royalist forces at Marston Moor on 2 July.

Royalist hopes now centred on Montrose, who conducted a brilliant campaign in Scotland before being decisively defeated at Philipaugh by David Leslie (nephew of Alexander Leslie) in September 1645. In the preceding June the royalist cause in England had been lost at the battle of Naseby. The Scots were now less necessary to the English Parliamentarians, who (especially with the growth of the Independents) became increasingly resentful of the Scottish aim of establishing presbyterianism as the sole religion everywhere and increasingly reluctant to pay the Scottish army its promised expenses. The Scots in their turn became disillusioned with the prospect of establishing presbyterianism in England. Charles, sensing that in these circumstances he would be better off with the Scots, surrendered to the Scottish army at Southwell near Newark on 5 May 1646. The Scots urged Charles to accept the Covenant as a condition of supporting him, but Charles consistently refused. The English Parliament, determined both to get rid of the Scots and to get possession of the King, paid the Scots a proportion of the vast arrears of expenses due them and the Scots delivered the King to the Parliamentary forces.

Edinburgh naturally reflected the tensions provoked by these tremendous national events, with the large majority of its citizens on the side of the Covenanters. But an outbreak of plague in 1645 turned their minds to more immediate problems. This is the last recorded outbreak of bubonic plague in Edinburgh, and it was one of the worst. The High School was closed in April and remained closed for eleven months. The University moved to Linlithgow. Parliament fled to Stirling. Prisoners in the Tolbooth and the Castle were set free because of fear of an uprising among them. All work came to a standstill and it is said that grass grew around the Mercat Cross. The death toll was enormous, especially in Leith where fewer than 1,600 inhabitants survived out of a total of about 4,000. Graveyards were overcrowded, and orders were given that the dead should be buried in pits wherever it was convenient. The sick were huddled in huts on the Burgh Muir or in the King's Park or in the grounds of the ruined convent of St Catherine of Sienna to the south of the city. Punishment for those who concealed plague in their homes was ruthless: parents who concealed the fact that a child of theirs had the plague were searched out by a special official with a white St Andrew's Cross on the front and back of his gown: a guilty father could be hanged at his own door, and a guilty mother taken to be drowned in one of the quarry holes on the Burgh Muir.

National politics moved on. Charles, imprisoned in Carisbrooke Castle, was visited by three Scottish Commissioners with whom he made a secret treaty known as the 'Engagement', to establish Presbyterianism in England for three years and suppress Independents and all other sectaries in return for Scottish arms. On 2 March 1648 the Scottish Parliament met in Edinburgh, its members showing notably diminished support of the Covenant. The result was a decision to invade England in support of the King, in spite of considerable opposition in Edinburgh and elsewhere: supplications against the decision poured into Parliament and the women of Edinburgh stoned both the Provost and Hamilton, now a Duke and leader of the 'Engagers'. Hamilton led a Scottish army into England on 8 June, which in three days' fighting (17 to 19 August) was destroyed by Cromwell at Preston, Wigan and Warrington. Hamilton's defeat (and subsequent trial and execution in England) gave encouragement to the Scottish Anti-Engagers whose leaders now marched on Edinburgh with a force of 6,000 men drawn mostly from the south-west of Scotland: Edinburgh received them with open arms. Cromwell himself arrived in Edinburgh on 5 October and supped with the Earl of Argyll at Moray House in the Canongate (built about 1628 by the Dowager Countess of Home).

The situation changed abruptly with the execution of Charles on 30 January 1649. Scotland, and especially the Covenanters, had had their quarrels with him, but he was after all their lawful King and descendant of a long line of Kings of Scots. Six days after the execution the Scottish Estates (i.e., Parliament, though strictly not a Parliament but a Convention when not summoned by the King) proclaimed his son King of Great Britain, France and Ireland. The young Charles was required to pledge allegiance both to the National Covenant and the Solemn League and Covenant, which, desperate for Scottish aid, he consented to do. So now the Scots, under David Leslie, found themselves in military support of Charles II fighting against the English under Cromwell. Cromwell invaded Scotland, and utterly defeated Leslie's army at Dunbar on 3 September 1650. Cromwell entered Edinburgh on 7 September and, remembering his comfortable entertainment there nearly two years before, took up his residence at Moray House.

Meanwhile Montrose, who had fled abroad after his disastrous defeat at Philiphaugh and returned to Scotland with a small Royalist force in March 1650, had been defeated once more at Carbisdale and this time he was captured and taken to Edinburgh for execution. (He had already been sentenced to death for high treason in his absence in 1644.) His great enemy the Earl of Argyll was at Moray House celebrating the wedding of his eldest son to a daughter of the Earl of Moray when the condemned Montrose, bound on a cart drawn by a horse on which the hangman sat in his livery, passed by on his deliberately humiliating procession along the Canongate and High Street to execution at the Mercat Cross. He had been condemned 'to be carried to Edinburgh Cross, and hanged up on a Gallows Thirty Foot high, for the space of Three Hours, and then to be taken down, and his Head to be cut off upon a Scaffold, and hanged on Edinburgh Tolbooth; his Legs and Arms to be hanged up in other public Towns of the Kingdom, and his Body to be buried at the Place where he was executed'. Argyll's party, watching the fatal procession from a balcony of Moray House, had it stopped for a while so that they could gloat, and Lady Argyll is said to have spat in Montrose's face. But, says a contemporary account, Montrose 'astonished them with his looks, and his resolution confounded them'. He died with composure and dignity, leaving an Edinburgh legend of heroism and nobility in the face of malice and barbarity.

The man who commanded the Town Guard that escorted Montrose to his execution, Major Thomas Weir, was to become an Edinburgh legend of a very different kind. He lived unmarried with his sister in the West Bow, outwardly a strict Presbyterian with a reputation for eloquence in prayer. But on becoming severely ill he proceeded to confess to acts of incest, bestiality and varied wizardry, in partnership with his sister. Both were rushed off to prison, tried and sentenced to death. His sister, who seems to have been even more severely mentally disturbed than the Major, freely and garrulously confessed to the most extraordinary activities connected with the Devil and with her brother's magic staff. She was hanged in the Grassmarket in April 1670, while her brother was strangled and burnt between Edinburgh and Leith near what is now Picardy Place. For over a century after Major Weir's death his house in the West Bow remained uninhabited and people claimed to have seen his apparition at midnight mounted on a black horse without a head. Little James Boswell, who started attending James Mundell's private academy in the West Bow in 1746, listened in fascinated horror to these stories which were perhaps the beginning of his life-long obsession with capital punishment and public executions.

We return to Cromwell in Edinburgh in September 1650. His soldiers dominated the city and did great damage. John Nicoll recorded in his diary: 'The College kirk, the Gray Freir kirk, and that Kirk callit Lady Yesteris kirk [built in 1644 at the corner of the High School Wynd], the Hie Scule, and a great pairt of the College of Edinburgh wer all wasted, thair pulpites, daskis, loftes, saittes, windois, dures, lockes, bandis [hinges] and all uther thair decormentis [ornaments], war all dung doun to the ground by these Inglische sodgeris, and brint to asses.' The larger part of Cromwell's troops were quartered at Holyroodhouse, where on 13 November they accidentally caused a disastrous fire which destroyed much of the building. (Cromwell later rebuilt the destroyed parts, in an inferior style.) On Christmas Eve 1650, after a three months' siege and much correspondence between its Governor, Colonel Walter Dundas of Dundas, and Cromwell, Edinburgh Castle fell to Cromwell. Dundas was entertained to dinner by Cromwell at Moray House on the actual day of the surrender: no malice seems to have been borne by either party.

The political and religious situation was in fact rather peculiar. The stricter Covenanters, who had never regarded Charles II's acceptance of the Covenants as genuine, saw Cromwell's victory at Dunbar as a divinely appointed chastisement, and in a 'Remonstrance' to the Committee of Estates presented on 30 October 1650 rejected Charles as their King until he had given 'convincing evidences to the realitie of his profession'. This drove Argyll to the support of the young King, who was crowned at Scone on 1 January 1651, Argyll himself placing the crown on his head. Before his coronation Charles once more subscribed to the Covenants, so that one group of Covenanters as well as traditional Royalists were now on the King's side. A Scottish army consisting of elements of both of these (but without Argyll) marched into England in July to be decisively defeated by Cromwell at Worcester on 3 September. This 'crowning mercy', as Cromwell called it, put Scotland at his feet. And the people in Scotland whom he naturally preferred to work with were the Remonstrants, those Covenanters who had not accepted Charles.

Cromwell's General Monck pushed north to take Stirling and Dundee and complete the Cromwellian conquest of Scotland. So after Cromwell's expulsion of the Rump Parliament at Westminster in 1653 he and his army were in control of all Britain and by the 'Instrument of Government' he became Lord Protector of a unified Commonwealth of England, Scotland and Ireland. The Ordinance for Union promulgated by Cromwell on 12 April 1654 stated:

> His Highness the Lord Protector of the Commonwealth of England, Scotland and Ireland, &c., taking into consideration how much it might conduce to the glory of God and the peace and welfare of the people in this whole island, that after all those late unhappy wars and differences, the people of Scotland should be united with the people of England into one Commonwealth and under one Government, and finding that in December, 1651, the Parliament then sitting did send Commissioners into Scotland to invite the people of that nation into such a happy Union, who proceeded so far therein that the shires and boroughs of Scotland, by their Deputies convened at Dalkeith, and again at Edinburgh, did accept of the said Union, and assent thereunto [they had in fact no choice]; for the completing and perfecting of which Union, be it ordained, and it is ordained by his Highness the Lord Protector of the Commonwealth of England, Scotland and Ireland, and the Isles of Orkney and Shetland ... that all the people of Scotland ... are and shall be, and are hereby incorporated into, constituted, established, declared and confirmed one Commonwealth with England; and in every Parliament to be held successively for the said Commonwealth, thirty persons shall be called from and serve for Scotland.

The monarchy and parliament of Scotland were abolished; the St Andrew's Cross was incorporated into the Arms of the Commonwealth; and complete free trade was allowed between Scotland and England, with Scottish access to English (now Commonwealth) colonial markets. (This last provision was largely frustrated by the jealousy of English merchants.) Cromwell found men in Scotland to participate in his imposed government: Johnston of Warriston was given his former position of Lord Clerk Register in 1657 and later joined the English Council of State. Imported English judges administered justice impartially (because, it was said, they 'had neither kith nor kin' and so were not influenced by family prejudice). In religion there was (to the dismay of many pious Covenanters) toleration, except for supporters of Popery and Prelacy and those who, 'under the profession of Christ, hold forth and practise licentiousness'. Feudal services and heritable jurisdictions throughout Scotland were abolished. Cromwell's rule was not unenlightened. But it was an imposed rule, a usurpation, and under it Edinburgh was no longer a capital city.

Edinburgh was quiet, even sullen, under the Commonwealth. Two significant developments of the period were the introduction of a regular service of stage coaches between Edinburgh and London, running once in three weeks at a charge of four pounds ten shillings a seat, and the appearance in 1652 of the first newspaper to be printed in Scotland, *A Diurnal of Passages of Affairs*, which was reprinted at Leith from a London publication. John Nicoll noted in his diary three other events. One was the appearance in late 1654 and early 1655 of 'great numbers of that damnable sect of the Quakeris; quha, being deludit by Sathan, drew mony away to thair professioun, both men and women, sindrie of thame walking throw the streities all naikit except thair schirtis, crying, "This is the way, walk ye into it". Another was the heavy taxation imposed on Edinburgh citizens in 1656, "extending to thrie scoir thouwsand pund, swa that the Tounes burdings daylie increst, burding eftir burding; and quahairas thair wes ony deficiency, they war compellit, and sodgeris quarterit upone thame till thair proportiounes wer payit" '. The third was more acceptable:

At this tyme, thair was brocht to this natioun ane heigh great beast, callit ane Drummodrary, quhilk being keipit clos in the Cannongait, nane hade a sight of it without thrie pence the persone, quhilk producit much gayne to the keipar ... Thair wes brocht in with it any lytill baboun, faced lyke unto a naip.

With the death of Cromwell in September 1658 and the quickly proved ineffectiveness of his son Richard, events proceeded rapidly towards the restoration of Charles II to all his lost kingdoms. On 15 November 1659 General Monck summoned representatives from the burghs and shires to Edinburgh and told them he was about to march into England to restore the liberties of the three nations, charging them to keep public order in his absence. In February 1660 a Convention of the Shires and Burghs met in Edinburgh and appointed a joint commission to represent them in any future dealings with England. The Restoration of Charles II, however, made any such representations unnecessary. The Restoration was achieved from England and accepted by Scotland, whose representatives played no part in achieving it, though they welcomed it. On 14 May Charles II was proclaimed at the Mercat Cross of Edinburgh 'with all solempniteis requisite, by ringing of bellis, setting out of bailfyres, sounding of trumpetis, roring of cannounes, touking of drumes, dancing about the fyres, and using all uther takins of joy for the advancement and preference of thair native King to his croun and native inheritance'.

This report by John Nicoll represents a genuine surge of royalism in Edinburgh at the end of the Cromwellian Commonwealth. Yet by common consent the Commonwealth had meant for Scotland a time of peace, order and justice, if not of prosperity or any conspicuous public happiness. The Restoration opened a more turbulent and in many respects a more distressing chaper in Edinburgh's history.

CHAPTER 4

The Restoration and After

We are fortunate in having a splendidly detailed impression of
Edinburgh in the mid-seventeenth century in the bird's eye view
made by James Gordon of Rothiemay, in 1647. James Gordon,
minister of Rothiemay, received five hundred merks from the Town
Council for drawing this view, which was engraved by Jacobus
de Wit at Amsterdam on a large scale: it is a view from the south,
and it measures forty-one and a quarter inches long by sixteen
inches broad. We see with great clarity the houses and wynds
on either side of the broad High Street, the Castle, the Tolbooth,
St Giles', the Tron Kirk and the Netherbow Port. We see Parliament
House immediately to the south of St Giles and Greyfriars' Kirk and
graveyard standing by itself to the south-west, outside the Flodden
Wall. That wall itself is clearly shown and we can trace its course
with great precision. Parallel to the High Street and south of it, considerably narrower, we see the Cowgate, broadening out into the
Grassmarket (marked as 'Horse market street') on the west. South-
west of Greyfriars', surrounded by gardens, Heriot's Hospital stands
in lonely dignity. Gardens, with the ornamental patterns of their
lay-out clearly shown, are abundant south of the Flodden Wall, and
are numerous also immediately north of it, surrounding 'The colledg'
which is seen precisely drawn just behind the wall on the north.
More surprising are the massive areas of ornamental gardens on
either side of the Canongate. Although the Canongate is seen as
flanked by houses, these do not extend anything like as far back as
they do from the High Street, and immediately behind them lie
these large garden tracts, 'pleasances' belonging for the most to the
houses of the nobility who reside there. Indeed, Gordon's view shows
the Canongate as very much a garden city, clearly divided from
Edinburgh proper by St Mary's Wynd and its northern extension
Leith Wynd, which form a continuous street running from the
'Suburbs of Plaisance' in the south past the Netherbow Port to
Trinity Hospital and St Paul's Work in the north. At the eastern end
of the view we see 'The palace of holy-rood-house with the south and
north gardens' and, immediately to the right of it, 'The Abbey kirk
with the kirkyard'. At the western end of the Grassmarket, below

the Castle, we see the West Port and beyond it an attractive looking westward-running group of houses and gardens that Gordon calls 'the West port suburbs'. (The name 'Pleasance', incidentally, given to the district south of St Mary's Wynd, has nothing to do with 'pleasant' but derives from St Mary of Placentia whose convent stood just south of Cowgate Port: hence also 'St Mary's Wynd'.)

St Mary's Wynd was the main road south. Gordon's map shows it flanked by houses at its more southern part (the Pleasance) – its western flank on its more northerly part was the Flodden Wall. Few of these houses survived Cromwell's invasion of Scotland in 1650, for, as John Nicoll reported in his diary, 'the toun demolished the haill houssis in St. Marie Wynd, that the enymie sould haif no schelter thair, bot that thai mycht haif frie pas to thair cannoun, quhilk thai haid montit upone the Neddir Bow'. For all the devastation wrought by Cromwell's troops, and for all the high taxation he imposed to maintain his army and government, the Town Council eventually acquiesced in his rule to the point of ordering a large block of stone for the purpose of erecting a huge statue to him in Parliament Close. Cromwell's death, however, occurred just after the block had been landed at Leith, and enthusiasm for the statue evaporated immediately. When Charles II was proclaimed in May 1660 amid scenes of great enthusiasm the Town Council obviously had other ideas: they eventually erected an equestrian statue of Charles on the site earlier intended for Cromwell. We have already quoted Nicoll's description of the lively scene at the Mercat Cross on 14 May, when the King was proclaimed. An abundance of wine flowed at the Cross, 'the magistrates and counsell of the toun being present, drinking to the Kinges helth, and breking numberis of glasses'. This was a very different scene from that which had occurred at the Mercat Cross on 30 September 1652 when, as again Nicoll recorded, 'two Englisches, for drinking the Kingis helth, war takin and bund to the gallous at Edinburgh Croce, quhair ather of thame resavit threttie nyne quhipes upone their naiked bakes and shoulderis, thairaftir their luggis wer naillit to the gallous. The ane haid his lug cuttit from the ruitt with a resour; the uther being also naillit to the gibbet, haid his mouth skobit [kept open by the insertion of two crossed sticks], and his tong being drawn out the full length, was bund togidder betuix twa stickes hard togidder with ane skainzie threid [pack thread] the space of half ane hour or thairby.'

David Buchanan, the first (and inaccurate) editor of John Knox's *Historie of the Reformatioun in Scotland*, wrote in Latin a descrip-

tion of Edinburgh intended to accompany Gordon of Rothiemay's
bird's-eye view, but it remained in manuscript until 1836. Buchanan
describes the growth of the city down the slope from the Castle, and
continues (in Hume Brown's translation):

> If we include the suburbs of the canons [the Canongate], either
> side of the slope from summit to base is lined with lofty buildings,
> a long line of them stretching in a spacious street along the middle
> of the ridge from one extremity to the other. The buildings are
> separated from each other by streets and closes, almost all of
> which are narrow. The houses on the opposite side of the street,
> therefore, are so close that there is hardly space for fresh air, and
> for this reason they are mutually harmful. I am not sure that you
> will find anywhere so many dwellings in so small space as in this
> city of ours ... On the south side of the Canongate, not far from
> the public cross [the Canongate Cross, not the Mercat Cross of
> Edinburgh: it stood nearly opposite the Canongate Tolbooth,
> erected in the reign of James VI], are the house and gardens of the
> Earl of Moray, of such elegance, and cultivated with such dili-
> gence, that they easily challenge comparison with the gardens of
> warmer climates, and almost of England itself. And here you may
> see how much human skill and industry avail in making up for the
> defects of nature herself. Scarcely would one believe that in
> severe climates such amenity could be given to gardens.

For over a century there was no significant change in the shape of
Edinburgh as shown in Gordon of Rothiemay's plan, though there
was considerable rebuilding on existing sites. The last quarter of the
seventeenth century was an important period of rebuilding: many
of the mediaeval tenements or 'lands' were rebuilt, and the timber-
fronted and thatched houses with their wooden balconies and stairs
that came out on to the High Street (as Dunbar had complained)
were largely removed. This period also saw the introduction of a
water supply into Edinburgh. In 1674 the Town Council agreed to
pay a German engineer called Peter Bruschi the sum of £2,950 for
laying a three-inch lead pipe with water from Comiston, about four
miles to the west of the city, to supply a reservoir to be made on the
Castle Hill. From the reservoir it was conveyed by pipes to five public wells, to which five more were soon added. Other developments in
this period included the building of a meal market in the Cowgate,
an Exchange for Merchants in Parliament Close, and a flesh market
and slaughter house beside the North Lock. There was also a stricter

enforcement of street-cleaning and the Town Council undertook the public lighting of streets.

Meanwhile, Edinburgh was much involved with public events after the Restoration, which the city, like the rest of Scotland, seems to have genuinely welcomed. Had not Charles II after all signed both Covenants? The 'Resolutions' at least were optimistic on these grounds, even though the other group in the Church, the 'Protesters' (who were in the minority), trusted Charles no more than they had ever done. Among the people in general there was relief at the end of the Cromwellian usurpation and an expectation of happier times. The Town Council sent Charles £1,000 and in return Charles gave them the power to levy ⅔d. on a pint of ale and 2d. on a pint of wine consumed within the city. As Hugo Arnot, Edinburgh's eighteenth century historian, remarked in recording this, 'it has always been equally unfortunate for its inhabitants, whether the magistrates testified their loyalty or sedition.'

The change in political atmosphere was vividly illustrated by the ceremonial rehabilitation of the executed Marquis of Montrose in January 1661. His dismembered body was re-assembled and the coffin containing it was deposited in the Abbey Church of Holyrood after a solemn procession with music and the firing of guns. The following May the remains were brought from the Abbey in another solemn procession and deposited in a vault in the south-east side of St Giles'. Citizens in armour, with banners displayed, lined the street from the Palace of Holyrood to St Giles'; twenty-six boys clad in deep mourning bore the Marquis's arms, and they were followed by the magistrates and all the members of Parliament, also dressed in mourning. John Nicoll, who described the ceremony, saw this period as auguring well for Scotland's future:

At this tyme [1661], our gentrie of Scotland did luik with such gallant and joyfull countenances, as gif thai haid bene the sones of princes; the beastes also of the feild, the numberis of the fisches of the sea, and flowers of the feild, did manifest Godis goodnes towardis this kingdome; and it wes the joy of this natioun to behold the flower of this kingdome, quhich for sa mony yeiris hath bene overcloudit, and now to sie thame upone brave horses, pransing in thair accustomat places, in telting, ryneing of races, and suchlyke.

For those with less appreciation of aristocratic sports, however, the Restoration soon brought disappointment and frustration. By nominating the members of the Scottish Privy Council before a meeting of Parliament (which constitutionally had a claim to be consulted) Charles gave notice of his intention of going his own way, and he soon made it clear that he had no intention whatever of adhering to the Covenants he had signed so long ago but would impose an episcopalian form of church government and make no compromise with the Covenanters. The fact is that the Restoration had been achieved on English initiative and the Scots had accepted it unconditionally, leaving themselves entirely at Charles's mercy. As in England, Charles's main objectives were to go as far in achieving absolute rule as he could without being sent 'on his travels again' and to provide a religious climate hospitable to Roman Catholics. He ruled Scotland by Commissioners whose policies reflected those of his English ministers.

The Parliament that met at Edinburgh on 1 January 1661, with the Earl of Middleton, the Commissioner, representing the King, restored the Lords of the Articles (who as royal nominees effectively limited the independence of Parliament and asserted royal influence), restored to the King the sole power of appointing the chief officers of state and the Lords of Session and of deciding when to summon Parliament, and wiped out all legislation since the Parliament of 1633. It also passed an Act leaving the religious settlement to the King's discretion, and the following year Charles imposed on Scotland the episcopal system that had been abolished in 1638. At the same time the sub-structure of presbyterian church government, through kirk session, presbytery and synod, was allowed to continue, with the bishops working with the synods: the General Assembly, however, the apex of this structure, was not allowed. This might have produced a workable compromise, but the Privy Council's insistence that all ministers appointed since 1649 should obtain formal re-appointment by a bishop produced a walk-out of 270 ministers throughout Scotland and a consequent hardening of attitudes on both sides. Middleton was now succeeded as Commissioner by the drunken and semi-literate Earl of Rothes, who in turn was succeeded by the Duke of Lauderdale, who virtually ruled Scotland for Charles from 1667 until 1680. Edinburgh saw vividly the consequences of the confrontation between royal policy and Covenanting principle that developed under these Commissioners.

One significant portent of this confrontation was the execution of the Marquis of Argyll at Edinburgh on 24 May 1661. Though it was

Argyll who had crowned Charles at Scone in 1651 he was made an exception to the Act of Oblivion passed to allow exemption from punishment to those who had been in rebellion against Charles I and, on the evidence of those who had been even more in favour of Cromwell's rule than Argyll had been, tried and condemned to death for his compliance with Cromwell's government. As he lay imprisoned in Edinburgh Castle awaiting his execution he heard the trumpets sounding and the guns roaring for the ceremonial rehabilitation and re-burial of his old enemy Montrose. 'I could die as a Roman,' he said as he was being led to the scaffold, 'but choose rather to die as a Christian.' He was executed at the Mercat Cross and his head was later fixed above the Tolbooth.

The 'outed' ministers formed a nucleus of disaffected Covenanters who came more and more into conflict with the Government. In 1662 the Scottish Parliament passed Acts against the Covenants ('unlawfull oaths ... taken by and imposed upon the subjects of this kingdome against the fundamentall lawes and liberties of the same') and against 'unlawfull meitings and conventicles' that 'may tend to the prejudice of the publick worship of God in the Churches'. Obstinate Covenanters were brought to Edinburgh for trial and punishment. In July 1663 the elderly Johnston of Warriston, who had supported Cromwell's Government and had fled abroad at the Restoration, was arrested in Rouen and brought back to Edinburgh for trial, even though, in the words of his nephew Gilbert Burnet, 'he was so disordered both in body and mind, that it was a reproach to a government to proceed against him'. He was hanged in Edinburgh in the Grassmarket on 22 July, having twice read a speech on the scaffold in which, says Burnet, 'he justified all the proceedings in the covenant, and asserted his own sincerity; but condemned his joining with Cromwell and the sectaries, though even in that his intentions had been sincere for the good of his country and the security of religion'. Other less distinguished persons suffered a variety of punishments for attending conventicles and failure to attend the parish kirk (the latter punishable by a fine in accordance with an Act passed in 1663). Torture and imprisonment were also commonly inflicted on the more recalcitrant Covenanters, many of whom regarded any compromise with Government on the question of religion as wicked Erastianism and a betrayal of the Covenants. The revival in 1664 of the Court of High Commission, originally set up by James VI to enforce his ecclesiastical views, provided a further weapon for the persecution – as they deemed it – of obstinate Covenanters, but its measures of petty oppression only increased their obstinacy while at the same time arousing a general repugnance among law-abiding citizens, and it was abolished within two years.

The Covenanting opposition was especially strong in Fife and in Galloway, but Edinburgh had a large number of supporters, who watched with horror and indignation what they considered to be the diabolical persecution of saintly men for their religious views. In 1666 a group of Covenanting rebels from the south-west, ill-armed peasants for the most part and numbering no more than 3,000, marched on Edinburgh, but they were crushed by General Thomas Dalyell (who had fought for the Czar of Russia against the Poles and Turks) at Rullion Green in the Pentland Hills before they reached the city. Nevertheless the Government was badly frightened, and showed their fright by their savage treatment of the seventy prisoners brought to Edinburgh for trial. Sir John Nisbet, the Lord Advocate, prosecuted for the Crown. Ten of the leaders were prosecuted first, and their argument that they had surrendered to quarter was not accepted by the prosecution, who argued that they had been taken in active rebellion and the quarter granted applied only to the moment of surrender. They were duly hanged in the Grassmarket, and were followed by five others a week later. Other survivors of what became known as the Pentland Rising were subjected to torture to make them reveal the true nature of what was believed to have been a conspiracy against the Government and to recant. A young man called Hugh M'Kail stood up to torture in a mood of high religious exaltation, and when he went to the scaffold the sympathy of the Edinburgh crowd was with him.

The brutal murder of Archbishop Sharp of St Andrews in 1679 by a group of fanatical Covenanters exacerbated the conflict, with a fiercer hunting down of the intransigent Covenanters on the Government side and a stronger conviction that they were persecuted saints on the part of the Covenanters. The Government sent James Graham of Claverhouse to enforce the law against the Covenanters, and he hunted down attenders at open-air conventicles with zeal. The Covenanting army was finally destroyed on 1 June 1679 at Bothwell Brig by a royal army with troops from England under the command of the Duke of Monmouth, and this was the end of any possibility of power for the Covenanters. Once again Edinburgh witnessed the spectacle of Government reprisals: two ministers captured at Bothwell Brig, named John King and John Kidd, were hanged at the Mercat Cross and a thousand other prisoners, bound two by two, were taken to Edinburgh and confined under wretched conditions in Greyfriars churchyard, most of them for nearly five months. Those who refused to sign a bond declaring that they would not again rise against the Government – more than two hundred and fifty – were sent off to the Barbados in a ship from Leith; but the ship split on a rock off the Orkney Islands in a storm, and the prisoners, who had been secured under hatches, went down with it.

In 1680 and again in 1681 Charles II sent his brother James, Duke of York to Edinburgh as Royal Commissioner. He settled at the Palace of Holyroodhouse with his second wife Mary of Modena and his daughter Anne and set out to make himself agreeable. While he gave some scandal to the orthodox by holding masked balls and the presentation of theatrical performances, he pleased others by playing tennis and being 'frequently seen in a party of golf on the Links at Leith with some of the nobility and gentry'. Many years later William Tytler of Woodhouselee, who was not born until 1711, recalled that in his youth he had 'often conversed with an old man named Andrew Dickson, a golf-club maker, who said that when a boy he used to carry the Duke's clubs, and to run before him and announce where the balls fell'. There was a great deal of royal celebration. Lord Fountainhall recorded some of it : 'Novembris 15, 1681, being the Quean of Britain's birth-day, it was keeped by our Court at Holyruid house with great solemnitie, such as bonfyres, shooting of canons, and the acting of a comedy called *Mithradates, King of Pontus*, before ther Royall Hynesses, &c., wheirin Lady Anne, the Duke's daughter, and the ladies of honour ware the onlie actors.'

But James had more serious objectives in view. On 28 July 1681 he opened a Parliament, the first that had met for nine years, which, at his insistence, passed the Act of Succession, declaring that no difference in religion could 'alter or divert the right of succession and lineal descent of the Crown'. (James was a Roman Catholic, and was anxious to ensure his succession to his brother Charles, to whom he was heir presumptive.) It also passed an Act imposing a tortuously self-contradictory test oath on all who held office in central or local government, all members of Parliament, and all bishops, ministers and teachers. The oath simultaneously renounced Popery and subscribed to the long outdated Confession of Faith of 1560, while promising to 'bear faith and true allegiance to the Kings Majestie his heirs and laufull successors' and to 'assist and defend all rights, jurisdictions, prerogatives, privileges, preheminencies and authorities belonging to the Kingis Majestie his heirs and laufull successors'. It also renounced both Covenants. The Earl of Argyll, son of the executed Marquis, said that he would subscribe to the oath, so far as it was 'consistent with itself'. This qualification was regarded by James (who had a deep suspicion of Argyll) as treasonable and he had Argyll brought to trial and condemned to death. Argyll's step-daughter, in a picturesque incident, managed to smuggle him in disguise out of Edinburgh Castle, where he was imprisoned awaiting execution, and he escaped to Holland. He did not however finally escape his father's fate, for he returned to Scotland to support Mon-mouth's rebellion against James in 1685, and was captured and executed without further trial on 30 June. He made an address to the Edinburgh crowd before laying his head on the Edinburgh variety of guillotine known as the 'maiden'. His severed head was placed on the Tolbooth gable.

The prosecution of Covenanters and others accused of plotting against the Government was conducted in Edinburgh by the Lord Advocate, Sir George Mackenzie of Rosenhaugh, who boasted in 1680 that he never lost a case for the King. He is execrated in Covenanting history as 'the Bluidy Mackenzie', but he was a man of culture and legal scholarship whose *Discourse upon the Laws and Customs of Scotland in Matters Criminal*, published in 1674 – two years after the creation in Edinburgh of the Court of Justiciary as a central criminal court – remained a standard work for 130 years. Mackenzie also wrote *Aretina*, a romance, and other works of law as well as books on ethics and political philosophy. His most signifi-cant contribution to Edinburgh and to the nation was his founding of the Advocates' Library (now the National Library of Scotland) to which he left his own collection of 1,500 books. Mackenzie brought his logical legal mind to bear on the prejudice and superstition sur-rounding the prosecution of people accused of practising witchcraft, and must get some credit for the decline of this appalling practice.

In spite of religious and political conflicts, this was the period in which Edinburgh began to assert itself as the home of a powerful and well organized legal fraternity who were to dominate the city's social and intellectual life in the next century. Though some of the credit for this goes to Mackenzie, more must go to James Dal-rymple, later first Viscount Stair, who in 1681 published his *Institu-tions of the Law of Scotland*, known to generations of students of Scots law as 'Stair's Institutes', which effectively erected Scots law into a coherent system with an underlying philosophy. Stair became Lord President of the Court of Session in 1671, but resigned in 1681 rather than take the Test Oath. He went to Holland, returning to Britain with William of Orange to be re-appointed Lord President.

This period also marked the emergence of Edinburgh as a centre of medical studies. Sir Robert Sibbald, physician and botanist, was born in Edinburgh in 1641 and studied medicine at Leyden. He returned to Scotland in 1662 and devoted himself mainly to botany. Together with Dr Andrew Balfour, a St Andrews physician who moved to Edinburgh in 1670, he founded the Physic Garden in 1667 for which the magistrates gave him part of the garden of Trinity Hospital. This eventually became the Royal Botanic Gardens. Its early success was in part due to the supervision of the botanist James Sutherland who was Sibbald's assistant and head gardener at the Physic Garden before his appointment as the University's first Professor of Botany. In 1681 Sibbald, with Balfour and others, founded the Royal College of Physicians of Edinburgh, of which he became President three years later : in 1685 he became first Professor of Medicine at Edinburgh University. Balfour was the first in Scotland to introduce the dissection of the human body as part of medical education, and he first projected the great hospital that became the Royal Infirmary. He was created a baronet by Charles II and bequeathed his museum to the University on his death in 1694. It was twenty-five years after this, in 1719, that the brilliant young anatomist Alexander Monro showed what could be done with the legacy of Sibbald and Balfour : he was only twenty-one when he was appointed Professor of Anatomy at Edinburgh in that year, to attain worldwide fame as a teacher and establish Edinburgh University as a great world medical centre. His son and then his grandson successively held the Chair of Anatomy after him.

The year of the founding of the Physic Garden was also the year in which Charles II ordered that the chief magistrate of Edinburgh should be styled 'Lord Provost', rather than simply 'Provost', and the title has been in use ever since. (Previously, the Provost had occasionally been styled 'Lord Provost', but as a rule only when, as sometimes happened, he was a peer anyway.) Charles II also showed his esteem for Edinburgh by his concern for the improvement of the Palace of Holyroodhouse, which had been rebuilt, but hastily and inadequately, on Cromwell's orders after his soldiers had destroyed much of it. 'Wee doe hereby order you to cause that parte thereof which was built by the usurper, and doth darken the court, to be taken down,' ran the Royal Warrant, and the royal architect, Sir William Bruce of Balcaskie and Kinross, followed his instructions in re-building with, it is said, the Château of Chantilly in mind. Work began in 1671 and was completed in 1679.

Charles II died in 1685 and was succeeded by his brother James VII. James's first Scottish Parliament met in Edinburgh on 23 April 1685, with William, Duke of Queensbury as Royal Commissioner. James was readily granted the supplies he asked for, and at first it looked as though he would have no trouble in achieving his ends. The rising against him of Monmouth in England and Argyll in Scotland were easily put down and, as we have seen, Argyll was captured and executed. James Renwick, the last fanatical organizer of conventicles and a bitter opponent of royal claims, was executed in the Grassmarket on 17 February 1688. In pursuit of his aim of achieving complete toleration for Roman Catholics, James issued what were called Letters of Indulgence which had logically to be extended to Protestant dissenters as well, provided their doctrines did not threaten the state, which ruled out Covenanters. But he issued these Letters of Indulgence not by an Act of Parliament but through the Privy Council in virtue of the Royal Prerogative. This claim to a Royal Prerogative was known in England but had no precedent in Scotland, and James's use of it increased the suspicion that he was bent on establishing in Scotland two evils most hated by Scottish Protestants – Roman Catholic ecclestiastical rule and absolute power for himself or, in the terms of the day, Popery and Arbitrary Power. There was certainly some justification for the suspicion that dissenters on what might be called the Protestant Left were not likely to reap as much benefit from the Letters of Indulgence as those of the Catholic Right. An Act against conventicles provided that 'all such as shall hereafter preach at such fanatical houses or field conventicles, as also such as shall be present as hearers at field conventicles, shall be punished by death and confiscation of goods'.

Edinburgh citizens watched with dismay as James fitted out the old Abbey church at Holyrood as a Roman Catholic Chapel Royal. That church had long been used as the parish church of the Canongate, but now the King wanted it for other purposes – ostensibly, as he stated to the public, as a Chapel for the Order of the Knights of the Thistle, an order which he had recently revived. Citizens of the Canongate were allowed the use of Lady Yester's church, quite some distance away, on the other side of the Flodden Wall near the High School, while provision was made for building a new Canongate Church with the money left to the disposal of the Crown by an Edinburgh merchant called Thomas Moodie. This was begun in

1688 and is still 'the Kirk in the Canongate'.

A group of apprentices and others started a riot in 1686 on seeing officers of state returning from the celebration of Mass. A baker who was involved was arrested, tried before the Privy Council, and sentenced to be publicly whipped through the Canongate. But he was rescued by the crowd, who attacked the executioner (who was to do the whipping) and kept the town in a tumult all night. The military were eventually called in and fired on the rioters, killing three. Two others were arrested, of whom one was hanged and the other shot. The Town Council complied meekly with all royal demands for the punishment of offenders.

But James's time as King was almost up. The birth of a Prince of Wales to his Catholic wife Mary of Modena in June 1688 convinced England that James's policy of Roman Catholic absolutism would be continued after his death, and provoked what became known as the Glorious Revolution. James fled to France with his baby son. Between the landing of William of Orange at Torbay on 5 November 1688 and James's flight to France in December, Edinburgh was in a state of great excitement. On 10 December a mob attacked Holyrood, bent on destroying all vestiges of Popery. They wrecked James's private chapel and burned its contents and then broke into the Chapel Royal, tore down the woodwork, which they carried to the Mercat Cross where they burned it, and even broke open the royal burial vaults exposing the remains of long dead kings and princes. The mob also drove James's Chancellor the Earl of Perth from Edinburgh and on Christmas Day, infuriated by the news that James had landed in Ireland and the false rumour that a large Irish army had landed in Scotland, anti-Catholic rioters went into action again. Students marched with bands playing to the Mercat Cross, where they burned an effigy of the Pope.

The English Parliament proclaimed William and Mary joint sovereigns of England in February 1689. In Edinburgh a Convention of the Estates (not a Parliament, since it had not been summoned by a king) met to decide what to do about Scotland's throne. There were some supporters of the absent James (Jacobites) as well as a strong Williamite party. A Williamite President, the Duke of Hamilton, was chosen by a small majority. John Graham of Claverhouse, now Viscount Dundee, supported James and rode out of Edinburgh in disgust with a group of sixty horses to organize a Jacobite army in the Highlands. On 11 April 1689 the Convention, freed from pressure by Claverhouse and his Jacobite force, proclaimed that James VII

had forfeited the crown of Scotland ('being a profest Papist' and
having 'by advice of Evil and Wicked Councellors invaded the Fundamental Constitution of the Kingdom, and altered it from a Legal,
limited Monarchy, to an Arbitrair and Despotick Power') and resolved 'that William and Mary, King and Queen of England, France
and Ireland, Be, and Be Declared King and Queen of Scotland'.
They asserted their nation's 'ancient Rights and Liberties' in a
'Claim of Right', which was read over to William and Mary by Scottish representatives who went south for the purpose, and William (on
behalf of both Mary and himself) took an oath to maintain in Scotland the true religion of Christ and preserve all the rights and
privileges of the Crown of Scotland. Edinburgh Town Council, who
had been so pliant before James's demands, and had only recently
declared that they would 'stand by his sacred person upon all occasions' and prayed for 'the continuance of his princely goodness and
care', now fell over themselves in offering their services to King
William.

CHAPTER 5

The Road to Union

While the estates of the Kingdom of Scotland were meeting in Edinburgh in the spring and summer of 1689, becoming a regular Parliament in June, after the acceptance by William of their offer of the Crown, the Castle was being held for the departed King James by the first Duke of Gordon, who had been appointed Governor of the Castle by James in 1686. On 14 March, when the Convention of Estates first met, the Earls of Lothian and Tweeddale, acting on a decision of the Convention, went to the Castle and demanded that the Duke surrender it, with complete exoneration for himself and his garrison 'as to all bygones'. The Duke of Gordon sent a message back to the Estates offering to comply with their order if they met certain conditions, which included security and compensation for the garrison. This was the beginning of a series of loftily courteous exchanges between Gordon and the Estates, in which conditions were met with counter-conditions and proposals matched with counter-proposals. On 18 March, just as these exchanges were getting under way, Viscount Dundee, on his way out of Edinburgh, paid a secret visit to Gordon at the western postern gate of the Castle, climbing up the steep Castle rock to get there. He is said to have tried to persuade him to leave the Castle in charge of his second-in-command and join Dundee's Jacobite clans in the north, but Gordon refused to leave and Dundee went north without him, to meet his death at the battle of Killiecrankie on 27 July. Gordon promised Dundee to hold out for twenty days, at the end of which time Dundee hoped to be able to come to his relief with an army.

On the same day that Dundee left Edinburgh a large body of Cameronians, those extreme Covenanters from the south-west, were brought in under the Earl of Leven to lay siege to the Castle; these were relieved on 25 March by three regiments from England brought by Major-General Hugh Mackay of Scourie. Desultory firing went on from both sides, which did not prevent the continued exchange of letters and proposals. The siege became a blockade, with the object of starving out the small and hard-pressed garrison. On 11 June Gordon began negotiations for surrender, by asking for the names of 'the persons with whom his Grace might safely treat and who could give security for performances of articles'. The Duke of Hamilton was named, and the next day negotiations for a treaty began. On the 13th it was agreed that the Castle be delivered up upon a number of agreed articles. 'The Duke of Gordon hath so much respect to all the princes of K. James the Sixth's line, as not to make conditions with any of them for his own particular interest; so he renders himself entirely on King William's discretion.' But conditions were proposed and agreed for the Lieutenant Governor and all the garrison to 'have their lives, liberties, and fortunes secured'; for the garrison to 'march out with their swords and baggage belonging properly to themselves'; and for an amnesty for any residents of Edinburgh who had kept up a secret correspondence with the Castle during the siege. The surrender was effected on the 14th. The garrison (as we are told by one of them, who kept a detailed diary of the siege) 'marched out, but not in a body, that they might be the less noticed; however, some of them were very ill treated by the rabble'. Hamilton entertained Gordon to dinner and allowed him his freedom provided he did not leave Edinburgh without permission. King William, however, demanded that he be kept a close prisoner. Later Gordon made submission to William in London, but he afterwards served several terms of imprisonment on suspicion of Jacobite loyalties.

The Parliament sitting in Edinburgh in the summer of 1689 had more important things to do than worry about the terms of Gordon's surrender of the Castle. After passing Acts 'declaring the Meeting of Estates to be a Parliament' and recognizing the royal authority of William and Mary, they went on to abolish Prelacy in an Act calling it 'a great and insupportable Grievance to this Nation'. In the second session of this Parliament, which began on 25 April 1690, all 'outed' Presbyterian ministers were restored, Presbyterian church government was re-established, and the old Knoxian Confession of Faith re-affirmed (all thirty-three chapters of it, including the remarkable chapter III, 'Of Gods eternal Decrees', which affirms that God, 'according to his eternal and immutable Purpose, and the secret Counsel and good Pleasure of his Will' has elected and predestined some for eternal life 'without any Foresight of Faith, or good Words, or Perseverance in either of them, . . . Neither are any other redeemed by Christ, effectually Called, Justified, Adopted, Sanctified and Saved, but the Elect only'). A great deal of the intellectual life of Edinburgh in the next century was concerned with modifying, or getting round, or. re-interpreting, or simply ignoring or actually denying the implications of the bleak Calvinist theology of this document.

The same Parliament abolished the Lords of the Articles (which they had previously declared to be 'a great grievance to the nation' since 'there ought to be no committees of parliament but such as are freely chosen by the estates to prepare motions and overtures that are first made in the house'). This Act gave new vigour and independence to the Scottish Parliament, so that paradoxically in the years of great debate before it finally voted itself out of existence in the Union of 1707 it showed a vitality it had never showed when its existence was more assured. It was in this session, too, that Parliament passed an 'Act anent Murthering of Children' which provided that, if a mother has concealed the fact of her pregnancy, and has not summoned assistance at her child's birth, in the event of the child being found dead or missing 'the Mother shall be holden and reputed the Murtherer of her own Child'. This was the law under which Effie Deans was condemned in Scott's *Heart of Midlothian*.

These acts were of course all passed in the name of 'Our Sovereign Lord and Lady, the King and Queen's Majesties' (for William and Mary reigned jointly until Mary's death in 1694) and touched with the sceptre on their behalf by their representative, the High Commissioner. But in fact William had little interest in Scottish affairs, except to see that the Jacobites were kept down, that he got his taxes, and that he had Scottish support in what was virtually his private war against France. He never visited his Scottish capital, nor indeed did any monarch after James VII visit Scotland until Sir Walter Scott arranged George IV's visit in 1822. He expressed the wish for a union of both kingdoms, and meanwhile governed Scotland through a Secretary of State whose job was to manage Parliament, a job that became more difficult with the abolition of the Lords of the Articles. The Highlands were regarded as representing a Jacobite threat, and any policy that was seen as helping to eliminate this threat was welcomed: hence William's acquiescence in the notorious Massacre of Glencoe in 1692, planned by his Secretary for Scotland Sir John Dalrymple and executed by Captain Robert Campbell of Glenlyon who had his own reasons for wanting revenge on the Macdonalds, the victims of the massacre.

Edinburgh, which had no great love for Highlanders, was nevertheless indignant about Glencoe: Parliament held an inquiry which blamed Dalrymple among others, but nobody was punished. 1695, the year in which the commission of inquiry into the massacre was concluded, saw the publication by Parliament of 'the Quota of Supply, payable Monthly by the several Burghs of the Kingdom'. This showed the City of Edinburgh paying £3,880 Scots monthly, compared with £1,800 for Glasgow, £726 for Aberdeen and £556 for Dundee. So Edinburgh was clearly the wealthiest burgh in the kingdom. But Scottish foreign trade was severely hampered by the English Navigation Acts of 1660 and 1663, which excluded Scottish merchants from trading with the English Colonies. In spite of this, Glasgow merchants found ways of trading between the Clyde and America, and east coast ports, chief of which was Leith, were being increasingly challenged from the west. It was in an attempt to improve Scotland's foreign trade and break the monopoly of the East India Company that led to the Scottish Parliament's passing in 1695 an 'Act for a Company Trading to Africa and the Indies'.

The impulse that prompted this Act began with an Edinburgh merchant, Bailie Robert Blackwood, whose 'Accompt of Money Spent in Procuring the Act of Parlement for the Afrecane Tread' shows how he spent money to further the Act's progress. Another Edinburgh merchant, James Balfour, took over from Blackwood : his records show that he paid £55 to the Lord Advocate, Sir James Stewart, for drafting the Act and laid out another £24 for having 'several dubells' of it made. When the draft of the Act came before the parliamentary Committee of Trade for preliminary consideration on 10 June 1695 there was great excitement in Edinburgh. On 14 June, after the Act had been read in Parliament and officially referred ·to the Committee of Trade, the Provost, Bailies and a number of merchants attended a meeting in William Ross's tavern to discuss ways of promoting the Act, and on the same day the Committee of Merchants met in the Ship Tavern. Further meetings followed, and on 26 June a final triumphant evening at Michael's celebrated the touching of the Act with the sceptre.

The interests of the Edinburgh merchants in the formation of this new company was chiefly with the African side : they were anxious to break the East India Company's monopoly by establishing a base in Scotland for trade to the east and to Africa. Glasgow merchants were more concerned with the West Indies and America. But both groups viewed the Act with the highest expectations. It gave the new company many privileges, including a permanent monopoly in Scotland of trade with Asia and Africa. There were many in England too who were anxious to break the East India Company's monopoly and they quickly agreed to subscribe the £300,000 which was the amount allotted to England of the £600,000 fixed as the amount of share capital required. But they reckoned without the power of the English vested interests, notably the East India Company. These effectively put pressure on the King, the English Parliament, and English merchants at home and abroad to prevent the Scots from raising capital either in England or abroad. What had begun as a promising Anglo-Scottish venture was now reduced to being a purely Scottish venture desperately short of capital.

In anger and pride the Scots decided to go it alone, and managed to raise £400,000, a remarkable sum for such a small and relatively poor country. Shut off by English manoeuvring from trading in Africa, India and America, the Company of Scotland trading to Africa and the Indies decided (on the advice of the Scots-born William Paterson, founder of the Bank of England) to found a trading colony on the Isthmus of Darien, which connects North and South America and separates the Caribbean Sea from the Pacific Ocean. This was seen as a natural centre of world trade, and Paterson's vision of an expanding Scottish community thriving there and producing enormous wealth for Scotland was eagerly accepted throughout the country.

On 14 July 1689 the ships for the first Darien expedition arrived at Leith Roads from Burntisland where they had been fitting out. They were three large vessels, the *St Andrew*, the *Unicorn* and the *Caledonia*, with two tenders, the *Endeavour* and the *Dolphin*. Edinburgh citizens swarmed down to Leith to see the ships that carried the economic hopes of the nation. They set sail, amid scenes of great enthusiasm, on 18 July and reached Darien on 17 October.

Everything went wrong. A terrible error had been made in the matter of provisioning. On top of this the English Government circularized all their colonial officials asking them to make sure that the Scottish colonists received no provisions. The Spaniards asserted their claim to the territory, and the English Government supported the claim. Ill, under-nourished and under attack from Spain, the survivors left Darien in June 1690. Unaware of this, but disturbed by news of Spanish activities on the Isthmus, the directors of the company despatched two relief ships from the Forth, carrying provisions and three hundred recruits, in May 1699. They arrived to find the colony deserted: one ship and her cargo was destroyed by fire; the other went to Jamaica, where most of the would-be colonists died of fever. Another expedition left from Rothesay Bay on 23 September,

and yet another ship under Captain Campbell of Fonab arrived at
Darien in February 1700. Every possible disaster occurred. The
survivors, having been offered honourable terms by the attacking
Spaniards, were allowed to sail off on 30 March in their own four
ships. None of these ever reached Scotland.

The eighth session of the First Parliament of King William met at
Edinburgh on 21 May 1700, with the Duke of Queensberry as High
Commissioner. After passing an 'Act for Securing of the Protestant
Religion, and Presbyterian Government' and another 'for Preventing
the Growth of Popery', members, seething with indignation at the
consequences of royal and English opposition to the Darien scheme,
made a formal representation in which the melancholy history of the
Darien settlement was recited, with supporting petitions from a
number of counties and burghs, and then moved that 'there be an
Resolve of Parliament that our Colony of Caledonia in Darien is a
legal and rightfull Settlement in the terms of the Act of Parliament
[of 1695], and that the Parliament will Maintain and Support the
same, And that there be an Act brought in the next Sederunt accordingly'. But Queensberry had instructions from the King himself to
allow no such motion. Insisting that matters had arisen which required him to consult the King, Queensberry on 30 May adjourned
Parliament until 20 June, and it closed in confusion and Government
panic, not to meet again in fact until 29 October. On the day of the
adjournment there was published in Edinburgh a pamphlet entitled
*People of Scotland's Groans and Lamentable Complaints Pour'd out
before the High Court of Parliament*, a bitter and eloquent protest
against the violation of Scotland's freedom, laws and trade by the
Government and their behaviour over the Darien affair and an appeal
to Parliament for redress. The author and printer of this and other
pamphlets evoked by the Darien disaster were committed to the
Tolbooth. Popular feeling in Edinburgh was wholly on the side of
the imprisoned men, and the atmosphere in the city was electric.

At the same time a parliamentary deputation presented William
with an address signed by a wide range of noblemen, barons and
burgesses of Scotland expressing their 'Unspeakable Grief and
Disappointment' at the lack of any response to the address in Parliament and asking for redress of the nation's grievances with respect to
Darien. William was perplexed. 'People there [in Scotland],' he
wrote, 'are like fools on the subject of their Colony in Darien, which
they will not tolerate in England: this causes me great annoyance.'
Worse annoyance was to follow. Captain Campbell, who had ar-

rived in Darien in February had, with the assistance of friendly Indians, defeated a Spanish force at Toubacanti and, though this did not make any difference in the end to the melancholy story of Darien, when news of the victory reached Edinburgh on 20 June there was enormous excitement and citizens gathered to celebrate. Bonfires were lit; the word CALEDONIA (the name of the colony in Darien) displayed in large illuminated letters; and crowds swarmed through the streets. The celebration turned into a riot. The rioters secured the Netherbow Port to prevent the company of guards stationed at Holyrood from entering, and proceeded to break windows of houses which were not displaying a celebratory candle. They stormed the Tolbooth and liberated the author and printer of the Darien pamphlets together with others imprisoned for political offences or civil debt. Queensberry, asleep in the High Commissioner's quarters at Holyrood, knew nothing about the riot until the next morning. The Privy Council was summoned, troops were ordered into the town, and a proclamation was issued prohibiting 'all Illuminations or Bonefires used for Expression of publick Joy ... in any Burgh within this Realm on any Pretence whatsoever'. The instigators of the riot were never discovered, but eventually four minor characters who had been observed among the rioters were brought to trial before the Court of Justiciary: one was sentenced to be scourged and banished the realm, the other three to be pilloried and then banished. There is a tradition that such was the general sympathy with the men that those in the pillory were presented with flowers and wine as they sat there while the executioner gave only a token scourging to the man sentenced to that punishment.

William's reign ended in 1702 with a deep sense of Scottish grievance and a high degree of anti-English feeling in Edinburgh as elsewhere in the country. To the economic disaster represented by the failure of the Darien scheme and the impotence of the Company of Scotland trading to Africa and the Indies was added a series of disastrous harvests extending altogether over seven years. The 'seven ill years', as they were called, began in 1696. 'These unheard-of manifold Judgments continued seven Years,' Patrick Walker later recalled, 'not always alike, but the Seasons, *Summer* and *Winter*, so cold and barren, and the wonted Heat of the Sun so much withholden, that it was discernible upon the Cattle, flying Fowls and Insects decaying, that seldom a Fly or Gleg was to be seen: Our Harvests not in the ordinary Months; many shearing in *November* and *December*, yea, some in *January* and *February*.' Andrew

Fletcher of Saltoun wrote in 1698 of 'the condition of so many thousands of our people who are this day dying for want of bread'. Jacobites called this period 'King William's years'. The English Court looked nervously at Edinburgh, now at the centre of a nationalist anti-English feeling which might result in the Scots recalling the exiled Stewart line and thus opening a 'back door' to England through which rebellion and civil war might enter. Through English governmental eyes it seemed more and more clear that the only way to close this back door permanently was to bring about a union of England and Scotland into a single political unit governed from London. And Edinburgh now became the centre of the great struggle over the question of the Union.

Both the Scottish and English Parliaments had settled the crown on James VII's daughter Anne (sister of Mary, the wife of William) after William. The English Parliament went further and by the Act of Settlement of 1701 provided that if Anne died leaving no surviving offspring (which proved to be the case) the crown of England should go to Sophia, Electress of Hanover, a grand-daughter of James VI through the female line, and her descendants. That was how George I, Sophia's son, came to succeed Queen Anne on her death in 1714. Scotland, however, did not accept the English Act of Settlement. The Scottish Parliament preferred to keep the issue of succession to the Scottish crown open after the death of Anne, to use as a bargaining weapon in winning economic concessions from the English, so desperately needed after the failure of the Darien scheme and the disaster of the 'seven ill years'. The injury to Scottish pride, too, was deeply felt, and some guarantee of greater political consideration for Scotland was also demanded before Scotland would agree to share a monarch with England after Anne's death.

The problem of running two kingdoms under a single monarchy had proved increasingly intractable ever since the Restoration, and during the reign of William it became almost insoluble. This was partly because, with the abolition of the Lords of the Articles, the Scottish Parliament was now free to assert its own views of Scotland's requirements and partly because the policy of 'managing' Scotland in the interests of what was known as the Court Party of England, either through one of the rival Scottish 'magnates' (by this time the Dukes of Hamilton, Queensberry, Atholl and Argyll) or through able non-magnate characters such as the Dalrymples, the Marquis of Tweeddale and James ('Secretary') Johnston, had virtually broken down by 1696. By the end of William's reign more and more influential voices among his English advisers were saying that only an 'incorporating union' of England and Scotland under one monarch could solve the problem of governing Scotland and at the same time eliminate the threat to England posed by the existence of the Scottish back door. Anne came to the throne of both countries in 1702 committed to such a policy, and her Ministers worked for it until they obtained it.

The Scottish Parliament met in Edinburgh in June 1702 and, under the guidance of the High Commissioner Queensberry, who for his own reasons favoured union, passed an Act setting up Commissioners from Scotland and England to treat of union. But when the Commissioners met, Scottish insistence on proper privileges for the Company trading to Africa and the Indies and, when the English denied this, on compensation for its dissolution, resulted in deadlock. The Queen adjourned the session, while the Scottish Parliament, angered at the Commissioners' refusal of royal assent to an Act for securing the liberties of the Kingdom of Scotland, withdrew recognition of the Commission altogether. It was also argued that new parliamentary elections should be held in Scotland, since a new monarch was now on the throne (Queen Anne had merely re-assembled the Parliament that had sat under William). This was agreed, and amid a flurry of pamphlets arguing for and against (but mostly against) the cause of union, new elections were held, and the new Parliament met in Edinburgh on 6 May 1703.

This was the opening of the first session of what proved to be Scotland's last Parliament. On 6 May 1703 Edinburgh saw for the last time the traditional ceremony of 'riding the Parliament' – the ceremonial procession of the Lord High Commissioner and his entourage up the Canongate and the High Street from Holyroodhouse to Parliament Square. Queensberry's first objective after Parliament opened was to get an Act of Supply passed, to raise the taxation without which the Government could not be run. The Opposition, which ranged from avowed Jacobites to anti-Jacobite land-owners and burgesses, determined to make agreement to an Act of Supply conditional on Parliament's acting to redress Scottish grievances and atone for previous affronts by the Government to Scottish dignity. On the motion of the fiercely patriotic Fletcher of Saltoun it was agreed that no Act of Supply or any other business would be considered before the passing of an Act securing religion, liberty and trade in Scotland. Fletcher also angered Government supporters by introducing his famous 'Limitations' – conditions that would have to be accepted by the monarch before Scotland would agree to share the same monarch with England. These safeguarded the dignity of the Scottish Parliament and specifically refused the King the power of making peace and war or concluding any treaty with any other state without that Parliament's consent. Though Fletcher's twelve Limitations were not accepted by the House in the form in which he presented them, their main objective was incorporated into the Act of Security which, after long and fierce debate, was approved by the House on 13 August 1703. This Act provided that the successor to Queen Anne in Scotland should not be the successor to the Crown of England unless 'there be such Conditions of Government settled and enacted, as may secure the Honour and Sovereignty of this Crown and Kingdom; the Freedom, Frequency, and Power of Parliaments, the Religion, Liberty and Trade of the Nation from English or any other Foreign Influence ...' Both Queensberry and the Earl of Seafield, Lord Chancellor of Scotland, whose joint job was to manage the Scottish Parliament in the interests of the Court Party in London, were angered and nonplussed. The Act of Security was clearly quite unacceptable to the Government. Queensberry, in spite of the most eloquent pleadings that he should do so, refused to touch the Act with the sceptre thus indicating royal assent, and adjourned the session of Parliament on 16 September without having done so. Throughout the debate and after the adjournment Edinburgh remained in a state of high excitement.

Parliament reassembled on 6 July 1704, this time with the Earl of Tweeddale as Commissioner, though Seafield remained as Chancellor. The debate raged more violently than ever. But in spite of every kind of persuasion and use of influence, neither Tweeddale nor Seafield was able to get a majority to vote for an Act of Supply before the 'touching' of the Act of Security. Finally, with the Government desperate for money – the army in Scotland remained unpaid and there was the constant fear of a Jacobite rising with French assistance – the Government gave in. Tweeddale 'touched' the Act of Security on 5 August 1704 and the House passed unanimously an Act of Supply. Edinburgh cheered.

The Government responded by having the English Parliament pass the Alien Act in March 1705: this provided for Scotsmen to be treated as aliens in England and for the prohibition of Scottish exports to England after 25 December, and in the meantime authorized the Queen to nominate Commissioners for 'a nearer and more compleat Union' between Scotland and England. The hope was that the Scots would see the light and change their attitude before the deadline. News of the passing of the Alien Act enraged Edinburgh citizens, who grimly demonstrated their anti-English mood in their handling of the crew of an English ship, the *Worcester*, which had been put into the Forth for repairs. The *Worcester* was quite wrongly believed to have been responsible for the earlier loss of the Scottish African Company's ship the *Speedy Return* and the murder of its crew. The *Worcester*'s master, Captain Green, and members of his crew were imprisoned, tried in Edinburgh by the Court of Admiralty on 14 March, and found guilty on the slenderest evidence. The Edinburgh mob, fearing that Green and his men would be reprieved, demonstrated violently in the streets and threatened to break into the Tolbooth and execute the men themselves. Seafield's carriage was stopped outside the Tron church and its windows smashed, but he managed to escape into the house of a friend. Green, with the mate Mader and a gunner named Simson, were brought out to execution, followed by the abusive jeers of the mob. They died courageously, protesting their innocence: the other arrested members of the crew were quietly released some months later. This was in fact an anti-English riot, provoked by memories of Darien as well as by the belief that Tweeddale and Seafield were betraying Scotland in Parliament.

The next session of the Scottish Parliament opened on 28 June, after months of intrigue aimed at bringing the Scottish members into line with Government policy. This time the young second Duke of Argyll, an ardent supporter of Union, was Commissioner, with Seafield still Chancellor. The Duke of Hamilton, Leader of the Opposition, insisted that any proposal for union 'should no Ways derogate from any fundamental Laws, ancient Privileges, Offices, Rights, Liberties, and Dignities of this Nation'. Fletcher of Saltoun made passionate speeches about the affronts to Scotland's dignity. The Duke of Atholl came right to the point by moving that Commissioners for Union should not be authorized until the Alien Act had been repealed. Queensberry compromised: he agreed that the sense of Atholl's resolution should be presented as an address to the Queen. On this understanding the House read and approved a draft Act for a Treaty of Union and also – surprisingly, on a motion by Hamilton – that the nomination of the Scottish Commissioners for Union should be in the hands not of the Scottish Parliament but of the Queen. This, of course, assured the nomination of those believing in an 'incorporating union' rather than the conditional federal union that the bulk of the Scottish supporters of union much preferred. Why Hamilton, who had hitherto strenuously opposed an incorporating union and was to voice such opposition again in Parliament, proposed the motion he did remains something of a mystery. But the Government were delighted.

The Commissioners of both Scotland and England duly met at Westminster and, after the Scots had won considerable economic concessions from the English Commissioners (for the economic motive was the main motive of the pro-union Scots), agreed on twenty-five articles that would unite England and Scotland into the single kingdom of Great Britain with a single Parliament, meeting at Westminster, to which Scotland would send forty-five members, while the Scottish peers should elect sixteen of their number to sit in the House of Lords. From the English Commissioners' point of view, what had been agreed was essentially the subsuming of the Scottish Parliament into the much larger English Parliament in return for freedom of trade, some financial adjustments, and a guarantee of the continuance of the Church of Scotland and the Scottish legal system. The Scottish Commissioners regarded the proposals as forming a united Great Britain of which Scotland would be the northerly and England the southerly part, but in England, then and for centuries later, the implicit view was that Scotland was now part of a greater England.

The Scottish Commissioners may have been satisfied, but many of the people of Scotland, and especially of Edinburgh, were not. A new session of the Scottish Parliament opened at Edinburgh on 3 October 1706 amid popular rumblings of discontent with what was known of the proposals for union. Queensberry was now back as High Commissioner, charged with the task of piloting the Union through the House. Seafield was still Chancellor. On the opening day the twenty-five Articles of Union were presented and read, and ordered to be printed, and the House then adjourned for a week to give people time to study the articles. At this time fiercely anti-Union pamphlets were circulating in Edinburgh, and groups of people congregated in the streets to engage in fierce argument on the subject. Most of the views expressed were strongly hostile. Every time Queensberry appeared in the streets he was cursed and hooted; every time Hamilton appeared he was wildly cheered. The publications of the Articles of Union on 12 October increased popular hostility.

Daniel Defoe was now in Edinburgh, charged with promoting the prospects of union vigorously but discreetly and reporting regularly to his Government master Robert Harley in London. On 24 October he wrote to Harley reporting anti-Union riots in Edinburgh:

> We have had Two Mobbs since my last and Expect a Third and of these the Following is a short account.
>
> The first was in the Assembly or Commission of Assembly [i.e., the Commission of the General Assembly of the Church of Scotland] where Very strange things were Talk'd of and in a strange Manner...
>
> But we had the last Two Nights a worse Mob than this and that was in the street, and Certainly a scots Rabble is the worst of its kind.
>
> The first night [22 October] they Onely Threatned hard and follow'd their Patron D. Hamilton's Chair with Huzzas from the Parliament house quite Thro' the City – They Came up again Hallowing in the Dark, Threw some stones at the Guard, broke a few windows and the like, and so it Ended ...
>
> I went up the street in a Friends Coach in the Evening [of the 23rd] and some of the Mob Not then Gott together were heard to say when I went into a house, There was One of the English Dogs &c.
>
> I Casually stayd at the house I went then to Till Dark and Thinking to Return to my Lodging, found the wholl City in a Most Dreadful Uproar and the high street Full of the Rabble.
>
> Duke Hamilton Came from the House in his Chair as Usuall and Instead of Goeing Down the City to his Lodgings Went up the High Street *as was said* to Visit the D of Athol.

Defoe went on to report that the mob then turned to attack the house of the former Lord Provost, Sir Patrick Johnston, one of the Commissioners for Union:

> The Mob came up staires to his Door and fell to work with sledges to break it Open, but it seems Could not. His Lady in the Fright with Two Candles in her hand that she might be known, Opens the Windows and Cries Out for God Sake to Call the Guard.
>
> An Honest Townsman, an Apothecary, that Saw the Distress the Family was In went Down to the Guard which is kept in the Middle of the street, and Found the Officers Very Indifferent in the Matter, whether as to the Cause or is Rather Judg'd Thro'

Reall fear of the Rabble, but Applying himself to One Capt Richardson, a brave Resolute Officer, he told him he Could Not go from the Guard without the Ld Provosts Ordr but if he would Obtain that ordr he would go up – In short the Ordr was Obtain'd and the Capt went with a Party of the Guard and made his way Thro' the Rable to Sir Pat. Johnston's stair Case – The Generallity of them fled, some were knock't Down, and the stair Clear'd, and Three or four Taken in the Very assaulting the Door.

In an interlude of relative quiet Defoe was able to return to his lodging. He continued:

I had not been Long There but I heard a Great Noise and looking Out Saw a Terrible Multitude Come up the High street with A Drum at the head of Them shouting and swearing and Cryeing Out all scotland would stand together, No Union, No Union, English Dogs, and the like.

About midnight the rioters were joined by a number of sailors from Leith. Troops were sent down from the Castle and the riot finally ended in the early hours of the morning when the town was occupied by a battalion of Foot-Guards. The next day a proclamation was issued ordering the streets to be cleared if any future disturbance should occur and absolving the military from any blame if they should have to use violence. Elaborate precautions were now taken to prevent further rioting. The public was excluded from the immediate vicinity of Parliament House, outside which troops were stationed. The daily passage of the Commissioner from Holyroodhouse to Parliament House was secured by a double line of musketeers, and when he returned to Holyrood house after the day's sitting his coach was surrounded by a detachment of Horse-Guards and often also of Foot-Guards.

Meanwhile, Parliament continued to debate the Articles of Union clause by clause, to the accompaniment of turbulent protests in the streets, which went on in spite of the precautions taken. On 19 November the Chancellor reported to the House that the Commissioner had been attacked and insulted by a stone-throwing mob and the Lord Provost was summoned and asked 'why nothing was done against them who were prisoners for the last mob'. Nothing, however, could now prevent the steady passing of the Articles through the House. Every kind of pressure was brought to bear on members to vote for them, and in addition to a certain amount of direct bribery, a great variety of inducements were held out before any member thought to be capable of such persuasion. In the end, in spite of passionate patriotic speeches of protest by Lord Belhaven, Fletcher of Saltoun, the Duke of Hamilton and others, the Act 'Ratifying, Approving and at length Narrating the Articles of Union as Explained and Amended' received its second reading on 16 January 1707, passing by 109 votes to 69. 'Now there's an end of an auld sang', said Seafield, Scotland's last Lord Chancellor as he signed the exemplication of the Act and returned it to the clerk.

The Jacobites never accepted the Union, and one of the most remarkable evidences of the strength of anti-Union feeling is the plan formed for a joint rebellion of Jacobites and Cameronians – two extreme points of opposition in terms of the history of Scottish religion and politics – to stop the Union. The plan proved abortive, but in 1715 a Jacobite rising led by the Earl of Mar had as its aim not only the bringing to the throne of James Francis Edward, son of James VII, but also breaking the Union and restoring Scottish independence. The Earl of Mar had strongly supported the Union in Scotland's last Parliament, but when, on the accession of George I in 1714, his overtures to that monarch were rebuffed, he turned in indignation to the Jacobite movement.

The main theatre of war in the 1715 rising was north of the Forth, though there was simultaneously an unsuccessful campaign in Lancashire. Edinburgh's involvement was confined to the attempt by Lord Drummond, son of the titular (Jacobite created) Duke of Perth, to capture Edinburgh Castle for the Jacobites. On the night of 8 September 1715, with a body of about a hundred men, mostly Highlanders, Drummond attempted to scale the western slope near the sally port. A ladder with great hooks at the top had been specially prepared for the attempt, whose success was to be reported by the lighting of a beacon which would announce the news to Fife and the north. But one of Mar's men revealed the scheme to his brother, a doctor in the city, who volunteered to assist, but also incautiously mentioned the fact to his wife. She, alarmed for her husband's safety, sent an anonymous letter to the Lord Justice-Clerk, Sir Adam Cockburn of Ormiston, revealing the plot. Ormiston informed Colonel Stuart, the Deputy-Governor. The scaling party were surprised in the act, and managed to flee, leaving behind four wounded companions who were made prisoners by the City Guard. 'From this period,' notes James Grant, the nineteenth century historian of Edinburgh, in a sentence difficult to resist quoting, 'with the exception of a species of blockade in 1745, . . . the history of the Castle is as uneventful as that of the Tower of London, save a visit paid to it in the time of George I, by Yussuf Jumati, General and Governor of Damascus.'

Throughout all the anxieties, controversies, problems, alarms and riots of the late seventeenth and early eighteenth centuries, the civic life of Edinburgh continued in a surprisingly even tenor. The Town Council minutes record daily preoccupations with civic amenities and the rights of burgesses. It is reassuring to find, for example, that on 12 April 1704 the Council authorized the payment of £165. 14s. Scots to Gilbert Kirktoune for 'wryting and gilding burges tickets, and furnishing gold, wax, and parchment'. The Council was much exercised about this question of burgess tickets and also honorary burgess tickets. 'For all burges and gild brother ticketts, wher the persones names and designations are gilded in capitall letters,' runs a Town Council resolution of the same date, 'ther shall be payd the soume of three pound ten shilling for wryting and gilding therof. As also, for all other burges and gild brother tickets not gilded, the soume of fourtie shilling for wryting therof; and for single burges tickets, the priviledge wherof continues but for fyve years, the soume of twentie-nyne shilling Scots.' Duties as well as rights of members of merchant guilds were frequently emphasized. The fleshers (butchers), for example, were reminded in an ordinance of 29 March 1717 of their 'many usefull and necessary priviledges' and at the same time forbidden to slay their beasts 'within the freedom of the toun' but ordered 'to bring the same to the mercat dead and slain, under the penalties mentioned in that act, which is afterwards ratified by the parliament in the year 1693, together with other acts in favour of the fleshers'. The ordinance went on to observe that the regulation 'is not only usefull and necessary for the good and policy of the burgh, to prevent driving numbers of cattle through the toun, and many other inconveniences, but is plainly ane undoubted consequence of the freedom competent to the fleshers as an incorporation'.

The most important, and in many respects the most impartial, visitor to Edinburgh in the early eighteenth century was Daniel Defoe. Though he was there at the time of the Union debates in the interests of the Government, his natural interest and curiosity made him an excellent observer of the city. In the third volume of his *Tour Thro' the whole Island of Great Britain, Divided into Circuits of Journies*, published in 1726, largely from notes that he had made in earlier years, he gives us one of the best descriptions we have of early eighteenth century Edinburgh:

> When you stand at a small Distance, and take a View of it from the East, you have really but a confus'd Idea of the City, because the Situation being in Length from East to West, and the Breadth but ill proportion'd to its Length, you view under the greatest Disadvantage possible; whereas if you turn a little to the right Hand towards *Leith*, and so come towards the City, from the North you see a very handsome Prospect of the whole City, and from the South you have yet a better View of one Part, because the City is encreased on that Side with new Streets, which, on the North Side, cannot be ...

Defoe considered the street from Holyrood to the Castle 'perhaps the largest, longest, and finest Street for Buildings and Number of Inhabitants, not in *Britain* only, but in the World'. He comments on the steep slope to the north, adding that if it were not so steep and the North Loch were filled up, 'as might easily be, the City might have been extended upon the Plain below, and fine beautiful Streets would, no doubt, have been built there; nay, I question much whether in Time, the high Streets would not have been forsaken, and the City, as we might say, run all out of its Gate to the North'. Like many other visitors, he notes the 'Stench and Nastiness' of the streets, 'as if the people were not as willing to live sweet and clean as other Nations'. People live in 'a rocky and mountainous Situation, throng'd Buildings, from seven to ten or twelve Story high, a Scarcity of Water, and that little they have difficult to be had, and to the uppermost Lodgings, far to fetch ...' He observed that 'I believe ... that in no City in the World so many People live in so little Room as at *Edinburgh*'.

In spite of various 'Discouragements and Disadvantages', Defoe found Edinburgh 'a large, populous, noble, rich, and even still a Royal City. The main Street ... is the most spacious, the longest, and best inhabited street in *Europe*; ... the Buildings are surprizing both for Strength, for Beauty, and for Height; all, or the greatest Part of Freestone, and so firm is every Thing made, that tho' in so high a Situation, and in a Country where Storms and Violent Winds are so frequent, 'tis very rare that any Damage is done here. No blowing of Tiles about the Streets, to knock People on the Head as they pass; no Stacks of Chimneys and Gable-Ends of Houses falling in to bury the inhabitants in their Ruins, as we often find in *London*, and

others of our Paper built Cities in *England*; but all is fix'd and strong
to the Top, tho' you have, in that Part of the City call'd the
Parliament-close, Houses, which, on the South Side, appear to be
eleven or twelve Story high, and inhabited to the very Top.'

At the end of the Lawnmarket 'the High Street ends, and parting
into two Streets, one goes away South West, and descending gradu-
ally, leads by the West Bow, *as 'tis called*, to the *Grass-market*. This
Street, which is called the *Bow*, is generally full of wholesale Traders,
and those very considerable Dealers in Iron, Pitch, Tar, Oyl, Hemp,
Flax, Linseed, Painters Colours, Dyers, Drugs and Woods, and such
like heavy Goods, and supplies Country Shopkeepers, as our Wholesale Dealers in England do: And here I may say is a visible Face of
Trade, most of them have also Warehouses in *Leith*, where they lay
up the heavie Goods, and bring them hither, or sell them by Patterns and Samples, as they have Occasion.'

Defoe noted that since the Union St Giles' 'is divided into four
Parochial Churches' and he described admiringly the set of bells 'in
the great tower of that part of St Giles called the New Church'.
They were, he said, played with keys, 'like a Harpsichord; the
Person playing has great strong wooden Cases to his Fingers, by
which he is able to strike with the more Force, and he plays several
Tunes very musically, tho' they are heard much better at a Distance
than near at Hand; the Man plays every Day, Sunday and Fast Days
excepted, at twelve a Clock, and has a yearly Salary for doing it, and
very well he earns the Money'.

There is a tradition that on 1 May 1707, the day when the Union
came into force, an unauthorized person obtained entry into the
great tower and played on the bells the old Scottish folk-tune 'How
can I be sad on my wedding day?'.

CHAPTER 6

After the Union

The union of 1707 administered to Edinburgh what might be called a historical shock. The city was shocked into a re-examination of its history and significance as Scotland's capital and a centre of Scottish political and cultural life. It had lost its Court in 1603; now it also lost its Parliament. No political power was now centred there. What *was* centred there? Was Edinburgh to be the capital of North Britain while London was the capital of Britain as a whole?

The first instinct was to take comfort in what Edinburgh and Scotland had been in the past. Impotent politically, those who opposed an incorporating union now turned to cultural activities. The moment when Scotland's extinction as a separate political entity became assured might be a good moment in which to consider what kind of a cultural entity it could now preserve. In 1706, when the great debate on the Union was moving into its final stages, James Watson brought out the first of three volumes entitled *A Choice Collection of Comic and Serious Scots Poems both Ancient and Modern*. Watson was the Edinburgh printer who had been confined to the Tolbooth for printing a pamphlet bitterly attacking the Government for betraying the Scottish people over the Darien scheme. Throughout much of his turbulent life he was involved in a fight against the claims to a printing monopoly maintained by the widow of Andrew Anderson, the late King's Printer in Edinburgh. In her struggle to maintain her monopoly against Watson, Mrs Anderson charged that he had been bred a Papist and printed Popish and Jacobitical books, and it is true that (besides revering the memory of Charles I) he was an ardent Scottish patriot and no supporter of an incorporating union with England. What moved him to publish his three volumes (the other two appeared in 1709 and 1711) is suggested by his prefatory note to the first:

As the frequency of Publishing Collections of Miscellaneous Poems in our Neighbouring Kingdoms and States, may, in a great measure, justify an Undertaking of this kind with us; so 'tis hoped, that this being the first of its Nature which has been published in our own Native *Scots* Dialect, the Candid Reader may be the more eagerly induced, through the Consideration thereof, to give some Charitable Grains of Allowance, if the Performance come not up to such a Point of Exactness as may please an over nice Palate ...

The intention was patriotic, and in some degree nostalgic. Yet in selecting 'Poems both Ancient and Modern' Watson also looked forward: what his collection actually does is to present fairly accurately the different kinds of material available for the development or reconstruction of the Scottish poetic tradition in the eighteenth century. It is in many ways a curiously motley collection, and illustrates the degree to which the great tradition of the mediaeval makars and the Scottish Court poets had become attenuated as a result of pressure from an increasingly dominant English culture. Even before James VI had removed his Court and Court patronage from Edinburgh, the turning of a Protestant Scotland towards a Protestant England, and the use of English translations of the Bible (first the Geneva Bible of 1560 and then the Authorized Version in 1611) in Scottish kirks and homes, had fostered the notion that an educated Scot who wanted a proper audience for his work should write in standard English. The events of 1603 and 1707 speeded up a process that had already begun. The Scots language, once a proud literary language capable of a wide range of expression from high rhetorical formality to lively satirical 'flyting', began to degenerate into a series of regional dialects. For without a living literary tradition a language tends to lose its sense of identity and split into local vernaculars. Watson was the first of many eighteenth century editors (for he edited as well as printed his anthology) to try and make contact with an older Scottish literary tradition and to build a bridge between it and the writers of his own time.

There was an element of nostalgia and antiquarianism in Watson's volumes, and this characterizes one of the major responses to the Union throughout the eighteenth century. People looked back to the days when Scotland was a proud and independent country, with its own Scots language and literature (Gaelic language and literature presented different problems), and reprinted, collected, imitated or tried to re-create works in the old tradition. Since with the departure of the Court poets Scotland was left with its folk tradition rather than its courtly tradition dominant (except sometimes in the north-east, where Aberdeen in particular was a centre of old courtly song), and since even the folk tradition had in some degree been driven underground by the Kirk's hostility to popular songs and the festivities they accompanied, much of the imitation and re-creating centred on attempts to refurbish Scottish folk song, as Robert Burns was to do so spectacularly. From Watson's *Choice Collection* through Allan Ramsay's *Tea-Table Miscellany* of 1724 and David Herd's two-volume *Ancient and Modern Scottish Songs* of 1776 to Walter Scott's *Minstrelsy of the Scottish Border* of 1802 we see this movement of what might be called nostalgic patriotic antiquarianism at work in Edinburgh.

But Edinburgh also produced a very different sort of reaction to the Union, which began to develop somewhat later than the one started by Watson. This was to accept the Union, to accept standard English as the proper written speech for educated Scotsmen, and to show that Scotland, as the northern part of Great Britain, could represent Britain before the world with a special kind of brilliance. It was this attitude that produced the Scottish Enlightenment and that galaxy of men of letters and scientists, the 'literati', who made late eighteenth century Edinburgh one of the great cultural centres of Europe. These men were proud of being Scots, but at the same time concerned to show that the Scots were great Britons. They regarded the Scots language, which most of them used in some degree in their ordinary daily speech, as, in David Hume's phrase, 'a very corrupt dialect', and were likely to send their manuscripts to English friends for the elimination of 'Scotticisms'. They were 'Moderates' in religion, seeking to smooth away the rough edges of Calvinism in the interests of an optimistic Deism, where they were not outright sceptics like Hume. They believed in progress, in agricultural improvement, in town planning. The well planned New Town of Edinburgh had its origin in this complex of ideas: while the Old Town, running from the Castle to Holyrood, stood for the old, picturesque, violent Edinburgh beloved of the antiquarians, the New Town stood for elegance, order, peaceful progress, British reasonableness. The literati were interested in history as much as the antiquarians were, but they were more concerned with the philosophy of social and political change and the nature of progress than with the picturesque violence of the past. Walter Scott, who combined both these interests, was able as a result to invent the historical novel.

Between those who imitated Scots folk songs, wrote pastoral poems or wrote poems descriptive of low life in the city in a deliberately popular Scots, and those who cultivated the genteel enlightenment of the 'literati' there was not only a figure like Walter

Scott who was at home in both camps; there was also in the first half
of the eighteenth century a patriotic, largely anti-Union movement of
scholarship, a latter-day Humanism (in the Renaissance sense of
classical Humanism), exemplified in the career of Thomas Ruddiman, who came to Edinburgh from the north-east about the turn of
the century, and the Edinburgh printer and bookseller Robert
Freebairn. This movement of what might be called vernacular
Humanism produced not only aids to classical scholarship (the most
important of which was Ruddiman's *Rudiments of the Latin
Tongue*, 1714) but also edited and published significant older Scottish works, such as Gavin Douglas's great translation of the *Aeneid*
into Middle Scots, and published works of patriotic Scottish history,
such as Patrick Abercromby's *Martial Atchievements of the Scottish
Nation*. The movement, strong in Edinburgh in the second, third
and fourth decades of the eighteenth century, was eventually
swamped by the Scottish Enlightenment, just as the new building to
the south of the Cowgate, such as Brown Square (long since absorbed
by the west end of Chambers Street), Nicolson Square, George
Square and Buccleuch Place, represented a vernacular classical
architecture that gave way to the more imposing international classi-
cism of the buildings of the New Town north of the drained North
Loch.

So much for the larger pattern. To return now to the tradition
that began with Watson in 1706, we soon find it developed and
amplified in the career of Allan Ramsay, who arrived in Edinburgh
from his native Leadhills, Lanarkshire, about 1700, when he was
fifteen years old. He was apprenticed to a wig-maker and in July
1710 was admitted a burgess. (The wig-makers, incidentally, do not
appear as one of the incorporated crafts of Edinburgh, but since
those who completed their apprenticeship were admitted burgesses,
they must have had some kind of organization.) In May 1712
Ramsay joined with a number of other young men in founding the
Easy Club, 'in order that by a Mutual improvement in Conversation
they may become more adapted for fellowship with the politer part
of mankind and Learn from one another's happy observations'. It
seemed at first as though the members wanted to model themselves
on what they knew of genteel London life. A copy of the *Spectator*
was read aloud at each meeting. Each member took the name of
some symbolic literary figure, and Ramsay chose the name of Isaac
Bickerstaff. But later he changed to 'Gawin Douglas', thus illustrat-
ing his interest in Scottish poetry. And the Club fostered a Scottish

patriotism that sometimes expressed itself in anti-Union sentiments. All his life Ramsay was torn between wanting to be an Edinburgh equivalent of the wits of early eighteenth century London and wanting to represent and encourage a revived indigenous Scottish culture in Edinburgh. The fact that, having moved from wig-making to book-selling, he tried his hand at imitating English poets such as Pope and Prior and to writing in Scots in the old folk tradition as well as collecting older Scottish poetry both folk and art, well illustrates the duality and indeed the confusion of the situation. But in the end Ramsay emerged clearly as a champion of older Scottish traditions, belonging to the first of the two reactions to the Union that we have described.

In 1724, the same year that saw the publication of the first volume of his four-volume anthology, *The Tea-Table Miscellany*, he brought out another collection, entitled *The Ever Green*, in which he introduced his readers to the great poetry of mediaeval Scotland, that of Dunbar and Henryson in particular. Most of this he took from the Bannatyne Manuscript, that invaluable anthology of earlier Scottish poetry compiled by the prosperous Edinburgh burgess George Bannatyne to occupy an enforced leisure when he had to retire from the city during a severe visitation of the plague in 1568. Like Watson, Ramsay shows his patriotic intention in his preface:

> When these good old Bards wrote, we had not yet made Use of imported Trimming upon our Cloaths, nor of foreign Embroidery in our Writings. Their Poetry is the Produce of their own Country, not pilfered and spoiled in the Transportation from abroad: Their Images are native, and their Landskips domestick; copied from those Fields and Meadows we every Day behold.

Ramsay opened what is believed to be the oldest circulating library in Britain about 1725, much to the distress of the orthodox Calvinists. Robert Woodrow in his *Analecta* records under the date 1728 how Ramsay was corrupting Edinburgh:

> Besides this, profaneness is come to a great hight, all the villainous profane and obscene bookes and playes printed at London by Curle and others, are gote doune from London by Allan Ramsay, and lent out, for an easy price, to young boyes, servant weemen of the better sort, and gentlemen, and vice and obscenity dreadfully propagated. Ramsay has a book in his shope wherein all the names of those that borrou his playes and books, for two pence a

night, or some such rate, are sett doun; and by these, wickednes
of all kinds are dreadfully propagat among the youth of all sorts.

Ramsay also gave scandal to the orthodox by his involvement
with the theatre. Stage plays had been frowned on by the Presbyterian Church of Scotland, and with the removal of the Court to
London in 1603 royal counter-influence in their favour disappeared,
except for those few occasions between the Restoration and the
Revolution when the Royal Commissioner had a play put on in
Edinburgh, primarily for the entertainment of himself and his entourage. In 1725 an English actor called Tony Aston endeavoured
to break the taboo on stage performances in Edinburgh and seems
for a while to have received the approval of the Provost and bailies
for his venture. Ramsay wrote the Prologue for the opening of his
second season in 1726:

> 'Tis I, dear Caledonia, blythsome Tony,
> That oft, last winter, pleas'd the brave and bonny,
> With medley, merry song, and comic scene: ...

But when a new Provost and bailies took office, Aston was told to
go. We learn from the press of demonstrations against him. The
Caledonian Mercury (a tri-weekly founded in 1720) wrote on 14
December 1727: 'Yesternight an idle giddy mob got up a little
below the guard-house, who, without the least shadow of provoca-
tion, insulted several persons of quality and distinction as they were
passing the street to see the play called the *Earl of Essex* acted by
Anthony Aston's company of comedians.' Aston had hired the
Skinner's Hall for his plays, and the magistrates now fined him and
put a padlock on the door of the hall. Further, Lady Morrison, who
lived below the Skinner's Hall, complained that the plays 'bended'
her roof to such an extent that 'her house was in danger of being
destroyed by the fall of the floor'. Aston appealed to the Court of
Session against the magistrates' prohibition, and won, but the city
fathers appealed against the decision on the grounds that it would
create 'a precedent and would open doors, not only for multitudes
of players, comedians; but at the same time for Merry Andrews,
Rope Dancers, Tumblers, Leaders of Bears, Munkies and other
Shows'. In the end Aston was forced to leave Edinburgh, and left
Ramsay to continue the fight for a legitimate theatre in the city.

Between 1733 and 1735 we find references to the Edinburgh
Company of Players and their performances, with the information

that tickets were to be had at Allan Ramsay's shop, which suggests that he had some interest in the company. Ramsay was certainly managing a theatrical company in a new theatre in Carrubber's Close that opened on 8 November 1736. But in 1737 the Government passed the Licensing Act, prohibiting theatrical performances outside London and Westminster unless the sovereign was in residence, and though the intention was to stop attacks on Walpole it was also possible to use the Act to suppress the theatre in Edinburgh, and this the magistrates appear to have done, much to Ramsay's indignation. He wrote several poems protesting vigorously against the prohibition which severely limited the pleasures of Edinburgh citizens:

> Thus whore, & Bawd, Doctor, & Pox
> The tavern & a large white Ox,
> Are the whole Sum for Lord or clown
> of the Diversions of our Town,
> Since by a late Sour-snouted law
> which makes great Heroes stand in awe
> The morall Teachers of broad Truths
> have golden padlocks on their mouths ...

Ramsay long continued his vigorous campaign to legalize the theatre in Edinburgh, on one occasion writing to the Member of Parliament for Edinburgh, Patrick Lindsay, to urge his support in stopping those who were working 'towards impoverishing and stupefying the Good Town by getting every thing that tends towards politness and Good humour Banished that antichristian-Preistcraft & Gloomy Enthusiasm & Contention may prevail'. Eventually a way round the Licensing Act was found by charging admission to a concert followed by a free play, but by this time Ramsay was enjoying his retirement in his octagonal house by the Castle popularly known as the 'Goose-pie'. Ramsay died in 1758, six years before a theatre was licensed in Edinburgh.

The two most spectacular events that took place in Allan Ramsay's Edinburgh were the Porteous Riots of 1736 and the occupation of the city by Bonnie Prince Charlie's Jacobite army in 1745. The prelude to the Porteous Riots is well described by Alexander ('Jupiter') Carlyle, who witnessed it as a boy of fourteen:

In those days it was usual to bring the criminals who were condemned to death into that church [the Tolbooth Church], to attend public worship every Sunday after their condemnation, when the clergyman made some part of his discourse and prayers to suit their situation; which, among other circumstances of solemnity which then attended the state of condemned criminals, had no small effect on the public mind. Robertson and Wilson were smugglers, and had been condemned for robbing a custom-house, where some of their goods had been deposited; a crime which at that time did not seem, in the opinion of the common people, to deserve so severe a punishment. I was carried by an acquaintance to church to see the prisoners on the Sunday before the day of execution. We went early into the church on purpose to see them come in, and were seated in a pew before the gallery in front of the pulpit. Soon after we went into the church by the door from the Parliament Close, the criminals were brought in by the door next the Tolbooth, and placed in a long pew, not far from the pulpit. Four soldiers came in with them, and placed Robertson at the head of the pew, and Wilson below him, two of themselves sitting below Wilson, and two in a pew behind him.

The bells were ringing and the doors were open, while the people were coming into the church. Robertson watched his opportunity, and, suddenly, springing up, got over the pew into the passage that led in to the door in the Parliament Close, and no person offering to lay hands of him, made his escape in a moment – so much the more easily, perhaps, as everybody's attention was drawn to Wilson, who was a stronger man, and who, attempting to follow Robertson, was seized by the soldiers, and struggled so long with them that the two who at last followed Robertson were too late. It was reported that he had maintained his struggle that he might let his companion have time ...

Robertson escaped to Holland, while Wilson remained to await execution. The commander of the City Guard, whose duty it was to attend executions, was Captain John Porteous: 'he was a common soldier in Queen Anne's wars, but had got a commission for his courage', according to Carlyle. His roughness of manner made him highly unpopular with the Edinburgh mob. The Provost and bailies, fearing that an attempt to rescue Wilson might be made as he was being led to execution and not trusting the City Guard to be able to contain the mob, 'thought it a good measure to apply for three or four companies of a marching regiment that lay in the Canongate, to be drawn up in the Lawnmarket, a street leading from the Tolbooth to the Grassmarket, the place of execution, in order to overawe the mob by their being at hand'. Porteous is said to have been enraged at the implied suggestion that he and his Guard could not execute the law. His bad temper was increased by the fact that he had drunk heavily at dinner (then taken between one and two).

Wilson was executed without any attempt at rescue, but after the execution there was some growling and desultory stone-throwing by by-standers. There was no more violence than was usual on such occasions. Carlyle tells what now happened :

Porteous, however, inflamed with wine and jealousy, thought proper to order his Guard to fire, their muskets being loaded with slugs; and when the soldiers showed reluctance, I saw him turn to them with threatening gesture and an inflamed countenance. They obeyed, and fired; but wishing to do as little harm as possible, many of them elevated their pieces, the effect of which was that some people were wounded in the windows [crowded with on-lookers]; and one unfortunate lad, whom we had displaced, was killed in the stair window by a slug entering his head ... We had seen many people, women and men, fall on the street, and at first thought it was only through fear, and by their crowding on one another to escape. But when the crowd dispersed, we saw them lying dead or wounded, and had no longer any doubt what had happened. The numbers were said to be eight or nine killed, and double the number wounded; but this was never exactly known.

The ordinary people of Edinburgh were enraged by Porteous's murder of their fellow citizens, and expressed great satisfaction when Porteous was tried and condemned to be hanged. However, as he had been in the habit of playing golf with people of rank and influence in Edinburgh, pressure was brought on Queen Caroline (who was acting as Regent in the absence on the Continent of her husband George II) to reprieve him, which she did. This was regarded by the Edinburgh mob as an affront to their city and their country by a distant English Government, the kind of thing made possible by the Union of 1707. So their outrage mingled anti-Porteous with anti-Union and anti-English feeling. In such a mood, a mob assembled at the West Port after dark on 7 September: they overpowered and disarmed the City Guard which had been called out to disperse them and seized the city gates. They burned down the door of the Tolbooth, where Porteous was lodged in a cell, dragged him out, led him down to the Grassmarket, and there hanged him on a dyer's pole. The mob operated in uncanny silence, and did no other damage. They even gave a guinea to the shopkeeper from whom they obtained the rope for the hanging. Sir Walter Scott has brilliantly reconstructed the scene in *The Heart of Midlothian*.

The Government was in its turn outraged by the action of the Edinburgh mob and proposed to punish the city severely. They were particularly incensed that an investigation by the Scottish law officers was met by a conspiracy of silence. In February 1737 the Scots judges were made to stand at the Bar of the House of Lords and in the Commons an Act was passed disbarring the Lord Provost, Alexander Wilson, from holding further office and fining the city £2,000 to go to Porteous's widow. More drastic measures, including the imprisonment of the Provost (who had already spent three weeks in jail before being admitted to bail), the abolition of the City Guard and the dismantling of the city gates were dropped after the unanimous protest of the Scottish Members of Parliament and the influential opposition of the second Duke of Argyll. Large rewards were offered for the capture of the ringleaders of the Porteous execution, but none was ever discovered. Some of them appear to have been disguised as women, and one is said to have been the Earl of Haddington disguised in the clothes of his cook-maid.

Eight years later came the Jacobite occupation of Edinburgh. Charles Edward Stewart, grandson of James VII of Scotland and II of England and son of James Francis Edward, the Chevalier de St George, who lived in exile at Rome but still claimed the British throne as rightfully his, landed with a few followers on the island of Eriskay on 23 July 1745 in an attempt to regain the throne for his father. He gathered a Highland army, which approached Edinburgh from the west on 15 September. On the 16th they advanced to Corstorphine, three miles west of Edinburgh, and Gardiner's Dragoons and Hamilton's Dragoons, with a few hundred men from the hastily formed Edinburgh regiment and from the City Guard, who had been sent to stop their advance, retreated eastward towards Edinburgh and encamped in a field near Coltbridge. Coltbridge was then a little village on the Water of Leith with two bridges, an old and a new; it is now completely absorbed in the western New Town of Edinburgh.

On the evening of the 15th Brigadier Thomas Fowke had arrived at Edinburgh from England to take command of the two regiments of dragoons. When he reviewed them in their camp the next morning he found both men and horses in appalling condition and Colonel Gardiner depressed and fatalistic. It was decided to withdraw the men to Leith Links where they could join with Sir John Cope's forces, due to arrive at Leith from the north any moment. Before this could be done in an orderly manner, a small advance party of the Jacobite army advancing eastward to reconnoitre were mistaken by the rearguard of the dragoons for the whole Jacobite army, so they 'wheeled about, and rode off, carrying their fears into the main body' (in the words of John Home, minister and playwright, who served with the Government forces). What followed became known as the 'Canter of Coltbrigg': Brigadier Fowke and the two regiments of dragoons retreated eastward at speed along the Long Dykes (where Princes Street now runs) 'in full view of the people of Edinburgh' as far as Leith: shortly afterwards they withdrew to Musselburgh and then, on Gardiner's suggestion, to Prestonpans, near his own estate of Bankton. The Jacobite army encamped at Gray's Mill, near Slateford, two miles south-west of Edinburgh, and from there Charles sent a summons to the Provost and magistrates of the city ordering them to receive him and his army and promising protection and the preservation of all rights if they were peacefully received.

Meanwhile about four hundred volunteers had assembled in the College Yards and were addressed by Captain Drummond, who commanded the first company of volunteers, called the College Company. A strange scene occurred on Sunday the 15th:

> The volunteers loaded their pieces for the first time; the fire-bell was rung, as a signal for them to repair to the Lawn Market, which they did in a body. The fire-bell ringing in the time of divine service, emptied the churches in an instant; and the people rushing into the streets, were told that volunteers, who they saw under arms, were going out with the dragoons to fight the rebel army. As soon as the dragoons appeared, the volunteers huzzaed; and the dragoons clashing their swords against one another, as they marched on, returned the huzza. An universal consternation seized the minds of the people of every rank, age, sex, and party. The relations of the volunteers crowded about them, and mixed with their ranks. The men reasoned, and endeavoured to dissuade their friends: the women expostulated, complained, and, weeping, embraced their sons and brothers ...

Some dropped out, others agreed to march with the dragoons, and those who were willing marched to the Grassmarket where they were joined by forty-two men of the College Company under Captain Drummond. Home's eye-witness account continues:

> Soon after this junction was made, Dr Wishart, principal of the University of Edinburgh, with his brother George Wishart, (who was so well beloved,) and several other clergymen, came to the Grass Market, and addressing the volunteers with great earnestness, conjured them by whatever they held most sacred, to stay within the walls, and reserve themselves for the defence of the city ... When the Principal and his friends went away, Captain Drummond, after talking with his officers, sent a message to Provost Stuart ... to acquaint him, that unless he agreed to their marching out of town, the volunteers were determined not to proceed, and that they waited his answer. [The Provost replied] that as he was very much against the proposal of marching the volunteers out of town, he was very glad of their resolution not to march out of town. Captain Drummond having received this answer, put himself at the head of his company, and marched the volunteers back to the College-yards.

When Charles's letter was received by the Town Council, 'the cry against resistance became louder than ever; and it was proposed to send a deputation to the person from whom this letter came, to desire that hostilities might not be commenced, till the citizens had deliberated, and resolved what answer should be made to the letter'. News that Sir John Cope's army was in the Forth encouraged the Provost and magistrates to stall for time, and throughout the 16th they kept sending notes to Charles's emissary, Murray of Broughton, until Charles realized what they were up to and decided to take the city by force. Murray of Broughton recorded what then happened:

> With this view he ordered Locheil to putt his people under arms to be ready to march upon a minutes warning, and ordered Mr M[urray] to be their guide, as he was well acquainted with all the avenues to the place, giving strickt orders to behave with all moderation to the Inhabitants, and that the sogers should not be allowed to taste spirits, and to pay for wtever they got, promising them two shillings each so soon as they rendered themselves Masters of the place. The detachment ... passed without being observed by the garrison of the Castle, tho so near as to hear them distinctly call their rounds, and arrived at the nether bow

Port without meeting any body on their way, and found the wall
of the Town which flanks the Pleasants and St Marys wynd
mounted with cannon, but no person appeared. [They demanded
admission at the Netherbow Port, but this was refused, so] it now
being clear daylight Mr M. proposed to retire to a place called
St Leonards hills [Arthur's Seat], and after securing themselves
from the cannon of the Castle, to waite for orders from the
Chevalier where to attack the town, ... This retreat being thus
agreed to Mr M. went to the rear of the detachment to make them
march and guide them to the place proposed, but before they had
time to get so far, the coach which had returned with the deputies
[of the Town Council, who had come to ask for another suspension of hostilities] came down the High Street and obliged the
Guard to open the Port, upon which Locheil took the advantage
and rushed in, the guard immediately dispersing. Thus did the
Chevalier render himself master of the Capital without shedding a
drop of Blood, notwithstanding all the mighty preparations and
associations entered into for its defence.

This happened about 5 a.m. on the 17th. As soon as Lochiel's
men had entered the Netherbow gate 'they immediately sent parties
to all the other gates', as Home reported, 'and to the town guard,
who making the soldiers upon duty prisoners, occupied their posts as
quietly as one guard relieves another. When the inhabitants of
Edinburgh awoke in the morning, they found that the Highlanders
were masters of the city'.

The lawyers, clergymen and tradesmen of Edinburgh were on the
whole in favour of the Government, if only for the sake of peace and
quiet, though there were some who had Jacobite sympathies without
being willing to put themselves to any risk for their sake. Allan
Ramsay, in spite of the eloquent Jacobite and anti-Union poems he
had written (sometimes attributing them to older Scottish poets),
cannily took himself off to Penicuik where he suffered a diplomatic
illness that prevented him from returning to Edinburgh for several
weeks. The Jacobites seized his 'Goose-pie' house near the Castle
and used it as a vantage point from which to fire on the Castle
sentries. For the Castle remained in Government hands, defended
by the eighty-five-year-old Lieutenant-General Joshua Guest, officially designated 'Lieutenant-General and Commander-in-Chief of
all His Majesty's Forces, Castles, Forts and Barracks in Great
Britain'.

On midday of the 17th a manifesto proclaiming Charles as Regent on behalf of his father was read at the Mercat Cross. 'The populace of a great city, who huzza for any thing that brings them together, huzzaed; and a number of ladies in the windows strained their voices with acclamation, and their arms with waving white handkerchiefs in honour of the day.' Home adds that these demonstrations of joy were confined to the ladies; 'few gentlemen were to be seen on the streets, or in the windows; and even amongst the inferior people, many shewed their dislike by a stubborn silence'.

Charles and his army marched by Duddingston and the King's Park, below Arthur's Seat, to avoid fire from the Castle cannon, to the palace of Holyrood, where Charles took up residence. John Home was there:

> The Park was full of people, (amongst whom was the Author of this history,) all of them impatient to see this extraordinary person. The figure and presence of Charles Stuart were not ill suited to his lofty pretensions. He was in the prime of youth, tall and handsome, of a fair complexion: he had a light coloured periwig with his own hair combed over the front: he wore the Highland dress, that is a tartan short coat without the plaid, a blue bonnet on his head, and on his breast the star of the order of St Andrew. Charles stood some time in the park to shew himself to the people; and then, though he was very near the palace, mounted his horse, either to render himself more conspicuous, or because he rode well, and looked graceful on horseback.

On Saturday 21 September the Government forces of Sir John Cope were routed by the Jacobite army at Prestonpans. Charles returned to Holyrood, and, Murray of Broughton reports, 'being told that rejoicings and bone fires were intended for the victory, he gave positive orders against it, saying that he was far from rejoicing att the death of any of his fathers Subjects'. Charles 'likewise sent a message to the Presbiterian ministers, desiring them to preach as usual and that they might depend upon meeting with no disturbance'. When they asked if they could pray for King George, Charles replied that 'he could not pretend to give them that Liberty, which in its self would be a flatt Contradiction, but he would venture to assure them that no notice would be taken of any thing they said'. They decided it would be wiser to keep silent.

The Jacobite army was now partly encamped at Duddingston and partly quartered in Edinburgh and adjacent villages. Many of the men lay on straw in the Tron Church and in the lobby of Parliament House. Charles held court at Holyrood. He was determined to behave magnanimously, and issued proclamations expressing his anxiety that nobody should be prevented from passing to and from the city on business and granting formal protection to all the inhabitants and those living in the surrounding countryside 'from all insults, seizures, injuries, and abuses of our army against them respectively'. An order of 23 September strictly forbade pillaging. He issued proclamations forbidding anybody to attend the Parliament at Westminster summoned for 17 October and denouncing 'the pretended union of the two nations'. He levied taxes and customs in Edinburgh. He never succeeded in taking the Castle, though he tried to force its surrender by cutting off supplies, but when this resulted in General Guest's ordering the Castle guns to fire on the city with resulting civilian casualties he called off the blockade.

When Charles and his army left Edinburgh on 1 November for Dalkeith on their way into England there was relief in the city, though some landladies regretted their lost Highland officer lodgers and some ladies who had lost their hearts to the Bonnie Prince grieved secretly. News of the utter defeat of the Prince and his army at Culloden on 16 April 1745 was preceded by a false report that he had won, the Government forces defeated and their General, the Duke of Cumberland, taken prisoner. As the anti-Jacobite Whig Andrew Henderson reported, on this false report 'Balls and Dances were held by the disaffected Ladies, whose Mirth was interrupted, about One in the Sunday morning, by a Round from the great Guns of the Castle, answered by Discharges from the Men of War in the Road, on Receipt of quite contrary News. Next Thirsday was observed with the utmost Gaiety, as a Day of rejoicing for the Victory obtained: The most ingenious Devices, capable of striking the nicest Taste, were contrived . . . Satisfaction appeared in the Populace, who set Bonfires, brought forth Liquor, and celebrated the Era of their Freedom.' But Bonnie Prince Charlie remained a romantic memory in Edinburgh, a memory which grew stronger as Jacobite hopes faded away for ever.

Town Council elections had been prevented by the presence of the Jacobite army, and on their departure a new Council was chosen, which immediately demonstrated their loyalty to the Government by voting the freedom of the city to the Duke of Cumberland and presenting him with a massive gold box embossed with the city arms outside and engraved with the Duke's arms inside. A period of

fining, imprisonment and confiscation of goods for 'Papists, Jacobites, Episcopals, and disaffected persons' followed. Lord Provost
Archibald Stewart was suspected of being less than zealous in his
opposition to the Jacobites and was brought to trial, which lasted
from 27 October until 2 November. He was acquitted by the unanimous verdict of the jury. This was regarded by Jacobite sympathizers
as a triumph for Jacobite principle, and some went so far as to
announce a public meeting to celebrate it to be held the following
evening in the Baxters' Hall; but on hearing of the announcement
the magistrates summarily prohibited the meeting.

A few years after this Edward Burt journeyed from London to the
north of Scotland, spending a few days at Edinburgh on his way
north. He published an account of his experiences in 1754 in the
form of letters to a friend, which gives us a visitor's impression of
the city in mid-century:

When I first came into the High-Street of that City, I thought I had
not seen any thing of the Kind more magnificent; the extreme
Height of the Houses, which are, for the most Part, built with
Stone, and well sashed; the Breadth and Length of the Street, and
(it being dry Weather) a Cleanness made by the high Winds, I was
extremely pleased to find every Thing look so unlike the Descriptions of that Town, which had been given me by some of my
Countrymen.

Being a Stranger, I was invited to sup at a Tavern. The Cook
was too filthy an Object to be described, only another *English*
Gentleman whispered me and said, he believed, if the Fellow was
to be thrown against the Wall, he would stick to it ...

We supped very plentifully, and drank good *French* Claret, and
were very merry till the Clock struck Ten, the Hour when everybody is at Liberty, by beat of the City Drum, to throw their Filth
out at the Windows. Then the Company began to light Pieces of
Paper, and throw them upon the Table to smoke the Room, and,
as I thought, to mix one bad Smell with another.

Being in my Retreat to pass through a long narrow *Wynde* or
Alley, to my new Lodgings, a Guide was assigned to me, who went
before me to prevent my Disgrace, crying out all the Way, with a
loud Voice, *Hud your Haunde*. The opening up of a Sash, or
otherwise opening a Window, made me tremble, while behind and
before me, at some little Distance, fell the terrible Shower.

Well, I escaped all the Danger, and arrived, not only safe and sound, but sweet and clean, at my new Quarters; but when I was in Bed I was forced to hide my Head between the Sheets; for the Smell of the Filth, thrown out by the Neighbours on the Backside of the House, came pouring into the Room to such a Degree, I was almost poisoned with the Stench.

Like so many other visitors, Burt was struck not only by bad smells but also by the height of the tenements, with eight, ten and even twelve storeys having 'each a particular Family and perhaps a separate Proprietor'. He also described the caddies, Edinburgh messenger boys who performed an essential service in the city:

I then had no Knowledge of the *Cawdys*, a very useful Black-Guard, who attend the Coffee-Houses and publick Places to go of Errands; and though they are Wretches, that in Rags lye upon the Stairs, and in the Streets at Night, yet are they often considerably trusted, and, as I have been told, have seldom or never proved unfaithful.

These Boys know everybody in the Town who is of any kind of Note, so one of them would have been a ready Guide to the Place I wanted to find; and I afterwards wondered that one of them was not recommended to me by my new Landlady.

This *Corps* has a kind of Captain or Magistrate presiding over them, whom they call the Constable of the *Cawdys*, and in case of Neglect or other Misdemeanor he punished the Delinquent, mostly by Fines of Ale and Brandy, but sometimes corporally.

They have for the most Part an uncommon Acuteness, are very ready at proper Answers, and execute suddenly and well whatever Employment is assigned them.

The Edinburgh described by Burt was still the Old Town. But momentous changes were in prospect.

CHAPTER 7

The Eighteenth Century Vision

Archibald Stewart, suspected of Jacobite sympathies, was succeeded as Lord Provost in 1746 by George Drummond, who was not. Drummond had been active in raising volunteers for the defence of Edinburgh against the Jacobites whom he had fought in 1715 at the battle of Sherrifmuir, and he was present at the battle of Prestonpans. His real passion, however, was Edinburgh itself. He is perhaps Edinburgh's greatest Lord Provost, and he certainly did more for the city than any other individual of his century. He was born in Perthshire in 1687 and came to Edinburgh as a young man, to be appointed one of the Commissioners of Customs in 1715 and elected to the Town Council the following year. He was first elected Provost in 1725, and it was during his first term of office that he was active in raising funds to build an Infirmary. A small house was opened for patients in 1729 and in 1738, under a charter granted by George II, building of a Royal Infirmary began in what is now Infirmary Street, between the University and the old High School. This remained the Royal Infirmary until 1870, when a massive new building was begun on land in Lauriston belonging to George Watson's Hospital: it was completed in 1879.

Drummond served six terms as Lord Provost. After serving from 1725–7 he served again in 1746–8, 1750–2, 1758–60 and 1762–4. During his twelve years as Provost he was closely associated with the beginning of modern Edinburgh. Though there had for long been discussions about the possibility of bridging the valley to the north and so extending the city in that direction (we have seen how Defoe had considered what 'fine beautiful streets' could have been built to the north if the approach were not so steep and the North Loch were filled up), it was not until 1752 that precise proposals were made. In that year there appeared a pamphlet entitled *Proposals for carrying on certain Public Works in the City of Edinburgh*, which appears to have been written by Sir Gilbert Elliott of Minto under the inspiration of Provost Drummond. The Advertisement to the Reader, with which the pamphlet opens, pointed out that 'the narrow limits of the royalty of EDINBURGH, and the want of certain public buildings, and other useful and ornamental accomo-

dation in the city, have long been regretted' and went on to say
that the collapse the preceding September of 'the side-wall of a
building of six stories high, in which several reputable families lived'
had led to a survey of the condition of many old houses and the
pulling down of many that were revealed to be 'insufficient'. As a
result, 'several principal parts of the town were laid in ruins'. This
was the opportunity to make radical proposals for extending the
city. The proposals themselves begin with a reference to the 'striking
example' of London, whose growth had spread the spirit of industry
and improvement 'over the greatest part of SOUTH BRITAIN'. The
author continues:

To illustrate this further, we need only contrast the delightful
prospect which LONDON affords, with that of any other city,
which is destitute of all, or even of any considerable number of
these advantages. Sorry we are, that no one occurs to us more
apposite to this purpose, than EDINBURGH, the metropolis of
SCOTLAND when a separate kingdom, and still the chief city of
NORTH BRITAIN. The healthfulness of its situation, and its
neighbourhood to the *Forth*, must no doubt be admitted as very
favourable circumstances. But how greatly are these overbalanced
by other disadvantages almost without number? Placed upon a
ridge of a hill, it admits but of one good street, running from east
to west; and even this is tolerably accessible only from one
quarter. The narrow lanes leading to the north and south, by
reason of their steepness, narrowness, and dirtiness, can only be
considered as so many avoidable nuisances. Confined by the small
compass of the walls, and the narrow limits of the royalty, which
scarcely extends beyond the walls, the houses stand more crowded
than in any other town in *Europe*, and are built to a height that is
almost incredible. Hence necessarily follows a great want of free
air, light, cleanliness, and every other comfortable accomoda-
tion. Hence also many families, sometimes no less than ten or a
dozen, are obliged to live overhead of each other in the same
building; where, to all the other inconveniences, is added that of
a common stair, which is no other in effect than an upright street,
constantly dark and dirty. It is owing to the same narrowness of
situation, that the principal street is incumbered with the herb-
market, the fruit-market, and several others; that the shambles
are placed upon the side of the *North-loch*, rendering what was
originally an ornament of the town, a most insufferable nuisance.

No less observable is the great deficiency of public buildings. If the parliament-house, the churches, and a few hospitals, be excepted, what other have we to boast of? There is no exchange for our merchants; no safe repository for our public and private records; no place of meeting for our magistrates and towncouncil; none for the convention of our burghs [the Convention of Royal Burghs],which is intrusted with the inspection of trade ... To such reasons alone it must be imputed, that EDINBURGH, which ought to have set the first example of industry and improvement, is the last of our trading cities that has shook off the unaccountable supineness which has so long and so fatally depressed the spirit of this nation ...

The magistrates and town-council, the college of justice, and several persons of rank who happened to be in the neighbourhood of this place [therefore make a number of proposals of which the first two are the building of an exchange 'upon the ruins on the north side of the high street' and the erecting of a building for law courts, and town council, the advocates' library, etc., 'upon the ruins in the parliament-close'. The next two are:]

3 To obtain an act of parliament for extending the royalty; to enlarge and beautify the town, by opening new streets to the north and south, removing the markets and shambles, and turning the *North-Loch* into a canal, with walks and terrasses on each side.

4 That the expense of these public works should be defrayed by a national contribution.

The extending the royalty, and enlargement of the town, make no doubt the most important article. So necessary and so considerable an improvement of the capital cannot fail to have the greatest influence on the general prosperity of the nation.

The author goes on to say that it is no wonder that people of rank prefer to reside in their country seats or make frequent visits to London rather than stay in Edinburgh. 'Let us improve and enlarge this city, and possibly the superior pleasures of LONDON, which is at a distance, will be compensated, at least in some measure, by the moderate pleasures of EDINBURGH which is at home.' The pamphlet concludes by pointing out that there are already signs of increased activity in manufacturing, commerce and road-repairing in Scotland:

The little detail of an established commerce, may ingross the attention of the merchant: but it is in prosecution of greater objects, that the leading men of a country ought to exert their power and influence. And what greater object can be presented to their view, than that of enlarging, beautifying, and improving the capital of their native country? What can redound more to their honour? What prove more beneficial to SCOTLAND, and by consequence to UNITED BRITAIN?

This is the voice of Scottish patriotism combined with the voice of British 'improvement'. The planners and improvers were for the most part North Britons dedicated to the task of making Edinburgh a great British city to compensate for the loss of its position as capital of a separate kingdom of Scotland. Drummond was an enlightened Whig anti-Jacobite who did not look back to Edinburgh's violent independent past but forward to its great British future.

There had been some magnificent developments before this, but none conceived in this spirit. The Earl of Mar, writing in exile after his defeat in the Jacobite rebellion of 1715, had discussed the possibility of bridging the ground 'betwixt the North Loch and the Physic Garden' and building 'many fine streets' and gardens. Earlier still, in the last decade of the seventeenth century, Milne's Court (designed by the master mason Robert Mylne) had been built at the top of the Lawnmarket and to the west of it James's Court, eight storeys high, where David Hume lived for a while and where Boswell welcomed Johnson in 1773, was built in the 1720s. These were improvements within the old Royalty, conceived in terms of the Old Town. Later we find Brown Square and Adam Square built beyond the Royalty south of the Cowgate: these belong to what we have called in the previous chapter the 'vernacular classical' style of Edinburgh building, motivated by simple need and utility rather than by any grand vision of expansion and improvement.

The first of the proposals made in the pamphlet was put into effect almost immediately. In 1753 an Act was passed 'for Erecting several Public Buildings in the City of Edinburgh; and to impower the Trustees therein to be mentioned to purchase Lands for that Purpose; and also for Widening and Enlarging the Streets of the said City, and certain Avenues leading thereto'. In September work was begun on the Royal Exchange, with a loan from the Bank of Scotland and the Royal Bank of Scotland (founded respectively in 1695 and 1727) secured on the revenue from the ale duty as well as by personal guarantee by members of the Town Council jointly and severally. The architect was John Adam. This formal classical building, with a pediment supported by four Corinthian pilasters, stands well back from the High Street at the end of a court with a piazza for merchants along the whole of the north side; it was intended to accommodate not only a Custom House but also shops, coffee houses and dwellings. It was completed in 1760. But the Edinburgh merchants did not use it: they preferred to continue their old practice of discussing their deals in the street. In 1811 it became the City Chambers.

Another building in the Old Town, less spectacularly conceived, but proudly modelled on the Opera House at Parma, was St Cecilia's Hall, at the Cowgate end of Niddry's Wynd that ran between the Cowgate and the High Street. It was built in 1763 for the Musical Society (founded in 1728), inspired by Provost Drummond, and designed by Robert Mylne, of the well-known Edinburgh family of master-masons, surveyors and architects.

But the real vision of enlightened Edinburgh was to the northward. Drainage of the North Loch began in 1759 and in July 1763 tenders were invited for a bridge across it. The advertisement inviting them began:

> As it is greatly desired, for the public utility, that a road of communication be made betwixt the High-street of Edinburgh, and the adjacent grounds belonging to the city and the other neighbouring fields, as well as to the port of Leith, by building a stone bridge to the east end of the North Loch, at least forty feet wide betwixt the parapets of the said bridge, and upon an equal declivity of one foot in sixteen from the High-street ... this advertisement is publicly given to all who are willing to undertake the said work ...

In October 1763 Provost Drummond laid the foundation stone, though there was still no detailed architect's plan. It was not until 1765 that William Mylne's plan, with alterations by John Adam, was accepted, after a previous plan by David Henderson had been declared winner of the prize offered for the best design. The first arch, at the north end, was completed by 1 June 1768 and early the following year the bridge was open to pedestrians. In August 1769, however, part of the side-walls of the south abutment collapsed, burying five people. Financial problems and disputes about responsibility complicated matters but at last the bridge, with additional

'Ballusters' to prevent pedestrians being blown off, was completed in 1772.

By this time all sorts of other developments had taken place. Lord Provost Drummond died in 1766 in his eightieth year, having signed the contract for the North Bridge but not having had the satisfaction of seeing the fulfilment of his grand scheme for the extension of the Royalty. But his successor, Gilbert Laurie, pursued this vigorously, with the result that a Bill was presented to the House of Commons on 31 Janary 1767 entitled 'An Act for Extending the Royalty of the City of Edinburgh over certain adjoining Lands; and for giving powers to the Magistrates of Edinburgh, for the Benefit of the said City; and to enable His Majesty to grant Letters Patent for establishing a Theatre in the City of Edinburgh, or Suburbs thereof.' It passed on 16 April and received the royal assent on 20 May. A New Town to the north (to say nothing of a Theatre Royal) now became an immediate practical possibility.

The site of the intended New Town was determined partly by the physical features of the area and partly by existing boundaries of property. It extended from east to west for about three quarters of a mile along the top of a low, broad ridge just north of the North Loch. The western boundary of the extended Royalty was marked by the road to Queensferry. On the east, the Town Council were unable to acquire the property known as Cleland's Yards, which lay below Calton Hill to the south-west, with the 'Foot Walk to Leith' running between it and the hill. From the eastern end, crossing what was known as Multree's Hill just south-west of Cleland's Yards, ran a lane known as the 'Lang Gait' or 'Lang Dykes', crossing the whole length of the site from east to west to link the main roads to the west and north-west with the roads to Leith and the east. The northern boundary of the site ran from 'Lord Barjarg's Feu' on the west in an irregular line to what is now the east end of Queen Street. On the south, there was the North Loch and the boundary of the ancient Royalty that followed the shore of the loch westward as far as St Cuthbert's graveyard.

In March 1766, anticipating the passing of the Act of 1767, Lord Provost Drummond and the Town Council had published an advertisement announcing a competition for a plan to fill this site to the north of the North Loch:

Whereas the Bridge building over the North Loch of this City, (whereby an early and commodious communication will be made

between the city and the fields on the north,) is already considerably advanced, the Magistrates and Town-Council are now taking
the necessary measures for the further improvement of the city,
by feuing out the said fields for the purpose of building houses
thereon; they have accordingly ordered a survey and plan to be
made of the said fields, which will be ready about 14 days hence
and will then publish another advertisement inviting Architects
and others to call for copies of the said plan at the Council-
Chamber, that from them they may make plans of regular streets
and buildings, to be built upon the above-mentioned grounds, and
will then also be ready to grant feus thereof.

On 9 April the Magistrates and Town Council published a further
notice 'inviting Architects and others to give in Plans of a New Town
marking out streets of a proper breadth and by-lanes, and the best
situation for a reservoir, or any other public buildings, which may
be thought necessary; they will be furnished in the Council-Chamber
with a survey of the grounds, and their heights or risings upon a
proper scale'. On 17 April 1767 it was announced that James Craig
was 'entitled to the primum for the best plan of a New Town in
terms of the advertisement in the newspapers for that purpose' and
on 6 June the Council minutes recorded that 'the Magistrates of
Edinburgh conferred upon Mr James Craig, Architect, a gold medal,
with the freedom of the city in a silver box, as a reward for his merit
for having designed the best plan of the New Town'.

Craig's plan was a perfect visual embodiment of those ideas of
progress, prosperity, order and elegance that were represented by the
Scottish Enlightenment; its object was to make the chief city of
North Britain worthy of the reputation it was increasingly winning
as a centre of intellectual excellence. The vision had been described
by Craig's uncle, the poet James Thomson, in a poem entitled
Liberty, and at the head of his plan Craig put these lines from that
poem:

> August, around, what Public Works I see!
> Lo! stately Streets, lo! Squares that court the breeze!
> See long Canals and deepened Rivers join
> Each part with each, and with the circling Main
> The whole enlivened Isle.

These words are spoken by the Goddess of Liberty, who recom-
mends, as necessary for establishing liberty in Great Britain,

'Sciences, Fine Arts, and Public Works'.

The New Town did not develop precisely in accordance with Craig's plan, but it did keep to his general lines. It was designed as a self-contained residential area, the assumption being that most business and traffic would remain in the Old Town. After all, the Royal Exchange had been built in the High Street. The principal street of the New Town was to be George Street, running east and west on the top of the ridge to the north of the North Loch, and each end was closed by a square. (On Craig's design they are shown as St Andrew's Square at the east and St George's Square at the west. St George's Square became Charlotte Square, designed by Robert Adam in 1791 as the first treatment of a block of houses as a whole: on Adam's death the following year various alterations to his plan were allowed by the Town Council.) Craig intended to preserve the North Loch in the form of a 'long canal' as described in his uncle's poem, flanked by tree-lined walks, with the whole valley laid out as a formal park. In general his whole conception was more formal and symmetrical than was finally found practicable or desirable. Nevertheless, the formality and symmetry were not abandoned, and are visible even to the casual eye today.

Another point on which Craig's original intentions were frustrated was the naming of the streets. His original plan shows the street running parallel to George Street to the south of it (the present Princes Street) as St Giles Street, but George III, who had never heard of St Giles, objected to the name when he was shown the plan. 'Hey, hey— – what, what— – St Giles Street— – never do, never do—' So the name was altered to Princes Street, after the future George IV and the Duke of York. Craig's Forth Street, running parallel to George Street to the north, became Queen Street. What Craig called Queen Street, running north and south between Forth Street and St Giles Street, became Frederick Street. The only name with a specific Scottish association that remained of those given in Craig's original plan was St Andrew's Square (now St Andrew Square). St David Street, which runs north and south just east of St Andrew Square, was not so called in ironic compliment to the sceptical philosopher David Hume (who built himself a house on the south-west corner of St Andrew Square which was entered from the side street running south to Princes Street), as the legend has it: though unnamed in Craig's map, it was called St David Street in compliment to the patron saint of Wales. This was part of the deliberate all-British association of New Town names.

The northward extension of the Royalty gave the Magistrates and Town Council the opportunity to fulfil a project discussed since at least as early as 1722 – the provision of a worthy building to house the Public Records of Scotland. It was agreed to build it on 'the area at the end of the New Bridge'. The brothers Robert and James Adam were appointed architects, and the foundation stone of Register House (as it was and is called) was laid at the east end of Princes Street on 27 June 1774. Difficulty with finance caused some long delays in its completion. Robert Reid carried on the rear portion after Robert Adam's death in 1792, and this was finished in 1822. Almost opposite the Register House stood the Theatre Royal, built in 1768 where the General Post Office now stands, a legal theatre authorized by the Act of 1767. Around it grew up between 1772 and 1778 what James Grant in his *Old and New Edinburgh* described as 'the grim little enclosure named Shakespeare Square,' which closed the east end of Princes Street. It was, says Grant, 'simply a place of lodging-houses, a humble inn or two, like the Red Lion tavern and oyster shop'.

Other public buildings in the first phase of the New Town were Craig's own Physicians' Hall in George Street, and the Assembly Rooms designed by John Henderson, also in George Street. The foundation stone of the Physicians' Hall was laid by Dr Cullen assisted by all the medical professors on 27 November 1775, and it was completed in 1777. It survived for something over sixty years. The Assembly Rooms were built by public subscription between 1784 and 1787.

Building in the New Town did not proceed without controversy. The Town Council invited the public to purchase lots from them and laid down regulations to ensure that all buildings on the lots purchased should be according to the approved plan. But, complained Hugo Arnot in 1778, the magistracy did not consider that they themselves were bound by these regulations, and they deviated from the plan by building on 'the spot which in the plan was dilinaeted into terraces, and a canal, ... mean and irregular buildings'. Purchasers in the extended Royalty complained to the Court of Session, but the Court of Session upheld the Town Council. But the House of Lords reversed this decision on appeal, and remitted the cause to the Court of Session. 'After an expensive litigation,' Arnot reported, 'differences were compromised, chiefly by the mediation of Mr Stoddart, then Lord Provost of Edinburgh [James Stoddart was Lord Provost from 1774–6, and was responsible for the laying out of Leith

Walk in 1774: in 1776 he laid the foundation stone of the Observatory on the Calton Hill] who, in every thing respecting public works, and the improvement and decoration of the city, showed himself an excellent magistrate'. The compromise was established by a 'decreet-arbitral' dated 20 March 1776. It provided that on the south side of Princess Street there should be no buildings from a point as far west as the intended street called in the plan Hanover Street, as the large buildings on the south side of Princes Street, fronting north and west, is east from St Andrew's Square. The intermediate spaces were to be laid out in terraces and a canal.

Arnot concluded his account of the New Town up to his own time with some satisfaction:

> Notwithstanding these discouragements, the progress of the New Town has been rapid. The buildings along Princes Street have run to a considerable length. St Andrews square, and the streets connected with it, are almost compleat.... The prospect from the New Town is as beautiful as almost any country can afford. There is a supply of excellent water from the general reservoir; and, in the neighbourhood, there is an inexhaustible fund of free and whinstone quarries, the first for building houses, the last for paving the streets. The New Town, however, is, in a special manner, exposed to very violent winds, which rage in Edinburgh with incredible fury. Houses blown down, large trees torn up by the roots, people carried off their feet, are no uncommon circumstances in Edinburgh.

In 1785 an Act was passed authorizing the building of the South Bridge, which spanned the Cowgate Valley south of the North Bridge, the road between the North and South Bridges crossing the High Street at right angles. The South Bridge was finished in 1789, the year in which the new University building, designed by Robert Adam, was begun; this building was not completed until 1815, according to a modified design by William Playfair. A so-called second New Town, laid out by Robert Reid and William Sibbald to the north of Queen Street in 1802, produced Heriot Row, where R. L. Stevenson was to grow up (complaining, as Arnot did, of the New Town winds), parallel to Queen Street on the north side of Queen Street Gardens, and its continuation to the east, Abercrombie Place, the first curved street façade in Edinburgh, with parallel streets further north centering on Great King Street. Plans for building around Calton Hill to the east ran into difficulties and the terraces on

the hill – Royal Terrace, Carlton Terrace and Regent Terrace –
were not completed until the middle of the nineteenth century.
Calton Hill itself, which patriotic Edinburgh citizens regarded as
Edinburgh's Acropolis, seemed a splendid site for classical buildings.
Playfair's observatory and his never finished (because of lack of
money) National Monument to those who fell in the Napoleonic
wars were deliberate imitations of famous ancient Greek buildings,
as were the monuments to Burns and Dugald Stewart built on the
hill in the early 1830s. At the west end of the New Town, by the
Glasgow approaches, there were new developments in the second
decade of the nineteenth century. The main road west crossed two
shallow crescents, Athol Crescent and Coates Crescent, and to the
north, parallel to this road, ran Melville Street. Finally, the original
New Town and the second New Town were connected with the
valley of the Water of Leith to the north-west, and together with the
opening of Thomas Telford's spectacular Dean Bridge in 1831 and
Sir Henry Raeburn's development of his land just to the north (giving among other streets the uniquely attractive Ann Street, called
after his wife), this completed the Georgian development of Edinburgh. Its completion coincided almost exactly with the end of
Edinburgh's Golden Age, symbolized by the death of 'the Scottish
Addison' (to whom Scott dedicated *Waverley*), the founder of the
sentimental novel Henry Mackenzie, in 1831 and of Scott himself in
1832. It is a unique story of the meshing of intellectual, artistic,
architectural and town-planning activity, extending from what may
be called the Age of Hume to the Age of Scott.

CHAPTER 8

Social Life in the Eighteenth Century

On 5 September 1750 the poet Robert Fergusson was born in the Cap-and-Feather Close, one of the alleys entering the High Street from the north that disappeared when the North Bridge was constructed. He died on 17 October 1774 in the Bedlam attached to the Edinburgh Poorhouse, at the south-east corner of the grounds of Darien House (dating from the ill-fated Darien Scheme) near the Bristo Port, his short life ending in mental derangement. But between January 1772 and the end of 1773 he produced poems in Scots, nearly all of which appeared in the *Weekly Magazine or Edinburgh Amusement* founded by Walter Ruddiman (nephew of Thomas) in 1768, that give the flavour of Edinburgh life with great vividness. This was not the life of the literati, but the colourful, noisy and dirty street life of the old town. At the same time his poems show how much eighteenth-century Edinburgh depended on its legal establishment, which controlled so much of its activities and determined its periods of bustle and of passivity.

The first of his poems to appear in the *Weekly Magazine* was in the issue of 2 January 1772. This was 'The Daft Days', celebrating festivities during the holiday period at the end of the old year and the beginning of the new. It begins with a vivid picture of winter laying its frozen hand on Edinburgh and its rural environs, then proceeds to contrast the cosy interior with the winter scene outside:

Auld Reikie! thou'rt a canty hole,	*cheerful*
A bield for mony a caldrife soul,	*shelter; sensitive to cold*
Wha snugly at thine ingle loll,	
Baith warm and couth;	*comfortable*
While round they gar the bicker roll	*make; drinking-cup*
To weet their mouth.	

'Auld Reikie' is Edinburgh, Old Smokey: it was said that observers in Fife across the Forth could tell the time by seeing the smoke rise from the chimneys when cooking for dinner began. But Fergusson is here using the term affectionately, not censoriously. He goes on to describe the prodigious eating and drinking, the music and the dancing and, finally he appeals to the God of Whisky to save any inebriated citizen from the clutches of the City Guard:

> And thou, great god of *Aqua Vitae*!
> Wha sways the empire of this city,
> When fou we're sometimes capernoity, *drunk, bad-tempered*
> Be thou prepar'd
> To hedge us frae that black banditti,
> The City-Guard.

The City Guard had declined both in numbers and effectiveness since the ill-fated John Porteous led them in 1736. Sir Walter Scott gave a good account of them in chapter 3 of *The Heart of Midlothian*:

They were chiefly veterans who enlisted in this corps, having the benefit of working at their trades when they were off duty. These men had the charge of preserving public order, repressing riots and street robberies, acting, in short, as an armed police, and attending on all public occasions where confusion or popular disturbance might be expected. Poor Fergusson, whose irregularities sometimes led him into unpleasant rencontres with these military conservators of public order, ... mentions them so often that he may be termed their poet laureate, ...

In fact, the soldiers of the City Guard, being, as we have said, in general discharged veterans, who had strength enough remaining for this municipal duty, and being, moreover, for the greater part, Highlanders, were neither by birth, education, or former habits, trained to endure with much patience the insults of the rabble, or the provoking petulance of truant schoolboys, and idle debauchees of all descriptions, with whom their occupation brought them into contact ...

On all occasions when a holiday licensed some riot and irregularity, a skirmish with these veterans was a favourite recreation with the rabble of Edinburgh. But the venerable corps, with whom the contention was held, may now [1818] be considered as totally extinct ... A spectre may indeed here and there still be seen, of an old grey-headed and grey-bearded Highlander, with war-worn features, but bent double by age; dressed in the old-fashioned cocked hat, bound with white tape instead of silver lace; and in coat, waistcoat, and breeches of a muddy-coloured red, bearing in his withered hand an ancient weapon, called a Lochaber-axe; a long pole, namely, with an axe at the extremity, and a hook at the

The Castle from the foot of Castle Street, 1909. *Edinburgh City Libraries*

Edinburgh from the North Loch, by Slezer. *Edinburgh City Libraries*

View of Edinburgh in 1650. *Edinburgh City Libraries*

John Knox. *National Galleries of Scotland*

James VI of Scotland and I of England. *National Portrait Gallery*

Sir George Mackenzie. *National Galleries of Scotland*

Engraving of New Bridge and part of the Castle. *Edinburgh City Libraries*

Edinburgh from the Glasgow Road, 1835. *Edinburgh City Libraries*

Allan Ramsay Junior. *National Galleries of Scotland*

Hugh Blair. *National Galleries of Scotland*

Engraving of Edinburgh from Carlton Hill, 1820. *Edinburgh City Libraries*

Robert Fergusson. *National Galleries of Scotland*

The University, 1819. *Edinburgh City Libraries*

David Hume, 1766. *National Galleries of Scotland*

Robert Burns, by Alexander Nasmyth, 1787. *National Galleries of Scotland*

Sir Walter Scott, by Sir Henry Raeburn, 1882. *National Galleries of Scotland*

Lord Francis Jeffrey, by William Bewick. *National Galleries of Scotland*

Dean Bridge Edin⁺

The Dean Bridge, 1835.
*National Galleries of
Scotland*

R.L. Stevenson, by
Nerli, 1892. *National
Galleries of Scotland*

OPPOSITE: 'The
Disruption', May 1834.
*Edinburgh City
Libraries*

THE
FREE ASS-EMBLY
FOR
EVER!!!

Every copy speaks, and I will not suffer

This is as will to secure the loaves and fishes however

This is the flag I saw our Commodore nail to the mast

Hurra for Torphid!

Ay, Candy, wait till we get to the Gov-work, and we'll blow up the Establishment!

The very sound of a Free Church hath a charm for me

The grandest display this in history of Christendom.

What a responsibility rests upon us

The smallest donation thankfully received.

NOT LEAVE A WRACK BEHIND!!!

CONTRIBUTIONS
TO
THE FREE CHURCH

Don't attempt to lead me, John. Mind, we don't recognise you for a Brother.

I'll marshal you the way that you should go.

Princes Street, by Hill and Adamson. *Edinburgh City Libraries*

Waverly Station, circa 1901. *Edinburgh City Libraries*

back of the hatchet. Such a phantom of former days still creeps, I have been informed, round the statue of Charles the Second in the Parliament Square, ... and one or two others are supposed to glide around the door of the guard-house assigned to them in the Luckenbooths, when their ancient refuge in the High Street was laid low.

Among other poems descriptive of Edinburgh festivities, Fergusson wrote 'The King's Birth-Day in Edinburgh', which appeared in the *Weekly Magazine* on 4 June 1772:

> Sing, then, how, on the fourth of June,
> Our bells screed aff a loyal tune,
> Our antient castle shoots at noon,
>   Wi' flag-staff buskit,   *decked*
> Frae which the soldier blades come down
>   To cock their musket.

There are fire-works:

> Now round and round the serpents whiz,
> Wi' hissing wrath and angry phiz;
> Sometimes they catch a gentle gizz,   *wig*
>   Alake the day!
> And singe, wi' hair-devouring bizz,   *hissing noise*
>   Its curls away.

All kinds of riotous behaviour occur, but in the end we are reminded that Edinburgh, even the Old Town, lies surrounded by nearby countryside, where one can go for relief after urban excesses:

> Next day each hero tells his news
> O crackit crowns and broken brows,
> And deeds that here forbid the Muse
>   Her theme to swell,
> Or time mair precious to abuse
>   Their crimes to tell.
> She'll rather to the fields resort,
> Where music gars the day seem short,   *makes*
> Whare doggies play, and lambies sport
>   On gowany braes,   *daisy-covered*
> Whare peerless Fancy hads her court,   *holds*
>   And tunes her lays.

The *Weekly Magazine* gave a more decorous account of the festivities in prose on 10 June:

> Friday last, being the anniversary of his majesty's birth-day, when he entered into the 36th year of his age, was observed here with the greatest demonstrations of joy. In the morning the flag was displayed from the castle, at noon there was a round of the great guns, returned by three vollies from a party of the military drawn up on the Castle-hill, and accompanied by the ringing of music-bells. [The Lord Provost, magistrates and Town Council with distinguished guests, drank the King's health in Parliament House.] After which the evening concluded with a brilliant assembly. – It is, however, to be regretted that, on such days of festivity, the lower class of people seldom indulges their mirth without mischief ...

Fergusson celebrated the consumption of fresh oysters from the Forth in Lucky Middlemass's tavern in the Cowgate (the site of which is now occupied by the south pier of the South Bridge). When the bells of St Giles' rang eight in the evening and merchants locked their shops was the time when Fergusson and his friends adjourned there:

When aud Saunt Giles, at aught o'clock,	
Gars merchant lowns their chopies lock,	*makes; shops*
There we adjourn wi' hearty fock	*people*
Ti birle our bodles,	*spend our money*
And get wharewi' to crack our joke,	
And clear our noddles.	

On 17 November 1772 a poem of Fergusson's in the *Weekly Magazine* celebrated Edinburgh's Hallow Fair, held at Hallowmass, the Season of All-Hallows at the beginning of November. He describes the lively activity at the stalls:

Here chapmen billies tak their stand,	*merchant fellows*
An' shaw their bonny wallies;	*'gewgaws', finery*
Wow, but they lie fu' gleg aff hand	*glibly*
To trick the silly fallows;	
Heh, Sirs! what cairds and tinklers come,	
An' ne'er-do-weel horse-coupers,	
An' spae-wives fenzying to be dumb	*fortune-tellers; feigning*
Wi' a' siclike landloupers,	*vagabonds*
To thrive that day.	

In 1772 Hallow Fair was held at Orcharfields, near Castlebarns, on the Falkirk Road about half a mile from the Grassmarket.

Edinburgh life was in considerable degree dominated by the activities of the Court of Session, which sat for two terms in the year, from 12 November to 12 March and from 12 June to 12 August, with a three weeks break at Christmas and New Year. Fergusson's two poems, 'The Rising of the Session' (which appeared on 18 March 1773) and 'The Sitting of the Session' (4 November 1773) give a vivid account of the bustle and business and drinking brought about by the opening of the Court and the emptying of the city (especially of its taverns) after it has risen. After the rising of the Court

Nae body takes a morning dribb	*drop of liquor*
O' Holland gin frae Robin Gibb;	
And tho' a dram to Rob's mair sib	*more closely related*
Than to his wife,	
He maun take time to daut his Rib	*pet his wife*
Till siller's rife.	*silver*
This vacance is a heavy doom	*vacation*
On Indian Peter's coffee-room,	
For a' his china pigs are toom;	*pitchers; empty*
Nor do we see	
In wine the sucker biskets soom	*sugar biscuits swim*
As light's a flee.	

Fergusson's most ambitious poem about Edinburgh, which gives a complete view of the life of the city, is 'Auld Reikie', a poem of 328 lines which was published as a separate pamphlet in 1773. A further forty lines were printed in the posthumous 1779 edition of his poems. He describes its aspects in different seasons; the different kinds of social life; the day time activities and the night life; the goings-on in Edinburgh clubs; the Sunday afternoon walks; the debtors who sought refuge in the precincts of Holyrood, where the ancient right of sanctuary could still be claimed; pays tribute to the late Lord Provost Drummond (whose work for Edinburgh, he says, at last made that city able to boast superiority to Glasgow in beauty and design); and ends by looking across at Edinburgh from the Fife side of the Firth of Forth:

Reikie, farewel— I ne'er cou'd part	
Wi' thee but wi' a dowy heart;	*gloomy*

Aft frae the Fifan coast I've seen
Thee tow'ring on thy summit green;
So glowr the saints when first is given
A fav'rite keek o' glore and heaven;   *glory*
On earth nae mair they bend their ein,   *eyes*
But quick assume angelic mein;
So I on Fife wad glowr no more,
But gallop'd to Edina's shore.

Fergusson's Edinburgh was a city of taverns, many of which, like
Rob Gibb's, were situated within a stone's throw of Parliament
House, now the centre of Scotland's legal establishment since the
Scottish Parliament ceased to exist in 1707. It was divided into
various court rooms until 1780; to reach them one entered by a
narrow passage where Peter Williamson's Coffee-House afforded refreshment to litigants, lawyers and judges alike. Williamson was
known as 'Indian Peter' because as a child at Aberdeen he had been
kidnapped while playing on the quay and taken to Philadelphia
where he was sold as a slave. He was fortunate in his master, who
was a fellow Scot and on his death left him money and his freedom,
so that he was able to marry and settle down as a substantial planter
in Pennsylvania. His house was attacked by a party of Indians, who
scalped him and carried him off as a prisoner. He eventually
escaped, and returned to Aberdeen in 1758. He then settled in
Edinburgh, where he opened a tavern before turning to bookselling,
printing and publishing. In 1776 he started a periodical called *The
Scots Spy, or Critical Observer*, which appeared every Friday. He
published an account of his own adventures as well as the first
Edinburgh Directory, and established the first penny-post in Edinburgh. He married again when he was settled in Edinburgh: his
wife, Jean Wilson, daughter of John Wilson, a bookseller in the city,
carried on mantua-making and advertised that 'orders given in at
P. Williamson's General Penny-Post Office, Luckenbooths, will be
punctually attended to'. She also carried on in less respectable ways,
and Williamson successfully brought proceedings for divorce, alleg-
ing among her other misdemeanours that she had recklessly spent all
his money. Williamson died in January 1799.

Fergusson's Edinburgh is still visibly the descendant of Dunbar's
Edinburgh, a lusty, dirty, bustling, vivid city pent up on the ridge
between the Castle and Holyrood. And Fergusson's convivial even-

ings at Walter Scott's tavern in Geddes Close with fellow members of
the Cape Club or taking his oysters and gin at Lucky Middlemass's
or his dish of rizzard haddock and bicker of tippeny at some other
Edinburgh howff – these were rather different from the formal
meetings of the Select Society which took place on Friday evenings
to discuss literary and philosophical topics and to enable its members to improve themselves in the art of public speaking. It is true
that social lines were not clearly drawn in eighteenth century Edinburgh when it came to matters of conviviality in taverns, and some
very highly placed people could be found enjoying plebeian food
and drink in some fairly low places of public resort. Nevertheless,
there was a clear difference between the Cape Club on the one hand
and the Select Society or the Poker Club on the other. It was not a
question of riotousness, for the clubs with the more distinguished
members could be very riotous indeed. Judges and advocates were
as deep drinkers as poor poets, and the goings-on in 'The Feast of
Tabernacles', a club composed of highly placed lawyers and men of
letters, proved that it had what Ramsay of Ochtertyre politely
called its 'frolicsome moments' as well as the Cape. But the Cape
Club was united by a sense of community which drew no social or
professional lines at all: in Fergusson's time it included David
Herd, the distinguished antiquary and song collector, a number of
painters, printers, musicians, and a large number of tradesmen
(shoemakers, tailors, glovemakers, smiths, saddlers, marblecutters,
barbers, brewers) as well as a few advocates, writers to the signet,
surgeons and physicians, shipowners and naval officers and a solitary
student of divinity.

There was a curious contradiction in the social and intellectual
life of eighteenth century Edinburgh: on the one hand, pulpits rang
with denunciations of such temptations to sin, lust and worldliness
as dancing and the theatre, while on the other hand there were
continuous attempts, often highly successful, to organize both formal
dances and theatrical performances. As early as 1710 the first 'assembly' for public dancing was opened, and though 'promiscuous
dancing' was regularly condemned by sections of the clergy who
regarded the assemblies as nurseries of vice, they proved increasingly
popular. Dancing masters were in great demand, and gave their own
balls which generally lasted from five in the afternoon until ten or
eleven at night; tickets cost 2s. 6d. There was also an assembly in
the West Bow, in a large room in a flat opposite the deserted house

of the notorious Major Weir. In 1720 dances began to be held in the Assembly Close off the High Street. A visitor from Banffshire wrote in 1727 to a friend at home:

They have an asembly at Edinburgh, where every Thursday they meet and dance from four till eleven at night. It is half-a-crown, and whatever tea, coffee, chocolate, biscuit, etc., they call for, they must pay as the managers direct; and they are the Countess of Panmure, Lady Newhall, the President's lady, and the Lady Drumpellier. The ministers are preaching against it, and say it will be another horning order. [A 'horning order' was an edict by which a person was 'put to the horn' and so proclaimed an outlaw.]

Captain Edward Topham, an English visitor, wrote from Edinburgh in May 1775 describing the balls given for their pupils by the dancing masters of the city. Each dancing master gave one or two balls or 'publics' a year. 'It is incredible the pleasure and satisfaction the inhabitants of this City take in this diversion. They seem to enjoy it much more than dancing themselves.' Topham continued:

At these balls all the children dance minuets; which would be very tiresom and disagreeable, as well from the badness of the performance, as from the length of time they would take up, were they regularly continued. But the Dancing-masters enliven the entertainment by introducing between the minuets their High Dances, (which is a kind of Double Hornpipe) in the execution of which they excell perhaps the rest of the World ... Besides all those common to the hornpipe, they have a number of their own, which I never before saw or heard of; and their neatness and quickness in the performance of them is incredible: so amazing is their agility, that an Irishman, who was standing by me the other night, could not help exclaiming in his surprise 'that by Jesus, he never saw children so *handy* with their *feet* in all his life.'

In another letter written during the same month Topham described the assemblies:

I assure you the Assemblies afford a very agreeable diversion: they are governed by seven Directors and seven Directresses, one of whom manages the dancing alternately, and performs the part of Mistress of the Ceremonies. As the room is too small for the company who generally frequent them, it is impossible for all to dance at the same time: to prevent, therefore, the inconvenience and confusion which must necessarily be occasioned, the Lady Directress is obliged to divide the company into Sets, and suit them according to their rank and quality, putting about twelve couple in a Set. After this *etiquette* is over, the first Set dance minuets, beginning in the order of the tickets which are distributed by the Lady Directress, and then one country dance, which is surrounded by chairs, to prevent the rest of the company interfering with the dancers. At the conclusion of this, the second Set begin, and then the third and fourth in their respective turns, till all the Sets have danced their minuet and country dance, and then the first begin again a country dance, and the other follows as at first ...

Ever since I have been in Edinburgh, the office of Lady Directress has been discharged by Mrs Murray [Miss Nicky Murray], sister to Lord Mansfield; who executes her part with so much success, that the other Ladies fear to attempt it after her; and, indeed, she deserves every encomium that can be bestowed on her. As long as Mrs Murray obliges the Public with her assistance, the City of Edinburgh cannot wish for a more agreeable entertainment, than their Assemblies; but if any thing should happen to deprive them of her abilities, it is imagined they would furnish themselves with a better room, where a different plan would be adopted ...

The company is so much the more obliged to Mrs Murray, as the task is by no means to be envied. The crowd which immediately surrounds her on her entering the room, the impetuous applications of *chaperons*, maiden-aunts, and the earnest intreaties of lovers to obtain a ticket in one of the first Sets for the dear object, renders the fatigue of the office of Lady Directress almost intolerable; and I am sensible, few would undertake it, did not Mrs Murray's zeal and endeavours meet with universal approbation.

Besides minuets and country-dances, they in general dance reels in separate parts of the room; which is a dance that every one is acquainted with, but none but a native of Scotland can execute in perfection ...

But besides the general Assemblies, there are a number of private ones given by societies, clubs, or subscription, and every week is productive of something new. Among the rest, the matrons and married Ladies give an Assembly and Entertainment to the young Ladies, to whom they distribute tickets to provide themselves partners ... In return for this Ball the Gentlemen of the Capilaire club give another equally elegant and polite, with a supper, ices, and every thing that luxury can invent. After the Ladies are withdrawn, the Gentlemen, in conformity with the manner of this Country, retire into a private room, where each sacrifices his understanding and health to wishing, in full bumpers, the health of his fair partner; ...

The opening of the Assembly Rooms in George Street in 1787 marked the move of fashion from the Old Town to the New. But a younger generation, looking back on the assemblies held in the older parts of the city, found them insufferably formal. Lord Cockburn, writing in the 1820s, looked back at the earlier time:

The ancient dancing establishments in the Bow and the Assembly Close I know nothing about. Everything of the kind was meant to be annihilated by the erection ... of the handsome apartments in George Street. Yet even against these, the new part of the Old Town made a gallant struggle, and in my youth the whole fashionable dancing, as indeed the fashionable everything, clung to George Square; where in Buccleuch Place (close by the southeastern corner of the square) most beautiful rooms were erected, which, for several years, threw the New Town piece of presumption entirely into the shade. [The 'George's Square Assembly Rooms' were opened in 1785: it was here that Walter Scott danced with his first love.] Here were the last remains of the ball-room disciplines of the preceeding generation. Martinet dowagers and venerable beaux acted as masters and mistresses of ceremonies, and made all the preliminary arrangements. No couple could dance unless each party was provided with a ticket prescribing the precise place in the precise dance. If there was no ticket, the gentleman, or the lady, was dealt with as an intruder, and turned out of the dance. If the ticket had marked upon it – say for a country dance, the figure 3.5; this meant that the holder was to place himself in the third dance, and fifth from the top; and if he was anywhere else, he was set right, or excluded. And the partner's ticket must correspond. Woe on the poor girl who with ticket 2.7, was found opposite a youth marked 5.9! It was flirting without a licence, and looked very ill, and would probably be reported by the ticket director of that dance to the mother. Of course parties, or parents, who wished to secure dancing for themselves or those they had charge of, provided themselves with correct and corresponding vouchers before the ball day arrived. This could only be accomplished through a director; and the election of a pope sometimes required less jobbing. When parties chose to take their chance, they might do so; but still, though only obtained in the room, the written permission was necessary; and such a thing as a compact to dance, by a couple, without official authority, would have been an outrage that could scarcely be contemplated. Tea was sipped in side-rooms; and he was a careless beau who did not present his partner with an orange at the end of each dance; and the oranges and the tea, like everything else, were under exact and positive regulation. All this disappeared, and the very rooms were obliterated, as soon as the lately raised community secured its inevitable supremacy in the New Town. The aristocracy of a few predominating individuals and families came to an end; and the unreasonable old had nothing for it but to sigh over the recollection of the select and elegant parties of their youth, where indiscriminate public right was rejected, and its coarseness awed.

Cockburn noted the paradox that 'there was far more coarseness in the formal age than in the free one'. He noted swearing and drunkenness as 'very prevalent, if not universal, among the whole upper ranks'. Until towards the end of the century merchants met their customers and advocates met 'writers' (solicitors) and writers met their clients in taverns. When the bells of St Giles' rang half-past-eleven in the morning it was the sign for citizens to adjourn to a tavern for their 'medidian' or mid-morning drink of ale or spirits. Hard drinking went on in the evening in the innumerable clubs of the city. The Poker Club met at Fortune's Tavern in the Stamp-Office Close. The Star and Garter, kept by a man called Clerihugh, was a favourite haunt of the magistrates and Town Council. Douglas's in the Anchor Close was a popular tavern. Robert Chambers has described it in his *Traditions of Edinburgh*:

You went a few yards down the dark, narrow alley, passing on the left the entry to a scale stair, decorated with 'THE LORD BE MY SUPPORT;' then passed another door, bearing the still more antique legend, 'O LORD, IN THE IS AL MY TRAIST;' immediately beyond, under an architrave calling out 'BE MERCI-FULL TO ME,' you entered the hospitable mansion of Dawney Douglas, ...

The frequenter of Douglas's, after ascending a few steps, found himself in a pretty large kitchen – a dark, fiery Pandemonium, through which numerous ineffable ministers of flame were continually flying about, while beside the door sat the landlady, a large, fat woman, in a towering head-dress and large-flowered silk gown, who bowed to every one passing. Most likely, on emerging from this igneous region, the party would fall into the hands of Dawney himself, and so be conducted to an apartment ... The house was noted for its suppers of tripe, rizzared haddocks, mince collops, and *hashes*, which never cost more than sixpence a-head. On charges of this moderate kind the honest couple grew extremely rich before they died.

It was at Douglas's that the club called the Crochallan Fencibles met, taking its name from the Gaelic song Douglas liked to sing to his customers, 'Crodh Chaillein', meaning 'Colin's Cattle'. (The 'Fencibles' part of the name derived from the voluntary military companies formed after the outbreak of the American War of Independence.) Robert Burns was introduced to Douglas's and the Crochallan Fencibles by the club's founder, the printer William Smellie, who printed the second (Edinburgh) edition of Burns's poems in 1787. Burns was in Edinburgh in the winter of 1786–7, to be shown off and patronized as a rustic genius by the gentry and literati, who for the most part showered him with bad advice about his future course as a poet. Smellie's office was very near Douglas's tavern, in the Anchor Close, and there Burns corrected the proofs of the Edinburgh edition sitting on a stool that came to be known as 'Burns's Stool'. His meeting with the Crochallan Fencibles, who were noted for what was then called 'sculduddery', was a refreshment after the patronizing ceremoniousness of the formal entertainments arranged for him. They were a bawdy lot, and it was probably for them that Burns assembled the bawdy songs that make up *The Merry Muses of Caledonia*.

Ale was the common drink especially of the ordinary people, but in 1779 Hugo Arnot sadly noted that instead of this 'the lower class of inhabitants have be taken themselves to tea and *whisky*. The first of these, to people who are not able to afford generous diet, and liquors, cannot be esteemed wholesome. The last ins equally pernicious to health and to morals.' Gentlemen drank vast amounts of claret or port at dinner, and were often carried to bed drunk. Henry Mackenzie, who was born in 1745, used to tell in his old age about a drinking session he attended as a young man at Kilravock Castle, but it might well have happened in Edinburgh. Cockburn recalled how Mackenzie told the story:

> Mackenzie was once at a festival there, towards the close of which the exhausted topers sank gradually back and down on their chairs, till little of them was seen above the table except their noses; and at last they disappeared altogether and fell on the floor. Those who were too far gone to rise lay still from necessity; while those who, like the *Man of Feeling* [Mackenzie, so called after the title of his famous novel, published in Edinburgh in 1771], were glad of a pretence for escaping fell into a doze from policy. When Mackenzie was in this state he was alarmed by feeling a hand working about his throat, and called out. A voice answered, 'Dinna be feared, Sir; it's me.' 'And who are you?' 'A'm the lad that louses the craavats.'

After a night of heavy drinking a Lord of Session would appear on the bench the next morning with no loss of dignity. Charles Hay, Lord Newton was one of the judges particularly noted for his heavy drinking. It is said that he often drank until seven in the morning, slept for two hours, and then appeared on the bench where he conducted himself perfectly. Cockburn described an eighteenth century practice that survived among older judges until the early years of the nineteenth:

> Black bottles of strong port were set down beside [the judges] on the Bench, with glasses, caraffes of water, tumblers, and biscuits; and this without the slightest attempt at concealment. The refreshment was generally allowed to stand untouched for a short time, as if despised, during which their Lordships seemed intent only on their notes. But in a little, some water was poured into the tumbler, and sipped quietly as if merely to sustain nature. Then a few drops of wine were ventured upon, but only with the water. But at last patience could endure no longer, and a full bumper of the pure black element was tossed over; after which the thing went on regularly, and there was a comfortable munching and quaffing to the great envy of the parched throats in the gallery. The strong-headed stood it tolerably well, but it told, plainly enough, upon the feeble. Not that the ermine was absolutely intoxicated, but it was certainly sometimes affected. This however was so ordinary with these sages, that it really made little

apparent change upon them. It was not very perceptible at a distance; and they all acquired the habit of sitting and looking judicial enough, even when their bottles had reached the lowest ebb.

James Boswell, who practised as an advocate in Edinburgh from 1766 until 1786, has left a more detailed account of his drunken bouts than any other Scot of the century. While Boswell can hardly be taken as typical of his fellow citizens of Edinburgh in temperament or behaviour, it is clear from the numerous accounts of drinking in his Journals that he readily found companions among men of his own class and that for two people to drink five bottles of claret at a sitting was not regarded as particularly monstrous. But only Boswell could write in his Journal such a passage as this: 'We sat till near ten. I was very drunk, roved the streets, and went and stayed above an hour with two whores at their lodging in a narrow dirty stair in the Bow.'

Early in the eighteenth century people were prohibited from staying on at taverns after the town drum had beaten its nightly tattoo in the High Street at ten o'clock, and though the regulation remained throughout much of the century, it came to be ignored by determined drinkers (including the city's magistrates) at club meetings in taverns. Once again Fergusson pictures the scene for us, in his 'Auld Reikie':

Now some to Porter, some to Punch,
Some to their Wife, and some their Wench,
Retire, while noisy Ten-hours Drum
Gars a' your Trades gae dancing Home.   *makes*
Now mony a Club, jocose and free,
Gie a' to Merriment and Glee,
Wi' Sang and Glass, they fley the Pow'r   *put to flight*
O'Care that wad harrass the Hour: ...

But they had to be careful going home at night, for at any moment the cry of 'Gardy-loo!' (gardez l'eau) could be heard from an upper window as a warning that a chamber pot was about to be emptied on to the heads of any unfortunate passing below unless he was quick-witted enough to shout out 'Haud yer hand' and briskly step out of the way. 'How long can it be suffered,' wrote John Wesley in his *Journal* in 1762, 'that all manner of filth should be flung into the streets? How long shall the capital city of Scotland and the chief

street of it stink worse than a common sewer?' In spite of regular
condemnation by visitors, the practice went on till the end of the
century. Even after the throwing of refuse from windows was prohibited the magistrates were able to enforce the prohibition only in
the principal streets, and as late as 1796 there was a complaint in the
Scots Magazine that the populous minor lanes of the city were
thoroughly foul, while people living in Princes Street had to put up
with a stagnant marsh at their front doors.

Meal times changed as the century progressed. Until after the
middle of the century the dinner hour was between one and two, but
after about 1760, when the fashionable dinner hour was two o'clock,
it grew steadily later, to three and by the 1780s to four or five. When
Cockburn wrote his *Memorials* in the 1820s it had been moved to
six or even half-past six, but he recalled how it had been postponed
from two until four and then reached five, 'which, however, was
thought positively revolutionary; and four was long and gallantly
adhered to by haters of change as "the good old hour". At last even
they were obliged to give in, and made a desperate stand at half-
past four.' With dinner served at four or five there was no longer
any question of returning to work after it. Then men sat long over
their wine, and when there were guests often went on until the small
hours. The exemption of claret from import duty in Scotland made
that the favourite wine, but after this exemption was withdrawn, in
1780, port began to replace it. Port and sherry were the only wines
drunk when he was young, Cockburn remembered, and champagne
was not introduced until after France was made accessible by the
peace of 1815. Punch (whisky punch, brandy punch or – the great
Glasgow drink – rum punch) was often consumed by the gentlemen
in large quantities after dinner. 'Early dinners begat suppers,' wrote
Cockburn, and in many households late suppers survived long after
the dinner hour had reached five: the supper party was a speciality
of Edinburgh convivial gatherings, and at least it postponed the hour
at which the men settled down to solid drinking.

In the later decades of the eighteenth century the drinking of
healths went on right through the meal, and ladies indulged freely as
well as gentlemen. Toasting, Cockburn recalled, was a serious
affair:

For one thing, the wine was very rare on the table. It had to be
called for; and in order to let the servant know to whom he was to
carry it, the caller was obliged to specify his partner aloud. All

this required some premeditation and courage. Hence timid men never ventured on so bold a step at all; but were glad to escape by only drinking when they were invited. As this ceremony was a mark of respect, the landlord, or any other person who thought himself the great man, was graciously pleased to perform it to every one present. But he and the others were always at liberty to abridge the severity of the duty, by performing it by platoons. They took a brace, or two brace, of ladies or of gentlemen, or of both, and got them all engaged at once, and proclaiming to the sideboard – 'A glass of sherry for Miss Dundas, Mrs Murray, and Miss Hope, and a glass of port for Mr Hume, and one for me,' he slew them by coveys. And all the parties to the contract were bound to acknowledge each other distinctly. No nods, or grins, or indifference; but a direct look at the object, the audible utterance of the very words – 'Your good health,' accompanied by a respect-full inclination of the head, a gentle attraction of the right hand towards the heart, and a gratified smile. And after all these de-tached pieces of attention during the feast were over, no sooner was the table cleared, and the after-dinner glasses set down, than it became necessary for each person, following the landlord, to drink the health of every other person present, individually.

Cockburn considered that 'this prandial nuisance was horrible'. Even more horrible, he said, were the rounds of toasts that took place after dinner and before the ladies retired, when each gentleman was expected to toast an absent lady and each lady an absent gentleman. And then there were 'sentiments'. 'The glasses being filled, a person was asked for his, or her, sentiment – "May the pleasures of the evening bear the reflections of the morning." Or, "May the friends of our youth be the companions of our old age." Or, "Delicate pleasures to susceptible minds." "May the hand of charity wipe the tear from the eye of sorrow." "May never worse be among us." "Guests could be terrified at having to produce a 'senti-ment', and one unfortunate dominie, when asked for his, 'after much writhing and groaning, he came out with – "The reflection of the moon on the cawm bosom of the lake."' '

Tea, taken at the 'four hours', was served when ladies went visiting. It eventually developed into afternoon tea; 'the meal of ceremony', as Henry Mackenzie recalled it, when he was a boy. Mackenzie reported that they had fifty-odd kinds of tea-bread. 'One Scott made a little fortune by his *milk-bakes*. His shop in

Forrester's Wynd ... was surrounded at five o'clock by a great con-
course of servant maids, – at that time there was scarce a footman
except in families of the first distinction. A similar reputation was
enjoyed by the rolls of one Symington, a baker of Leith.' Edinburgh
had thus acquired its reputation for varieties of tea-bread by the
eighteenth century. In that century, too, it had a reputation for its
bread (as early as 1655 Glasgow had sent for Edinburgh bakers to
advise on improving that city's bread) but Mackenzie reported in
1825 that Edinburgh bread had 'miserably fallen off' from what it
had been in his youth in the 1750s and 1760s.

When fashionable people went out to tea or dinner in Edinburgh
during this period they either walked or took sedan chairs, carried
almost invariably by Highland 'chairmen'. Mackenzie reported that
when he was a boy there were only three or four carriages kept in
Edinburgh. 'Indeed the state of the city at that time, its narrow
steep wynds and closes, did not admit of carriages; and like Bath
formerly ... the conveyance of fashionable people was by sedan
chairs. The proportion of carriages now, since the building of the
New Town, is in comparison with that former period, I really
believe, forty or fifty to one.' There was a general consciousness of
increasing refinement in the last three decades of the century. 'As
Edinburgh is not considerable for trade,' wrote Hugo Arnot in 1778,
'but depends chiefly for its support upon the college of justice, the
seminars of education, and the inducements which, as a capital, it
affords to genteel people to reside in it, these circumstances must
occasion the respective families to be pretty numerous. The manner
of living also has become more genteel, and the increase of wheel-
carriages must augment the number of domesticks.'

The number of separate families in Edinburgh and its immediate
environs was established by a survey of 1775 as 13,806. Arnot
worked out that on average each family consisted of six persons, so
he gave the total population as 80,836, adding a further 1,400 for
garrison, workhouse, hospitals, etc. 'The places comprehended in
this enumeration, are the city of Edinburgh and all its suburbs on
the west and south, within the respective toll-bars. On the east, the
Abbey-hill, Jock's lodge and Restalrig. Beyond the New Town, the
villages of Broughton and Picardy, the towns of South and North
Leith, and the east and west roads to Leith. Such parts of the city of
Edinburgh as constitutes the royalty, and also the Canongate, pay
cess or land-tax to government, *as the city of Edinburgh*.' The
writer of the account of Edinburgh in volume VI of the *Statistical*

Account of Scotland (1793) thought that Arnot's figure of six to a family was too high: he calculated on the basis of five to a family that 'the number of souls in the city and suburbs, including Leith, amounted in 1775 to 70,430'.

The village of Picardy to which Arnot refers (surviving now only in the name of Picardy Place) derived its name from the importation of French weavers from St Quentin, France, in the late 1720s. The Board of Trustees for Improveing Fisherys and Manufactures in Scotland decided in 1727 to bring over from France families 'skilled in making Cambricks & Looms &c & in Bleaching in order to Introduce these Manufactures into this Country'. Ten experienced weavers with their families were brought over by Nicolas D'Assaville of St Quentin, and after considerable argument and disagreement they obtained the site they wanted, adjacent to the villages of Broughton and Caltoun and at the same time near the city, from all three of which they expected to obtain spinners and apprentices. The bounds of the French weaver settlement of Picardy are marked in modern Edinburgh by Picardy Place on the south, Forth Street on the north, Broughton Street on the west and Union Street on the east.

CHAPTER 9

The Scottish Enlightenment

Mr Amyat, King's Chymist, a most sensible and agreeable English gentleman, resided in Edinburgh for a year or two. He one day surprised me with a curious remark. There is not a city in Europe, said he, that enjoys such a singular and noble privilege. I asked, What is that privelege? He replied, Here I stand at what is called the *Cross of Edinburgh*, and can, in a few minutes, take fifty men of genius and learning by the hand.

The speaker is the Edinburgh printer and founder of the Crochallan Fencibels, William Smellie in his *Literary and Characteristic Lives of Gregory, Kames, Hume and Smith.* Gregory was Dr John Gregory, Professor of the Practice of Physic at Edinburgh from 1766 until his death in 1773 and member of one of the most distinguished academic families of Scotland. His grandfather was James Gregory, friend of Newton and inventor of the reflecting telescope, first Professor of Mathematics at Edinburgh; his father Dr James Gregory was Professor of Medicine at King's College, Aberdeen and was succeeded in that position first by his older brother and then by John himself. John was in turn succeeded in his medical chair at Edinburgh by his son James. John's grandfather's brother David was an inventor and medical practitioner and his son, also David, was an astronomer who became Savilian Professor of Astronomy at Oxford in 1692. A third David Gregory was Professor of Mathematics in St Andrews: his death in 1765 produced one of Robert Fergusson's first Scots poems. Before him, Charles Gregory (a great-uncle of John) had also been Professor of Mathematics at St Andrews. The family record of the Gregorys surpassed even that of the Monros, three generations of whom held successively the Chair of Anatomy at Edinburgh for a combined period of 126 years (1719 to 1846).

Henry Home, Lord Kames, the second of the Edinburgh luminaries dealt with in Smellie's book, took his title on becoming a Lord of Session in 1752. During his long life he was regarded by many as the ideal cultivated Scottish man of law of the time. Ramsay of Ochertyre claimed that 'he did more to promote the interests of philosophy and *belles lettres* in Scotland than all the men of law had done for a century before'. He was an agricultural improver, moral philosopher, literary critic and historian, in which capacities he wrote respectively his *Gentleman Farmer* (1776), *Essays on the Principles of Morality and Natural Religion* (1751), *Elements of Criticism* (1762) and *Sketches of the History of Man* (1774), among many other miscellaneous works. He also wrote voluminously on legal subjects. There was an ease and elegance, an unruffled intellectual complacency about much of his writing on non-legal subjects: he was by no means a profound thinker, like David Hume, nor did he have the more solid learning of his eccentric colleague Lord Monboddo, who was once asked by Kames whether he had read his *Elements of Criticism* and received the reply: 'No, my lord. You write much quicker than I can read.'

The paradox of the co-existence in late eighteenth century Edinburgh of elegant formality and coarseness has already been noticed: Kames is a good example. The tone of elegant rumination that characterizes his writings was not matched by his personal behaviour. Ramsay of Ochertyre refers to his 'levity or prurience of speech' and there is other testimony to the raciness of his conversation. His favourite term, both of affection and reproach, applied to members of either sex, was 'bitch', and he once said of himself that 'I ken very weel that I am the coarsest and most black-a-vised bitch in a' the Court o' Session.' On his last visit to the Court shortly before his death in 1782 in his eighty-seventh year, he took farewell of his legal brethren with the exclamation 'Fare ye a' weel, ye bitches!'

Kames was one of many examples of the great Edinburgh phenomenon of the eighteenth century – the man of law as man of letters. Scotland retained its own legal system after the Union and Edinburgh was Scotland's legal centre. This gave the law a certain patriotic appeal, and many of the most active investigators of Scotland's past were lawyers. Sir David Dalrymple, who became a Lord of Session as Lord Hailes in 1766, was, as well as judge, historian, antiquary, editor, essayist, and general man of letters, author of the *Annals of Scotland* and *The Canons of the Church of Scotland*, editor of the Bannatyne Manuscript, contributor to Henry Mackenzie's periodical *The Mirror* and collector of ballads (in which activity he assisted Bishop Percy). Many writers and others trained for the law and 'passed advocate' without actually practising. 'The Gentlemen who are styled Advocates in this country,' wrote the Englishman Captain Topham from Edinburgh in 1774, 'are almost innumerable; for every man who has nothing to do, and no better name to give himself, is called Advocate. Of those, however, who practise and get business the number is extremely few; but amongst these few, are some men whose abilities are not only an honour to the profession, but to the country itself: Men who make the bar a school of eloquence, and not, as I am sorry to say with us, a jargon of barbarous and almost unintelligible words, and who preserve, in their debates, the manners and sentiments of Gentlemen.'

Peter Williamson's Edinburgh Directory for 1773–4 arranges the citizens by rank as follows: Lords of Session, Advocates, Writers to the Signet [a somewhat exclusive company of solicitors], Lords' and Advocates' Clerks, Physicians, Noblemen and Gentlemen, Merchants, Grocers, Ship-Masters, Surgeons, Brewers and down through the various trades to end with School and Writing Masters, Milliners and Room Setters (those who let out 'digs'). Clergymen, as might be expected, were classed as gentlemen, as were university professors whose rank soared far above that of mere schoolmasters. Many of the literati were clergymen or professors: some, like Hugh Blair, who was minister successively of Canongate, Lady Yester's and the High Kirk of Edinburgh, was appointed Professor of Rhetoric at Edinburgh University in 1760 and Professor of Belles Lettres in 1762. The historian William Robertson was a leader of the Moderates in the Church of Scotland, Principal of Edinburgh University from 1762 to 1792, and Moderator of the General Assembly in 1763. The fact is that (for economic as much as social reasons) there was no professional class of writers in Scotland in the eighteenth century: booksellers and patrons did not, as they did in eighteenth-century London, both make possible and tyrannize over a class of professional writers. There was no Edinburgh Grub Street. Gentlemen turned to writing from secure positions in the law, the church or the university or a combination of the last two of these. Ladies of leisure wrote ballads and lyrics, often concealing their authorship. This tradition died hard. When Walter Scott, a professional man of law, turned to novel writing in 1814 he maintained his anonymity partly because he did not want to be seen as a professional writer who looked to writing to make his money. And much later in the nineteenth century Robert Louis Stevenson's father made it quite clear to young Louis that writing was all very well as an elegant recreation but a man must have a solid profession, and since Louis didn't take to his father's profession of engineering they compromised on the law.

William Smellie's third Edinburgh luminary is David Hume, the greatest of them all. He was born in Edinburgh in 1711 of a Berwickshire family and spent his childhood at his family's Berwickshire home. He attended Edinburgh University, where he briefly studied law, but finding it 'nauseous', turned to a wider course of reading to equip himself, as he put it, as 'a Scholar & Philosopher'. He then lived for some years in France, where he prepared himself for his career as philosopher. In 1744 he applied unsuccessfully for the Chair of Ethics and Pneumatical Philosophy at Edinburgh University. The Town Council, who made such appointments, having regard to Hume's reputation as a sceptic (he had published his *Treatise on Human Nature* in 1738–40 and his *Essays Moral and Political* in 1741), appointed instead a Mr William Cleghorn. Hume lived for a while in Berwickshire but in 1751, in his own words, he 'removed from the Countrey to the Town; the true Scene for a man of Letters'. Though he was to reside temporarily both in Paris and London after this, he remained an Edinburgh citizen until his death in 1776. He first lived at Riddle's Land, on the south side of the Lawnmarket near the head of the West Bow, then moved to Jack's Land beyond the Netherbow in the Canongate (it is now no. 229 Canongate). In 1762 he moved to James's Court, on the north side of the Lawnmarket. He built himself a house in St Andrew Square in 1770–71, removing there from James's Court in 1771 and leasing his former residence to James Boswell. But Boswell, requiring larger quarters, moved to another 'house' on the same stair two years later and sub-let Hume's to Lady Wallace: Boswell's removal involved Hume in a lawsuit brought before the Baillie Court by a mason called Adam Gillies who had been employed by Mrs Boswell to replaster the kitchen.

Hume was elected Librarian to the Faculty of Advocates in January 1752 and made good use of the books there in working on his *History of England*. He resigned the position, for reasons that remain obscure, in January 1757. Thenceforward his life in Edinburgh as the genial and sociable sceptic, *le bon David*, a man whose goodness and humanity confounded those who believed that only the profession of a revealed religion could produce such virtue, went on agreeably until his calm and stoical death in his house in St David Street on 25 August 1776. Boswell had visited the dying Hume on

7 July to prove to himself that no one could maintain a religious scepticism in the immediate prospect of death. But to his bewilderment he found Hume perfectly cheerful and relaxed and at the same time quietly but firmly sceptical. 'He said he never had entertained any beleif in Religion since he began to read Locke and Clarke ... I asked him if the thought of Annihilation never gave him any uneasiness. He said not the least; no more than the thought that he had not been, as Lucretius observes ... The truth is that Mr Hume's pleasantry was such that there was no solemnity in the scene; and Death for the time did not seem dismal. It surprised me to find him talking of different matters with a tranquility of mind and clearness of head, which few men possess at any time.'

Adam Smith, the last of the literati written about by Smellie, was a Kirkcaldy man educated at Glasgow University and Balliol College, Oxford. But he spent much time in Edinburgh, where he was a friend of Hume and others, even after his appoinment to the Chair of Logic in 1751 and the Chair of Moral Philosophy in 1755 at Glasgow. He (like Hume) was a member of the Poker Club, originally founded in 1762 to stir up the question of reviving the Scottish militia that had been disbanded after the rising of 1745 but soon developing into a general discussion club consisting, as Dr Alexander ('Jupiter') Carlyle of Inveresk recalled, 'of all the literati of Edinburgh and its neighbourhood'. General James Murray, a much travelled man of the world, visited the Club in 1762 and paid it an interesting compliment. Carlyle remembered the occasion:

> When we broke up, between seven and eight o'clock, it being summer, and I was proceeding down street to take my horse to Musselburgh, he came up with me, and exclaimed, 'Ah, Doctor! I never was so much disappointed in all my life as at your club, for I expected to sit silent and listen to a parcel of pedants descanting on learned subjects out of my range of knowledge; but instead of that, I have met with an agreeable, polite, and lively company of gentlemen, in whose conversation I have joined and partaken with the greatest delight.'

This compliment reflected something characteristic of the intellectual life of Edinburgh in the latter half of the eighteenth century. It was what George Davie has called, with respect to the characteristic theory and practice of the Scottish universities, 'the democratic intellect' and involved the refusal to use specialist jargon in the discussing of even the most profound subjects. This sometimes involved superficiality or at least a rhetorical urbanity of style that could not do justice to the complexities of the subject discussed (as sometimes in Lord Kames and Beattie); but it also enabled writers like David Hume and Adam Smith to convey their searching and original ideas to a larger audience than would today read the works of philosophers and political economists.

Adam Smith was also a member of the Select Society, and it was he who, at its inaugural meeting on 22 May 1754, under the chairmanship of Allan Ramsay the painter (son of the poet) presented the proposals that gave the Society its name – that it should maintain a select membership and free discussion. The Society met in the Advocates' Library from six to nine on Wednesday evenings from mid-November to mid-August. Smith spent the years 1766 to 1776 in his native Kirkcaldy working on his monumental book, *An Inquiry into the Nature and Causes of the Wealth of Nations*, published in 1776. In 1778 he settled in Edinburgh on his appointment as one of the Commissioners of Customs for Scotland.

To the names of William Robertson, Lord Kames, Hugh Blair, Lord Hailes, David Hume and Adam Smith as members of the Edinburgh literati active in the Scottish Enlightenment we could add among many others those of the philosopher and historian Adam Ferguson and the versatile philosopher and social thinker Dugald Stewart, whose eloquent lecturing deeply impressed his students who carried his influence into the age of Scott, Jeffrey and Cockburn. Nor must we forget the scientists: the geologist James Hutton, whose *Theory of the Earth* (1785) has been described as 'the foundation work of modern geology', the chemist Joseph Black whose Edinburgh M.D. thesis in 1754 laid the foundations of quantitative analysis. If we add the architect Robert Adam (to say nothing of his father and brothers), the portrait-painters Sir Henry Raeburn and Allan Ramsay and the achievements of the doctors and medical professors of eighteenth century Edinburgh who made the University's medical school internationally famous, we can begin to see why Dr Lewis, writing from Edinburgh in Smollett's novel *Humphry Clinker* (1771), proclaimed simply that 'Edinburgh is a hot-bed of genius.'

It took some time for the University (or College) of Edinburgh to reflect the achievements and ambitions of the Scottish Enlightenment. Throughout most of the century it occupied the old buildings that had been begun in 1581. In 1788 – the year before the foundation stone of the new building was laid – an Italian visitor described it:

What is called the college is nothing else than a mass of ruined buildings of very ancient construction. One of them is said to be the house which was partly blown up with gunpowder at the time it was inhabited by Lord Darnley, ... The college serves only for the habitation of some of the professors, for lecture rooms, and for the library. Here resides, with his family, the celebrated Dr William Robertson, who is head of the university, with the title of principal. The students, who amount annually to some seven or eight hundred, do not live in college, but board in private houses, and attend the lectures according as they please. Dr Robertson thinks this method more advantageous to youth than keeping them shut up in colleges, as at Oxford and Cambridge.

But in spite of the primitive accommodation, by the time of Robertson's principalship Edinburgh University attracted students from all over the world. The Italian visitor went on to say: 'The results are such, that young men are sent here from Ireland, from Flanders, and even from Russia; and the English of the true old stamp prefer having their sons here, than in Oxford or Cambridge, in order to remove them from the luxury and enormous expense which prevail in these places.'

As early as 1703, when William Carstares was elected Principal, ambitious hopes for the enhancement of the status of the University were expressed. Carstares himself dreamt of a great revival of learning achieved through the importing of professors from abroad, and though he was unable to achieve this he did succeed in some important modernization of the curriculum, which had not changed significantly since the university's foundation. The old system of 'regents', under which the same teacher took the students through the whole curriculum, was replaced in 1708 by specialist professors, following the example of the universities of Leyden and Utrecht. Even before this some important advancement had been made. David Gregory (the Gregory who later became Savilian Professor of Astronomy at Oxford) became Professor of Mathematics at Edinburgh in 1684, at the age of twenty-three, and a few years later began to lecture on Newton, making Edinburgh the first University in Europe where Newton's *Principia* were publicly taught. And, as we have seen, the appointment of Robert Sibbald as the first Professor of Medicine at Edinburgh in 1685 marked the beginning of the University's march to pre-eminence in medical subjects.

When David Hume entered Edinburgh University in 1722 at the

age of 12 (not as ridiculously early as might be thought today : in the eighteenth century students entered Edinburgh University between the ages of twelve and fourteen) there was a first year Humanity (Latin) class, a second year Greek class, a third year class in logic and metaphysics and a fourth year class in natural philosophy (physics). Much of the teaching was conducted in the form of drilling and interrogating of the kind we today should associate with more elementary kinds of education. The first degree, as in all Scottish universities to this day, was the Master of Arts, though many students did not bother to take the degree but attended individual courses according to their preference. When James Boswell entered the University in 1752 he took classes in Latin, in which, like many students, he was already well drilled, Greek, which he started from scratch and in which he made little progress, and, Logic, which was taught by John Stevenson, who first introduced Locke's philosophy to Scottish students. Jupiter Carlyle had attended the University some twenty years before Boswell, and recorded his opinion of Stevenson, who had been appointed in 1730 :

I went to the Logic class, taught by Mr John Stevenson, who, though he had no pretensions to superiority in point of learning and genius, yet was the most popular of all the Professors on account of his civility and even kindness to his students, and at the same time the most usefull; for being a man of sense and industry, he had made a judicious selection from the French and English critics, which he gave at the morning hour of eight, when he read with us Aristotle's *Poetics* and Longinus *On the Sublime*. At eleven he read Heineccius' *Logic*, and an abridgement of Locke's *Essay*; and in the afternoon at two – for such were the hours of attendance at those times – he read to us a compendious history of the ancient philosophers, and an account of their tenets. On all these branches we were carefully examined at least three times a week.

Henry Mackenzie who entered the University in 1757 when he was only eleven, left a recollection of the Greek class :

So little was Greek taught when I went to College, that at the logic Class, where Aristotle and Longinus were used as text-books, only another lad and I were able to read them in the original. I had an advantage over the other lads, having had a good private master for Greek for several months before I entered to the class. That class was taught by Mr Hunter, himself a keen scholar both in Greek and Latin, but indolent and indulgent, and inspired no zeal or spirit in his pupils. He was a great man for politics and news ... At the end of the class-room, opposite to and furthest from the professor's chair, was a wall so loosely wainscotted that a blow on it sounded like the report of a distant cannon. When the lads, many of whom were from the indolent inattention of the professor idle enough, wished to get out at ten or twelve minutes before the end of the hour, one of them struck his back against the wainscot, which the professor taking for the report of a gun, and anxious to hear the news, made some apology for adjourning the class, that he might hurry to the Cross to know the cause of the firing of the Castle guns.

Walter Scott first attended classes at Edinburgh University in 1783, and attended the Latin and Greek classes (the latter unsuccessfully). He was at the University for three years, and then there was a gap, and when he returned to attend classes from 1789 to 1792 he concentrated on legal and historical subjects. He was particularly impressed with the lectures on Scots Law given by Professor David Hume (nephew of the philosopher) and paid tribute to the historical logic of the presentation:

I can never sufficiently admire the penetration and clearness of conception which were necessary to the arrangement of the fabric of law, formed originally under the strictest influence of feudal principles, and innovated, altered, and broken in upon by the changes of times, of habits, and of manners, until it resembles some ancient castle, partly entire, partly ruinous, partly delapidated, patched and altered during the succession of ages by a thousand additions and combinations, yet still exhibiting, with the marks of its antiquity, symptoms of the skill and wisdom of its founders and capable of being analyzed and made the subject of a methodical plan by an architect who can understand the various styles of the different ages in which it was subjected to alteration. Such an architect has Mr Hume been to the law of Scotland, neither wandering into fanciful and abstruse disquisitions, which are the more proper subject of the antiquary, nor satisfied with presenting to his pupils a dry and undigested detail of the laws in their present state, but combining the past state of their legal enactments with the present, and tracing clearly and judiciously the changes which took place, and the causes which led to them.

'The changes which took place and the causes which led to them'; this sums up Scott's own interest in history, the kind of interest that lay behind his historical novels. It shows that his mind and imagination, already nourished on historical ballads and anecdotes, received significant further nourishment from lectures at the University. History entered deeply into university studies in Edinburgh throughout the eighteenth century, and the reason was that the national trauma produced by the Union of 1707 sent Scotsmen to pondering on the nature of their past and its relation to their present, and so to consider further the nature of historical process in general. The first Professor of History at the University began in 1719 as Professor of Universal History and Scottish History – a reversal of the more usual development. William Robertson, the most wide-ranging historian of his time, began with a *History of Scotland* in 1759 before moving on to other countries and continents. In the same year that saw the publication of Robertson's *History of Scotland*, William Tytler published his defence of Queen Mary, *The Inquiry into the Evidence against Mary Queen of Scots*; his son, Alexander Fraser Tytler, became Professor of Universal History at Edinburgh University in 1780 and Scott attended his lectures in 1789–90. The movement from Scottish particularism to more general historical interests reflected in the relation between Tytler *père et fils* is seen also in the development of Scott's own historical concerns. It was an Edinburgh mood.

Philosophy and 'belles lettres' were taught at the University in the latter part of the eighteenth century by what might be called gifted amateurs. History, law and medicine were taught by internationally famous professionals. Among the many distinguished medical teachers at the University was William Cullen, who was elected Professor of Chemistry in 1765, Professor of the Theory of Physic in 1766 and President of the Edinburgh College of Physicians in 1773. When he died in 1790, Henry Cockburn, then nine years old, 'learned his look from the number of heads of him which, out of respect to his memory, were instantly set up as signs for druggists' shops; all respresenting him with a huge wig and an enormous under lip'.

The foundation stone of the new University building – now known as the Old College – was laid on 16 November 1789 amid high ceremony. The Lord Provost and all the magistrates in their robes were present, with the regalia of the city, Principal Robertson and the entire Senatus Academicus were there in their robes, and there were also 'all the students wearing laurel in their hats, Mr Schetkey's band of singers, and all the Masonic lodges, with their proper insignia'. But lack of funds postponed the completion of the building until 1834: the dome (by Rowland Anderson) was not added until 1884.

Of Edinburgh's schools at this period the most important was the High School, which remained in the old building erected in 1578 until in the 1770s, disturbed by the lack of accommodation for the increased number of pupils, a number of prominent citizens organized a subscription to build a new school. The new school was built on the old site enlarged by a piece of ground from their garden presented by the managers of the Royal Infirmary and another given from their garden by the Corporation of Surgeons. The foundation stone was laid on 24 June 1777 by Sir William Forbes, Grand Master Mason of Scotland, accompanied by the usual high ceremony. The Rector at this period was the celebrated Alexander Adam, a distinguished classical scholar and the first to introduce Greek into the school curriculum in 1772. Edinburgh University conferred on him the degree of LL.D in 1780, and henceforth he was universally known as Dr Adam.

Henry Mackenzie attended the old High School from 1751 until 1757. He later recalled his school years:

The scholars went through the four classes taught by the undermasters, reading the usual elementary Latin books (for at that time no Greek was taught at the High School) and so up to Virgil and Horace, Sallust and parts of Cicero. They were then removed to the Rector's Class, where they read portions of Livy along with the other classics above mentioned. In the highest class some of the scholars remained two years.

The hour of attendance was from seven to nine, and, after an interval of an hour for breakfast, from ten to twelve; thereafter another interval of two hours for dinner, latterly I think in my time of three; returned for two hours in the afternoon. They wrote *Versions*, translated from Latin into English, and at the annual examination in August recited *Speeches*, as they were called, from some of the Roman poets.

Walter Scott began attendance at the second class of the High

School in 1779, soon after the new building was opened, and there learned Latin from 'Mr Luke Fraser, a good Latin scholar and a very worthy man'. After three years with Fraser Scott went to Dr Adam, to whom he later paid eloquent tribute. 'It was from this respectable man that I first learned the value of the knowledge I had hitherto considered only as a burdensome task.' He went on:

> He remembered the fate of every boy at his school during the fifty years he had superintended it, and always traced their success or misfortunes entirely to their attention or negligence when under his care. His 'noisy mansion' which to others would have been a melancholy bedlam, was the pride of his heart; and the only fatigues he felt, amidst the din and tumult, and the necessity of reading themes, hearing lessons, and maintaining some degree of order at the same time, were relieved by comparing himself to Caesar, who could dictate to three secretaries at once; – so ready is vanity to lighten the labours of duty.

Scott went on to deplore the persecution of Adam by a member of his staff, William Nicol, a good Latin scholar but a brutal teacher. Nicol had his lively and convivial side, and it was this that attracted Burns to him when the poet was in Edinburgh: the two became good friends and went on a Highland tour together. But at school he was a thorn in the Rector's flesh and (in Cockburn's words) 'as bad a schoolmaster as it is possible to fancy' driving on the boys 'by constant and indiscriminate harshness'. Scott recalled that Nicol 'carried his feud against the Rector within an inch of assassination, for he waylaid and knocked him down in the dark'. After the outbreak of the French Revolution Nicol was responsible for bringing Adam under suspicion of having revolutionary political views, but this eventually blew over. In 1809 Dr Adam suffered a stroke while teaching. Again in Scott's words: 'He survived a few days, but becoming delirious before his dissolution, conceived he was still at school, and after some expressions of applause or censure, he said, "But it grows dark – the boys may dismiss" – and instantly expired.'

Among the tributes paid to Adam by his former pupils a sentence of Cockburn's stands out: 'He was born to teach Latin, some Greek, and all virtue.' Adam had begun his career as headmaster of Watson's Hospital, Edinburgh. This was founded by an Edinburgh merchant George Watson, 'for the maintenance and education of the offspring of decayed merchants; for boys, the children or grandchildren of decayed merchants in Edinburgh'. Watson died in 1723 and building of his 'hospital' began in 1738. Twelve boys were admitted in 1741 and thirty in 1744. 'At present,' wrote Hugo Arnot in 1778, 'double that number of boys are maintained and educated in the hospital. These, as well as those in Heriot's, have becoming attention paid to them.' The funds of Watson's Hospital were 'vested in the Merchant Company of Edinburgh, for behalf of the hospital'. In time Watson's, like Heriot's, grew to be one of the great schools of the city.

Arnot also refers to the 'Merchant Maiden Hospital' established 'at the end of the last century, by voluntary contribution, to which the company of merchants in Edinburgh, and Mrs Mary Erskine, a widow gentlewoman, lent particular assistance. It is destined for the education and maintenance of young girls, daughters of the merchant burgesses of Edinburgh'. The name was later changed to 'Edinburgh Ladies' College', but was known to generations of Edinburgh citizens as simply 'Queen Street', from its location; in 1944 it became The Mary Erskine School for Girls.

The intellectual life of late eighteenth century Edinburgh was not confined to the writings and discussions of the literati and the educational activities of the University and the schools. There was also a lively interest in the performed drama. In spite of the official ban on the threatre, there was, as we have seen, a successful use of the device of giving performances free as an adjunct to concerts for which alone admission was formally charged. The most successful practitioner of this method was the actor-manager West Digges who took over the management of what his advertisements referred to as 'the Theatre in the Canongate' in the middle 1750s. 'Concert Hall in the Canongate, Will be presented gratis (after the several Concerts), the following Dramatic performances': – this was a common way of announcing theatrical performances, which in the 1750s included many plays of Shakespeare, *The Beggar's Opera* and Ramsay's *The Gentle Shepherd*. On 4 December 1756 the *Edinburgh Evening Courant* (a tri-weekly founded in 1718) carried the following announcement:

A *New Tragedy* called DOUGLAS, written by an ingenious gentleman of this country, is now in rehearsal at the Theatre, and will be performed as speedily as possible. The expectations of the public from the performance are in proportion to the known talent and ability of the Author, whose modest merit would have suppressed a Dramatic work, which we think by the concurrent testimony of many gentlemen of taste and literature will be an honour to this country.

The author was John Home, minister of the East Lothian parish of Athelstaneford. For a minister of the Church of Scotland to produce a play, even though it was a moral and sentimental tragedy, gave great offence to the orthodox and provided new stimulus for the struggle between the Moderates and the Orthodox or 'High Flyers' that was so important a part of eighteenth century Edinburgh intellectual life and in which the literati played so conspicuous a part on the Moderate side. Jupiter Carlyle was much involved in the struggle, and later told the story:

The play had unbounded success for a great many nights in Edinburgh, and was attended by all of the literati and most of the judges, who, except one or two, had not been in use to attend the theatre. The town in general was in an uproar of exultation that a Scotchman had written a tragedy of the first rate, and that its merit was first submitted to their judgment. There were a few opposers, however, among those who pretended to taste and literature, who endeavoured to cry down the performance in libellous pamphlets and ballads (for they durst not attempt to oppose it in the theatre itself), and were openly countenanced by Robert Dundas of Arniston, at that time Lord Advocate, and all his minions and expectants. The High-flying set were unanimous against it, as they thought it a sin for a clergyman to write any play, let it be ever so moral in its tendency. Several ballads and pamphlets were published on our side in answer to the scurrilities against us, one of which was written by Adam Ferguson, and another by myself ... The zeal and violence of the Presbytery of Edinburgh, who had made enactments and declarations to be read in the pulpit, provoked me to write this pamphlet, which, in the ironical manner of Swift, contained a severe satire of our opponents ... This pamphlet had a great effect by elating our friends, and perhaps more in exasperating our enemies; which was by no means softened by Lord Elibank and David Hume, etc., running about and crying it up as the first performance the world had seen for half a century.

Carlyle, who was minister at Inversek, attended the performance on the third night and was prosecuted by the Presbytery of Dalkeith not only for attending the play but also because 'he ... did, without necessity, keep company, familiarly converse, and eat and drink with West Diggs (one of the actors on the unlicensed stage of theatre at the head of the Canongate of Edinburgh, commonly called the Concerthall), in the house of Henry Thomson, vintner in the Abbey . . . , or in some other house or tavern within the city or suburbs of Edinburgh . . . ; at least he, the said Alexander Carlyle, did, without necessity, at the time or times, place or places above libelled, converse in a familiar manner with the said West Diggs, or with Miss Sarah Ward, an actress on the said theatre, or with some other of the persons who are in the course of acting plays in the said theatre – persons that do not reside in his parish, and who, by their profession, and in the eye of the law, are of bad fame, and who cannot obtain from any minister a testimonial of their moral character . . .' Thomas Whyte, minister of Liberton, submitted to six weeks' suspension for having attended the play, his sentence being mitigated because, although he did attend, he tried to conceal himself behind a pillar. Home himself withdrew from the Church. Carlyle fought vigorously and was eventually acquitted. The effect was to strengthen the case for the theatre:

> Although the clergy in Edinburgh and its neighbourhood had abstained from the theatre because it gave offence, yet the more remote clergymen, when occasionally in town, had almost universally attended the playhouse; and now that the subject had been solemnly discussed, and all men were convinced that the violent proceedings they had witnessed were the effects of bigotry or jealousy, mixed with the party-spirit and cabal, the more distant clergy returned to their usual amusement in the theatre when occasionally in town. It is remarkable, that in the year 1784, when the great actress Mrs Siddons first appeared in Edinburgh, during the sitting of the General Aseembly, that court was obliged to fix all its important business for the alternate days when she did not act, as all the younger members, clergy as well as laity, took their stations in the theatre in those days by three in the afternoon.

The official licensing of the Theatre Royal in 1767 put an end at last to the great debate on the Edinburgh theatre. Henceforth the story of the theatre in the city is full and continuous, occupying over three hundred large pages in James Dibdin's *Annals of the Edinburgh Stage* which takes the story up to 1877. Young James Boswell, a passionate lover of the theatre, wrote a prologue to the performance on 9 December 1767 of a play entitled *The Earl of Essex*, which Dibdin called with some exaggeration the first legally performed play in Scotland:

> While in all points with other lands she vied,
> The Stage alone to Scotland was denied:
> Mistaken zeal, in times of darkness bred,
> O'er the best minds its gloomy vapour spread;
> Taste and religion were suppos'd at strife,
> And 'twas a sin to view the glass of life! ...
>   This night, lov'd George's free enlightn'd age
> Bids Royal favour shield the Scottish stage;
> His Royal favour ev'ry bosom cheers;
> The Drama now with dignity appears ...

Early in the next century Walter Scott's enthusiastic support of the theatre gave further impetus to its development in Edinburgh.

There was never the hostility to music that there was to the theatre, as the presentation of free plays as an appendage to paid-for concerts indicates. Early in the eighteenth century Patrick Steil, a musical tavern-keeper (to whose tavern the Cross Keys, anti-Union members of Parliament adjourned after a furious debate of the evening of 16 July 1703) known as a popular singer of Scots songs and also as a violin-maker, was host to a weekly meeting of amateur musicians who performed Handel and Corelli. In February 1729 all the pictures, books and musical instruments of John Steil, who appears to have been Patrick's son and heir, were sold by auction and the musical centre of Edinburgh became the Musical Society, which established what became known as the Gentleman's Concert in 1728. The concerts were given 'in a middling-sized room in Niddry's Wynd, called St Mary's Chapel, belonging to one of the Corporations'. On the opening of St Cecilia's Hall in 1762 the concerts were transferred there. In May 1769 Edinburgh was enchanted by the arrival of the Italian *castrato* Giusto Ferdinando Tenducci to fulfil a contract with the Musical Society: he sang the role of Arbaces in Arne's opera *Artaxerxes* in St Cecilia's Hall in July and August, introducing into the performance three Scots airs with words by Robert Fergusson. 'Tenducci', reported Henry Mackenzie, 'in his zeal for music, established an Academy, at which his pupils, both male and female, sung. It was held in the morning and became a very popular amusement.'

Eighteenth century Edinburgh was passionately devoted to song, especially to Scots songs, and it was in Edinburgh that Burns was enlisted first by James Johnson and then by George Thomson to contribute so magnificently his collected, re-worked, re-created or wholly original Scots songs, set to traditional airs. 'The ladies of Edinburgh,' Henry Mackenzie recalled, 'used to sing those airs without any accompaniment (indeed they scarce admitted of counterpoint, or any but a slight and delicate accompaniment) at tea and after supper, their position at table not being interrupted as now by rising to the pianoforte.' Captain Topham writing from Edinburgh in May 1775, remarked that 'there are few places where [music] is made a more requisite part of female education than at Edinburgh: almost every one above the common rank of mankind have some knowledge and taste in it'.

Late eighteenth century Edinburgh was a city of contrasts: New Town and Old Town; elegance and filth; humanity and cruelty. Arnot gave a horrified account of the state of the Tolbooth in 1778:

In the heart of a great city, it is not accommodated with ventilators, with waterpipe, with privy. The filth collected in the jail is thrown into a hole within the house, at the foot of a stair, which, it is pretended, communicates with a drain; but, if so, it is so completely chocked, as to serve no other purpose but that of filling the jail with disagreeable stench ... When we visited the jail, there were confined in it about twenty-nine prisoners, partly debtors, partly delinquents; four or five were women, and there were five boys ... All parts of the jail were kept in a slovenly condition; but the eastern quarter of it, (although we had fortified ourselves against the stench), was intolerable. This consisted of three apartments, each above the other. In what length of time these rooms, and the stairs leading to them, could have collected the quantity of filth which we saw in them, we cannot determine. The undermost of these apartments was empty. In the second, which is called *the iron room*, which is distined for those who have received sentence of death, there were three boys; one of them might have been about fourteen, the other about twelve years of age. They had been confined about three weeks for thievish practices. In the corner of the room, we saw, shoved together, a quantity of dust, rags, and straw, the refuse of a long succession of criminals. The straw had been originally put into the room for them to be upon, but had been suffered to remain till, worn by successive convicts, it was chopped into bits two inches long. From this, we went to the apartment above, where were two miserable boys, not twelve years of age. But there we had no leisure for observation; for, no sooner was the door opened, than such an incredible stench assailed us, from the stagnant and putrid air of the room, as, notwithstanding our precautions, utterly to overpower us.

Arnot professed himself puzzled at the 'want of humanity' which, though not characteristic of the age, allowed such appalling conditions to prevail. But this was another side of Enlightened Edinburgh, part of its Jekyll-and-Hyde character, which was most precisely symbolized in the career of Deacon Brodie which first gave Stevenson the idea for his Jekyll and Hyde story. William Brodie, respectable Edinburgh citizen, Deacon of Wrights, member of the Town Council, talented cabinet-maker, was also by night a daring burglar, who in disguise acted out with relish the role of Captain Macheath in *The Beggar's Opera*. He went too far when he and an accomplice decided to rob the General Excise Office for Scotland on the night of 5 March 1788. Betrayed by his accomplice, he fled the country but was eventually arrested in Amsterdam and brought back to Scotland where, after a dramatic trial presided over by the formidable Lord Braxfield (on whom Stevenson modelled Weir of Hermiston), he was found guilty and condemned to death. On 1 October 1788 he was hanged on a gibbet that he had himself designed for the Edinburgh civic authorities.

Yet another paradox of Enlightened Edinburgh was its combination of pride and shame in its Scottishness. David Hume considered the Scots that he spoke (but did not write) to be 'a very corrupt Dialect of the Tongue which we make use of'. In the summer of 1761 Thomas Sheridan (father of the dramatist) gave two series of lectures on Elocution and the English Tongue, in an Irish brogue, at St Paul's Chapel, Edinburgh. These lectures were sponsored by the Select Society, and at a charge of a guinea a head three hundred gentlemen attended the lectures over a period of four weeks. Sheridan then gave a shortened course for ladies. The Select Society soon afterwards published a document in which they announced that 'gentlemen educated in Scotland have long been sensible of the disadvantages under which they labour, from their imperfect knowledge of the ENGLISH TONGUE, and the impropriety with which they speak it'. In 1787, the very year that Burns was in Edinburgh, being lionized for his *Poems chiefly in the Scottish Dialect*, there was published in the city a work by James Beattie entitled *Scotticisms, arranged in Alphabetical Order, designed to correct Improprieties of Speech and Writing*. Its object was to enable Scottish literati to rid themselves completely of any Scottish elements in their language and speak with the voice of North Britain rather than of Scotland.

CHAPTER 10

The Age of Scott and Cockburn

Walter Scott was born in Edinburgh in 1771, in College Wynd, 'a steep and straightened alley' (as a contemporary native described it) that rose southwards from the Cowgate to the old College. It was an insalubrious corner of the Old Town, and of the first six children born to Scott's mother not one survived infancy. On the advice of Scott's maternal grandfather, Dr John Rutherford, a distinguished medical professor, the family moved to 25 George Square when young Walter was still an infant, and there he spent his childhood and much of his early life until, after his marriage in December 1797 and brief residences in two temporary domiciles, the couple settled at 39 North Castle Street. Scott retained this house as his Edinburgh base during the years he lived first at Lasswade, then at Ashestiel and finally, from 1812, at Abbotsford, until the disastrous financial crash of 1826, when he had to sell it. As a Principal Clerk of the Court of Session from 1806 Scott had to be in Edinburgh during the sitting of the Court and, much as he loved Abbotsford and the Tweed, he remained throughout his life a distinguished Edinburgh figure as well as the Border laird he so passionately desired to be.

George Square was built in the 1760s by James Brown, who called it after his brother George. This square, which Professor Youngson has called 'the first truly modern house-building project in Edinburgh, and the first true square', quickly attracted distinguished residents; Scott's neighbours included Robert MacQueen, who took the title of Lord Braxfield on his appointment as a Lord of Session in 1776 and who became Justice Clerk (effective head of the High Court of Justiciary, the criminal court) in 1788 : this formidable character, on whom Stevenson modelled Weir of Hermiston, was a friend of the Scott family and Walter dedicated to him the Latin thesis on a legal subject that he was required to produce before being admitted to the Faculty of Advocates. Other residents of George Square were the beautiful and lively Duchess of Gordon (who when still Jane Maxwell caused a sensation by riding on a sow down the High Street), the Countess of Sutherland, Admiral (later Viscount) Duncan, whose house later became George Watson's Ladies' College, and Henry Dundas, first Viscount Melville, Lord

Advocate from 1775 to 1783 and later holder of a number of other important government positions, so that from 1782 until 1805 he was the most powerful man in Scotland, 'King Harry the Ninth'.

In 1805 Robert Forsyth produced, in five conscientiously researched volumes, a 'clear and full account' of the 'cities, towns, villages, &c.' of each Scottish county. His 241 pages on Edinburgh give a much fuller account of the city than the section on Edinburgh in the sixth volume of the *Statistical Account of Scotland*, published in 1793. Brown paid his tribute to George Square, 'very spacious and regular' with its buildings 'reared in the best taste'. He added: 'As the ground declines towards the southern side of this square, which is continuous to the public walk called the *Meadow*, it is one of the most chearful residences in Edinburgh, on account of its rural prospects, and of its receiving a very large portion of the rays of the declining sun – a circumstance not unacceptable in this climate during nine months of the year.' The Meadow, or the Meadows as it soon came to be known, lay on the site of the old Burgh Loch (or Straiton's Loch as it was known for a time after its being leased, partially drained, with its adjacent marshes to John Straiton in 1658). In 1722 it was let to Thomas Hope of Rankeillor at a moderate rent on the understanding that he would drain the loch completely and make a walk round it enclosed by a hedge, with a narrow canal on each side. Hope, who was president of 'The Honourable Society of Improvers in the Knowledge of Agriculture in Scotland' who met fortnightly in a house at Hope Park (at the eastern end of the Meadows, hence the present Hope Park Terrace), duly carried out the drainage and improvement, and it became a favourite place for walking. Henry Cockburn, who was born in 1779, spent much of his early life in 'the eastmost house' bought by his father on the south side of the Meadows, and remembered those who walked there:

There has never in my time been any single place in or near Edinburgh, which has so distinctly been the resort at once of our philosophy and our fashion. Under these trees walked, and talked, and meditated, all our literary and scientific, and many of our legal worthies.

South of the Meadows there was still, at the beginning of the nineteenth century, largely open country and isolated houses:

There were very few fences south of the Meadows. The lands of Grange, Canaan, Blackford, Braid, Mortonhall, and many other now enclosed properties, were all, except in immediate contact with the mansion houses, unenclosed; and we roamed at pleasure till we reached the Pentlands, or the deserts of Peeblesshire. A delightful region for wild and active boys. A part of the monastry of the nuns of Siena [the convent of St Catherine of Siena which stood near the north-west corner of the present St Catherine's Place], from which the neighbouring village, now part of Edinburgh, is called Sciennes or Sheens, stood in a field behind our house, which field my father always had in lease from Sir Andrew Lauder of Grange; and a fragment of the monastery still remains. A large portion, including the great window, of the Chapel of St Roque [a small chapel dedicated to St Roque, or St Roch, the patron saint of those afflicted with the plague, stood below Blackford Hill in the valley south of the present Grange Loan], on the northern base of Blackford Hill, then survived. There was a pond close beside it where I learned to skate – the most delightful of all exercises, and one which I have practised with unfailing ardour ever since.

Those who, like the present writer, were schoolboys in Edinburgh in the 1920s, will remember that on winter days of hard frost they sometimes got a 'skating holiday', when the school closed and boys went to skate, as Cockburn did, on Blackford Pond.

The development of the south side as a genteel residential area took place considerably later in the nineteenth century. For long the whole area stretching south from the Meadows to the Braid Hills was covered by the great Forest of Drumselch, home of numerous 'hartis, hindis, toddis [foxes] and siclike manner of beasties'. David I (1124–53) had gifted much of the forest to the City to form the Burgh Muir. The corner of the present Leven Street and Tarvit Street (just about where the King's Theatre stands) was the western edge of the original Burgh Muir. The boundary then went south-west along to Albert Terrace and west to Tipperlinn Road before turning south to the Pow Burn, or Jordan Burn, later covered over by the Suburban Railway, which formed the southern boundary. Its eastern boundary was the east side of Dalkeith Road. The boundary on the north was the lands of Drumdryan, where Tarvit Street now runs, the South Burgh Loch (which became the Meadows when drained) and the lands of St Leonards. At the centre of this area, but not part of the Muir as defined in David's gift, was the Grange of St Giles, originally a farm belonging to a religious order, then, together with the parish church of St Giles and the lands around the farm that became known as the Grange of St Giles, gifted by David I to Cistercian monks. The boundary of the Grange of St Giles on the north was the present Sciennes Road, on the south was Grange Loan, with Kilgraston Road and Marchmont Crescent on the east and on the west a line running south-east from no. 1 St Catherine's Place to Penny Well in Grange Loan.

In 1376 Robert II (1371–90) gifted the Grange of St Giles to John Earl of Carrick and Robert III (1390–1406) granted the lands of 'Preistisfield and St Gelie Grange' to Andrew Wardlaw, in whose family the Grange remained until 1506 when it was bought by the prosperous Edinburgh burgess John Cant and his wife Agnes Carkehill. In 1517 Cant gifted the rights of superiority in eighteen acres of the grange to the sisters of the Nunnery of St Catherine of Sienna. In 1632 John Cant sold the lands of St Giles Grange, except for the eighteen acres belonging to the Nunnery, to William Dick, a powerful and prosperous Edinburgh merchant who in the same year acquired also the estate of Braid and who was Provost in 1638–39. His son William acquired the eighteen acres that had belonged to the Nunnery of St Catherine, and his widow acquired all the property of the Nunnery (including 'yards', orchards and buildings) with money inherited from her first husband, Thomas Bannatine. *Her* son, also William Dick, succeeded to the property, but the Town Council claimed ownership of everything within the nearly two acres enclosed by the ruined walls of the Nunnery. It was only after long litigation, engaged in by Andrew Lauder Dick of Grange (whose mother, Isobel Dick, had married Sir Andrew Lauder, fifth baronet of Fountainhall) that in 1765 by a decree of the Court of Session, the Town Council's tenants were evicted from the two acres and the Dick family obtained possession. His son, Sir Thomas Dick Lauder, was legally confirmed in possession of all the original lands of the Grange of St Giles on 19 March 1821. The quiet and leafy streets and genteel villas of south Edinburgh, between Marchmont and Blackford Hill, bear witness by the names they now bear – Grange Road, Grange Loan, Lauder Road, Dick Place – to the history of the Grange of St Giles.

At the beginning of the nineteenth century, with Edinburgh south of the Meadows still undeveloped, the fashionable world was split between the 'spacious and regular' George Square and the still developing New Town to the north. The Cowgate, which had once been the fashionable street, was, as Robert Forsyth reported, 'now

rapidly falling into decay, in consequence of the extension of the
city into more favourable situations'. Forsyth saw Edinburgh as a
city built on three ridges connected by bridges 'which divide the
Old Town, or central ridge, from the New Town on the north, and
from the Southern District on the opposite side'. He continued:

> In consequence of its being divided in the way now mentioned,
> into a sort of three distinct cities, built upon separate parallel
> eminences, divided from each other by intervening valleys, there is
> no city of its extent which is less perplexing to a stranger, or where
> he is less likely to lose his way, than Edinburgh. After the slightest
> inspection, he cannot possibly mistake one division for another;
> because the Old Town, the New Town, and the Southern District,
> are each of moderate extent, and have no more resemblance to
> one another, than if they had been built by different nations, or
> in distant quarters of the globe.

Forsyth describes the New Town with admiration. 'George Street,
which runs from east to west along the summit of the ridge, and
forms the centre, is said to have no rival in Europe. It is 115 feet
broad: It terminates in a superb square at each end.' He gives a
detailed account of the structure of the houses:

> The whole houses are of an uniform height, three stories above
> the street independent of the roof, all executed of the finest hewn
> stone. In front of the houses there is a sunk area, which gives
> light to a lower story. The sunk areas are all enclosed by an iron
> railing of uniform height. The street is furnished, like all the
> principal streets of Edinburgh, with a broad smooth pavement of
> hewn stone on each side for foot passengers, and the centre with a
> strong causeway of basaltic blue stone, here called *whinstone*. It
> is obtained in abundance from the neighbouring rocks of Arthur
> Seat, and is used for paving the whole city and suburbs ...
>
> Parallel to George Street, and between it and Prince's Street, a
> meaner and narrower street, called *Rose Street*, has been judi-
> ciously interposed for the convenience of an inferior class of
> inhabitants. On the north, *Thistle Street* occupies a similar situa-
> tion between George Street and the Terrace or Row called *Queen
> Street*.

Forsyth was much interested in urban sociology (as we would call
it), which he discusses from the point of view of a class-conscious
gentleman of his time:

The state of society in Edinburgh is such as naturally results from the class of persons by whom it is inhabited or frequented. It is still regarded as the capital of a considerable division of the island; and all those families of the nobility and gentry, whose fortunes do not enable them to encounter the expence of a residence in London, resort to this city for the enjoyment of society, and for the education of their children. Hence persons of title and rank abound in Edinburgh. [Thus the hopes expressed by Sir Gilbert Elliot of Minto in 1752 were fulfilled.] As Scotchmen are accustomed to wander in quest of fortune to all quarters of the globe, considerable numbers of those who have returned with success from the pursuit are led to resort to the capital of their native country. Many English families have also of late years come hither, whose fortunes, though not adequate to the enormous expence requisite to a splendid establishment in the capital of the island, are yet sufficient to enable them here to gain admission into the society of persons of rank. Of those engaged in business in Edinburgh the members of the profession of the law take the lead. Including all denominations or orders, they are supposed to amount to between 2000 and 3000 persons, who with their families form a considerable part of the population of Edinburgh. When along with these we consider the numbers connected with the university, amounting to from 1200 to 1500, the character of society in Edinburgh must be evident. It is generally polite and intelligent; and there is probably no city in the world, of the same extent, in which so great a proportion of the inhabitants consist of well-informed persons. The trading part of the community consists chiefly of artists or shop-keepers, employed in supplying the wants and the luxuries of the numerous classes of wealthy inhabitants that have either a temporary or a permanent residence here. The general politeness and intelligence which evidently prevail among all ranks of persons seem to be produced, partly by the literature which is so universally diffused through Scotland, and is more general at the seat of a university; and partly also by the faculty with which persons of different ranks intermingle with each other, on account of the moderate extent of the circle of respectable society, which does not enable any class or rank to associate exclusively with its own members.

The 'politeness and intelligence' that Robert Forsyth found in Edinburgh Society in the opening years of the nineteenth century are well attested. The first twenty years of the century represented the second stage of the Scottish Enlightenment, of which the first stage had been the Age of Hume. This was the Age of Scott – and of Jeffrey and Cockburn, though both of these long outlived Scott. Cockburn had no doubt of its quality:

> The society of Edinburgh had never been better, or indeed so good, since I knew it, as it was about this time. It continued in a state of high animation till 1815, or perhaps till 1820. Its brilliancy was owing to a variety of peculiar circumstances which only operated during this period. The principal of these were the survival of several of the eminent men of the preceding age, and of curious old habits which the modern flood had not yet obliterated; the rise of a powerful community of young men of ability; the exclusion of the British from the Continent [because of the Napoleonic wars], which made Edinburgh, both for education and for residence, a favourite resort of strangers; the war, which maintained a constant excitement of military preparation, and of military idleness; the blaze of that popular literature which made Edinburgh the second city in the Empire for learning and science; and the extent and ease with which literature and society embellished each other, without rivalry and without pedantry ... Peace in 1815 opened the long closed floodgates, and gave to the Continent most of the strangers we used to get. A new race of peace-formed natives came on the stage, but with little literature, and a comfortless intensity of political zeal; so that by about the year 1820 the old thing was so much worn out, and there was no new thing, of the same piece, to continue or replace it. Much undoubtedly remained to make Edinburgh still, to those who knew how to use it, a city of Goshen, and to set us above all other British cities except one, and in some things above even that one. But the exact old thing was not.

The founding of the *Edinburgh Review* in October 1802 by Sydney Smith, Francis Jeffrey, Henry Brougham and Francis Horner marked the emergence of Edinburgh as a literary centre. Its publisher was Archibald Constable, to whom, said Cockburn, 'the literature of Scotland has been more indebted than any other of his vocation'. The city was already well supplied with booksellers – Constable began his career as a young assistant in the bookshop of Peter Hill: Elphinstone Balfour, Bell and Bradfute, William Creech and William Laing were other well known Edinburgh booksellers of the time – but a bookseller who would boldly venture into publishing on a lavish scale was a new phenomenon in the city when Constable branched out into this field. 'He took possession of the open field,' wrote Cockburn. 'Abandoning the old timid and grudging system, Constable stood out as the general patron of all promising publications, and confounded not merely his rivals in trade, but his very authors, by his unheard of prices. Ten, even twenty, guineas for a sheet of a review, £2000 or £3000 for a single poem, and £1000 each for two philosophical dissertations, drew authors from dens where they would otherwise have starved, and made Edinburgh a literary mart, famous with strangers, and the pride of its own citizens.'

Francis Jeffrey, the reforming Whig lawyer and later Lord of Session (like his contemporary Cockburn), took over sole editorship of the *Edinburgh Review* in 1803 and under his editorship its circulation rose rapidly – to 7,000 in 1807 and to 13,000 in 1812, to reach its highest level in 1818 with 14,000. It was an aggressively Whig periodical, but this did not prevent the Tory Scott (published by Constable) from writing for it until an article on the Spanish situation which appeared in 1808 seemed so politically intolerable to him that he wrote to Constable saying that he could no longer continue as a contributor and concerned himself actively with the foundation of a rival periodical, as strongly Tory as the *Edinburgh* was Whig, the *Quarterly Review*, started in 1809 by the London publisher John Murray. In Edinburgh the shrewd and ambitious publisher William Blackwood founded another Tory rival to the *Edinburgh* in 1817: this was *Blackwood's Magazine*, familiarly known to its readers as 'Maga'. Blackwood's team consisted of John Wilson ('Christopher North'), Scott's son-in-law (from 1820) J. G. Lockhart, and James Hogg, 'The Ettrick Shepherd'. 'Maga' opened with a bang in October 1817, with three highly controversial articles, all anonymous, as the custom then was. The first was a violent and unscrupulous attack on Coleridge, in the guise of a review of *Biographia Literaria*; the second (first of the notorious series on 'The Cockney School of Poetry') blasted the morals of Leigh Hunt; and the third, which excited the good citizens of Edinburgh to frenzy, was a mock biblical story entitled 'The Chaldee Manuscript', purporting to be a translation of a recently recovered ancient manuscript but in fact telling with thin disguise the story of the conflict between Whig and Tory literary characters in Edinburgh with a juicy revelling in personalities. In the words of Professor Ferrier, Wilson's son-in-law: 'The Chaldee Manuscript was the first trumpet-note which dissolved the trance of Edinburgh, and broke the spell of Whig domination ... It fell on Edinburgh like a thunderbolt ... The satellites of the [Whig] party were scandalized. They protested lustily against the outrageous personalities and profanities of the Chaldee ... Friends and foes were alike confounded: the Tories were perplexed; the Whigs were furious.'

The Whig domination referred to by Ferrier had lasted only since 1806. Before that Edinburgh had been in the firm grip of a band of anti-reformist politicians at whose head was the all-powerful Lord Melville. The French Revolution had provoked a fiercely reactionary mood on the part of the Government, and nowhere was this more actively illustrated than in Edinburgh. In 1793 and 1794 a series of trials for sedition showed how ruthlessly the Scottish administration of justice was prepared to implement its war against any suspicion of radical opinion. The most notorious of these trials was that of Thomas Muir, a middle-class Glasgow advocate, over whose trial in the High Court of Justiciary the Lord Justice Clerk, Lord Braxfield, presided with open prejudice over a court whose jury of fifteen men had been carefully picked by himself. Muir was predictably found guilty and transported to Botany Bay: three years later he was rescued by an American ship but died in 1799 from the belated effects of a wound received on a Spanish frigate in a fight with the English.

The classic description of the political situation in Edinburgh at the opening of the nineteenth century is that of Cockburn:

With the people suppressed and the Whigs powerless, Government was the master of nearly every individual in Scotland, but especially in Edinburgh, which was the chief seat of its influence. The pulpit, the bench, the bar, the colleges, the parliamentary electors, the press, the magistracy, the local institutions, were so completely at the service of the party in power, that the idea of independence, besides being monstrous and absurd, was suppressed by a feeling of conscious ingratitude. Henry Dundas [Lord Melville], an Edinburgh man, and well calculated by talent and manner to make despotism popular, was the absolute dictator of Scotland, and the means of rewarding submission and of extinguishing opposition beyond what were ever exercised in modern times by one person in any portion of the empire.

The true state of things and its effects may be better seen in a few specific facts, than in any general description. As to our

Institutions – there was no popular representation; all town councils elected themselves; the Established Church had no visible rival; persons were sent to the criminal courts as jurymen very nearly according to the discretion of the Sheriff of the county; and after they got there, those who were to try the prosecution were picked for that duty by the presiding Judge, unchecked by any peremptory challenge. In other words, we had no free political institutions whatever.

Likewise there was no free press. For a short time two newspapers, the *Scots Chronicle* [a bi-weekly founded in 1793] and the *Gazeteer* [founded in 1792, and suppressed after reporting a prosecution of the proceedings of the allegedly seditious organization the Friends of the People], raved stupidly and vulgarly, as if their real object was to cast discredit on the cause they professed to espouse. The only other newspapers, so far as I can recollect, were the still surviving *Caledonian Mercury* [tri-weekly, 1720–1867], the *Courant* [*Edinburgh Evening Courant*, tri-weekly, 1718–1886] and the *Advertiser* [*Edinburgh Advertiser*, tri-weekly 1764–1859]. The only other periodical publication was the doited *Scots Magazine* [monthly, 1739–1826]. This magazine and three newspapers actually formed the whole regular produce of the Edinburgh periodical press.

Nor was the absence of a free public press compensated by any freedom of public speech. Public *political* meetings could not arise, for the elements did not exist. I doubt if there was one during the twenty-five years that succeeded the year 1795. Nothing was viewed with such horror as any political congregation not friendly to existing power ...

Almost everything in the city was under the control of the town council; not merely what was properly magisterial, but most things conducive to public economy. Our light, water, education, paving, trade, including the port of Leith, the poor, the police, were all in the hands of the civic corporation. Hence in Edinburgh, as in all other royal burghs, the character of the municipal magistracy was symptomatic of the whole place.

The town council met in a low, dark, blackguard-looking room, entering from a covered passage which connected the north-west corner of the Parliament Square with the Lawnmarket ...

Within this Pandemonium sat the town council, omnipotent, corrupt, impenetrable. Nothing was beyond its grasp; no variety of opinion disturbed its unanimity, for the pleasure of Dundas was the sole rule for every one of them. Silent, powerful, submissive, mysterious, and irresponsible, they might have been sitting in Venice.

This, of course, is the view of a Whig reformer. There were humane and enlightened men – Walter Scott, for example, a friend of Cockburn's though differing from him on politics – who supported the Tory Establishment and found no threat to the life of the intellect and the imagination in the political atmosphere Cockburn describes. And indeed there was no threat; in philosophical, historical, antiquarian and literary research and speculation early nineteenth century Edinburgh could hold its own against any capital in Europe. True, there was some pretty savage politico-literary fighting, especially in the Tory *Blackwood's* – attacks always deplored by Scott, who kept trying to restrain his son-in-law Lockhart from indulging in the expression of party bitterness in his reviewing – but there was also vitality and colour and intellectual vigour. Lockhart and John Wilson were experts in attack, for, says Cockburn, 'they were both poor, ambitious, and of great talent, and they were cheered into the line of factious personality by the value of this article [their talent for aggression] to their party'. Yet, bitterly though he opposed them politically, Cockburn also admired and appreciated them. No one paid more generous tribute than Cockburn did to the remarkable series of dramatic dialogues in *Blackwood's* entitled *Noctes Ambrosianae*, supposed to be conversations that took place in Ambrose's tavern in West Register Street between Wilson, James Hogg and others, but largely invented by Wilson (as 'Christopher North'), 'a most singular and delightful outpouring of criticism, politics, and descriptions of feeling, character, and scenery, of verse and prose, and maudlin eloquence, and especially of wild fun'. They are, Cockburn concluded, 'bright with genius'.

It was Wilson's politics that won him election to the Chair of Moral Philosophy at Edinburgh University in 1820. He was wholly unqualified, but he was a Tory, and the Tories on the Town Council – with the powerful backing of Walter Scott and other influential Tories – used their large majority to secure his election (for the Professor of Moral Philosophy was, like so many of Edinburgh's professors before the Act of 1858, appointed by the Town Council) and the defeat of the best qualified candidate, Sir William Hamilton, who was a Whig. Wilson was at first jubilant at his election, but jubilation soon gave way to panic when he realized that he would have to give regular lectures on a subject of which he had the most superficially amateurish knowledge. He appealed for help to his old college friend Alexander Blair, a critic and philosopher who later became Professor of Rhetoric and Belles Lettres at University College, London, but who was now working at his father's soap factory near Birmingham. Blair responded by writing a series of long impersonal letters which contained the substance of a course in moral philosophy. Wilson kept writing Blair asking him for special lectures on particular aspects of the subject. He also passed on questions from students for Blair to supply the answer. 'I enclose a letter from one of my students. If the objections in it appear good and worthy of answer I wish you to state them as general objections to our Theory, and to refute them.' Another letter to Blair asked for 'a good leter-full on the effects of passion on association' and another asked for a specially effective one on General Education for the last day of term: 'Think for a day or two before you begin – treat the subject according to your own views – sent it off to me in letters, writing off-hand and vigorously, but not disturbing me for God's sake.' Wilson would prop a number of Blair's letters in front of him as he lectured – the students thought he was improvising from random notes jotted down on the backs of old envelopes – and, using them as the basis for his ideas, would thunder away in high rhetorical eloquence to the immense delight of his audience. Wilson's 'rich pseudo-philosophic medley', as the content of his lectures was called by David Masson, future Professor of English at Edinburgh, who attended Wilson's lectures as a student, established his reputation in Edinburgh as a marvellous lecturer. But when the post failed to arrive in time and no letter from Blair was available, he had to cancel his lecture. When the expected letter did not arrive until the morning of the lecture, Wilson would read it on the way to the University.

A less ambiguous literary figure was Francis Jeffrey, who on becoming editor of the *Edinburgh Review* in May 1803 received from Constable the assurance that he was to be wholly independent of all booksellers and that there would be an absolute rule that all contributors had to accept payment for their contributions. Jeffrey remained editor until 1829: under his editorship the *Edinburgh* became a leading factor in the formation of critical opinion throughout the country and at the same time in pursuing its editor's reformist interests. In an article in the Radical *Westminster Review* in 1824 James Mill argued cogently that, for all its opposition to Tory governments, Jeffrey's review was essentially an instrument for aristocratic predominance. This is true in a sense: like Cockburn, Jeffrey was a reforming Whig aristocrat for whom a full representative popular democracy was wholly unacceptable. But, as John Clive has well summed the matter up, 'when one reads through the *Edinburgh* during Jeffrey's tenure as editor . . . , one is continually struck by its tone of moral indignation about the indolence, opulence and frivolity of the upper classes, as contrasted with the industry of "all those who are below the sphere of what is called fashionable or public life, and who do not aim at distinctions and situations"'. Jeffrey's famous attack on Wordsworth's *Excursion*, beginning with the oft-quoted sentence 'This will never do', did not spring from rationalist or formalist objection to the Romantic poets' expression of personal feeling, but from a refusal to agree that the finest expression of such feeling came from the contemplation of pedlars, leech-gatherers and idiots. Like Cockburn, he loved the country life, and loved his country retreat at Craigcrook (then about three miles to the north-west of Edinburgh, on the eastern slope of Corstorphine Hill, between the hill and Queensferry Road) much as Cockburn loved his Pentland retreat at Bonaly.

Jeffrey spent the summers of thirty-four years at Craigcrook Castle, whose ancient building and grounds had been improved and modernized by its previous owner, Archibald Constable. Jeffrey himself, prompted by what Cockburn called 'that *earth hunger* which the Scotch ascribe to the possession of any portion of the soil', made further enlargements and improvements. Cockburn, in his biography of his friend, left a description of happy days at Craigcrook:

It was the favourite resort of his friends, who knew no such enjoyment as Jeffrey at that place. And, with the exception of Abbotsford, there were more interesting strangers than in any house in Scotland. Saturday, during the summer session of the courts, was always a day of festivity; chiefly, but by no means exclusively, for his friends at the bar, many of whom were under general invitations. Unlike some barbarous tribunals which feel no difference between the last and any other day of the week, but moil on with the same stupidity through them all, and would include Sunday if they could, our legal practitioners, like most of the other sons of bondage in Scotland, are liberated earlier on Saturday; and the Craigcrook party began to assemble about three, each taking to his own enjoyment. The bowling-green was sure to have its matches, in which the host joined with skill and keenness; the garden had its loiterers; the flowers, not forgetting the wall of glorious yellow roses, their worshippers; the hill its prospect seekers. The banquet that followed was generous; the wines never spared, but rather too various; mirth unrestrained, except by propriety; the talk always good, but never ambitious; and mere listeners in no disrepute. What can efface these days, or indeed any Craigcrook day, from the recollection of those who had the happiness of enjoying them?

Edinburgh Town Council, to whose subservience to a Tory government Jeffrey and Cockburn so objected, was essentially the representative of the merchants and of the fourteen incorporated trades, each of which had its deacon, six of whom were chosen by the outgoing Council to sit on the incoming Council. Together with the six deacons there were three merchant councillors, two trades councillors and eight 'extraordinary council deacons': these, together with the Lord Provost, the Dean of Guild, the Treasurer, and eight Bailies, were chosen annually by the Town Council itself. Robert Forsyth noted a paradox about the government of the city:

The office of Lord Provost of Edinburgh has at times been held by men of very great respectability, whose activity and public spirit have much contributed to the improvement of the city. At the same time it is to be remarked, that this city, from the account now given of its municipal constitution, can scarcely be expected to be at all times under the management of its most distinguished inhabitants. The merchants and the trades hold the government between them, and are in some measure balanced against each other. As Edinburgh is not a manufacturing town, but is supported by the families of rank which resort to it, by the practitioners of the law, by the officers of the national government, and by the university established in it, the tradesmen or manufacturers of Edinburgh necessarily hold a place of very inferior importance in the community ...

In the meanwhile, as the members of the learned professions, especially of the very wealthy and numerous profession of the law, together with the men of property who reside in Edinburgh, without devoting themselves to any particular profession, are all excluded from the rank of magistrates of Edinburgh; it sometimes happens that these magistrates possess less weight in the community than their situation might be expected to command. Their conduct and measures are frequently exposed to unmerited obloquy; and they find a difficulty in carrying into effect the most necessary measures. Their political importance, as electors of a member of parliament, is even perhaps hurtful to their respectability; because it operates as a temptation to statesmen, or to men of rank, to interfere in their elections, and to endeavour, if possible, to remove men of independent fortunes or character from the magistracy to make way for their own political or personal adherents.

This throws some light on the conditions described by Cockburn.

A scandal which caused great concern in the second and third decades of the century was the quarrying of Salisbury Crags, that impressive ridge of rock beside Arthur's Seat. Some quarrying by the city had gone on from an early period, 'to furnish calsey stanes', but it was the increased volume of quarrying for paving the streets that went on in the early nineteenth century and which visibly altered the appearance of the Crags that began to cause concern. Between 15 June 1815 and 4 June 1819 an estimated 15,950 tons of rock were quarried from the Crags for paving, and more than double that amount for other purposes. It was estimated that a total of between 45,000 and 50,000 tons of stone was removed from Salisbury Crags during these four years. In February 1819 legal action was commenced against Lord Haddington, hereditary Keeper of the King's Park (which seems to have been first enclosed by James V in 1540), to restrain him from authorizing or conducting quarrying in Salisbury Crags, which of course lay within the Park. The case dragged on for many years. It had still not been settled by 16 April 1825 when a leading article in the *Scotsman* (founded in 1817, as a moderately reformist newspaper, originally a weekly) pleaded eloquently for action to prevent the destruction of 'the finest natural beauties, the richest ornaments, the noblest monuments of the place' by the quarrying of Salisbury Crags. After further press publicity and considerable public clamour the case finally went to the House of Lords, who delivered their judgment against quarrying in 1831, since when no quarrying operations have been allowed within the Park.

One Edinburgh street that did not require stones from Salisbury Crags was the Mound, that 'elongated hill, like a huge railway embankment, a clumsy, enormous, and unremovable substitute for a bridge', as James Grant considered it, that crossed the valley of the drained North Loch. It is said that a clothier of the Old Town called George Boyd, curious to see the new buildings going up on the north side of the drained North Loch, provided stepping stones to take him across the marsh, and that others followed his example, providing stones or planks, to produce what was known as 'Georgie Boyd's Mud Brig'. Later, Lord Provost Grieve, who lived at the corner of Hanover Street, obtained leave to have the rubbish from the foundations of the various new streets deposited on the makeshift bridge. 'From that time,' James Grant recorded, 'the progress of the Mound proceeded with rapidity, and from 1781 till 1830 augmentations to its breadth and height were continually made, till it became the mighty mass it is.' Robert Forsyth, in his 1805 volume, noted the progress of the Mound and its dimensions. 'It is above 800 feet in length. On the north it is 58 feet in height, and on the south 92 : The quantity of earth above the surface is 290,167 cubic yards : and from the nature of the soil, it is supposed to have sunk to such a degree, that there is now below ground half as much as appears above, or that, in other words, one-third of the whole mass is concealed from the view. Hence, as it stands at present, it amounts to 435,250 cubical yards of travelled earth; and if a cubical yard is held equal to three cart-loads, it will be found that this mound contains 1,305,780 loads in all.'

Much controversy about the future of the Mound went on in the 1820s. The Bank of Scotland had its building at the top of the Mound, between the Old Town and New, completed by 1806, in spite of the difficulty of finding firm foundations in the travelled earth : it was in 'Roman Corinthian after Palladio's manner', by Robert Reid, and Richard Crichton. (The building was considerably altered by David Bryce in the late 1860s.) An imposing public building at the north end of the Mound was called for in 1822, and plans for such a building by William Playfair were approved. This building, originally the Royal Institution built for the Board of Manufacturers to house the museum of the Society of Antiquaries, the Royal Society and the Society for the Encouragement of Fine Arts in Scotland, was completed in 1826 after considerable controversy about the cost and the quarry from which the stone was to come (after other sources had proved inadequate, stone was brought from Craigleith Quarry). Considerably improved and enlarged by Playfair in 1835, it is now the Royal Scottish Academy. The adjacent National Gallery of Scotland, also by Playfair, was begun in 1850 and completed in 1857, the year of his death.

Civic improvements brought inevitable loss of rural amenity. Cockburn, whose *Memorials* give us such a vivid account of the

Edinburgh scene and of Edinburgh attitudes at this time that one cannot refrain from quoting him on so many critical issues, has a memorable passage recording his sense of loss as the city extended into the country:

> No part of the scenery of Edinburgh was more beautiful than Bellevue, the villa of General Scott. It seemed to consist of nearly all the land between York Place and Canonmills – a space now almost covered by streets and houses. The mansion stood near the eastern side of what is now Drummond Place; and a luxurious house it was. The whole place waved with wood, and was diversified by undulations of surface, and adorned by seats and bowers and summer houses. Queen Street, from which there was then an open prospect over the Firth to the north-western mountains, was the favourite Mall. Nothing certainly, within a town, could be more delightful than the Bellevue foliage gilded by the evening sun, or the blackbirds and thrushes sending their notes into all the adjoining houses on a summer morning. We clung long to the hope that, though the city might in time surround them, Bellevue in the east and Drumsheugh (Lord Moray's place) at the west end of Queen Street might be spared.
>
> But in 1802 Bellevue was sold. The magistrates, I believe, bought it; and the whole trees were instantly cut down. They could not all have been permanently spared; but many of them might, to the comfort and adornment of the future buildings. But the mere beauty of the town was no more thought of at that time than electric telegraphs and railways. [A rather jaundiced judgment.] Trees never find favour in the sight of any Scotch mason. I remember people shuddering when they heard the axes busy in the woods of Bellevue, and furious when they saw the bare ground. But the axes, as usual, triumphed; and all that art and nature had done to prepare the place for foliaged compartments of town architecture, if being built upon should prove inevitable, was carefully obliterated; so that at last the whole spot was made as bare and as dull as if the designer of the New Town himself had presided over the operation.

This is the voice of Cockburn the countryman, the passionate lover of the Pentlands and his retreat there at Bonaly, the Cockburn who, in the words of his fullest modern interpreter Karl Miller, 'feared the destruction of the past' and in his *Memorials* turned the past 'into a paradise'. There was also Cockburn the zealous reformer, the believer in change and progress, major architect of the Scottish Reform Act, who appears in the next chapter. The paradox was not uncommon among Edinburgh men of imagination and sensibility of this time. Scott, with his passionate interest in the past, was also a great believer in progress, in technological advance, in the refinements of modern civilization, combining nostalgia for the past with the optimistic looking to the future characteristic of the Scottish Enlightenment. His close association with the printing and publishing affairs of the brothers Ballantyne and his schemes for rapid financial gain in connection with his writing and with printing and publishing, involved him in the disastrous failure both of the publishing companies of Constable, Hurst and Robinson and of the printing firm of James Ballantyne in 1826, and this brought about his own ruin. Again Cockburn gives us the most vivid account of Scott's first appearance before his Edinburgh friends after the disaster had become known:

Well do I remember Scott's first appearance after this calamity was divulged, when he walked into Court one day in January 1826. There was no affectation, and no reality, of *facing it*; no look of indifference or defiance; but the manly and modest air of a gentleman conscious of some folly, but in perfect rectitude, and of most heroic and honourable resolutions. It was on that very day, I believe, that he said a very fine thing. Some of his friends offered him or rather proposed to offer him, enough money, as was supposed to enable him to arrange with his creditors. He paused for a moment; and then, recollecting his powers, said proudly – 'No! this right hand shall work it all off!' ...

Meanwhile, the social life of Edinburgh's New Town went on with an increasingly sophisticated liveliness. Elizabeth Grant of Laggan recalled in her *Memoirs* the winter of 1816–17 she and her family spent in 'Sir John Hay's house in George Street':

There were very few large balls given this winter. Lady Gray, Mrs Grant of Kilgraston, Mrs MacLeod, and a few others retained this old method of entertaining. A much more pleasant style of smaller parties had come into fashion with the new style of dancing. It was the first season of quadrilles, against the introduction of which there had been a grand stand made by old-fashioned respectables. Many resisted the new French figures altogether, and it was a pity to give up the merry country dance, in which the warfare between the two opinions resulted; but we young people were all bit by the quadrille mania, and I was one of the set that brought them first into notice ... People *danced* in those days; we did not merely stand and talk, look about bewildered for our vis-à-vis, return to our partners either too soon or too late, without any regard for the completion of the figure, the conclusion of the measure, or the step belonging to it; we attended to our business, we moved in cadence, easily and quietly embarrassing no one and appearing to advantage ourselves. We were only eight; Mr White Melville and Nancy Macleod opposite to Charles Cochrane and me, Johnnie Melville and Charles Macleod with Fanny Hall and Miss Melville. So well did we all perform, that our exhibition was called for and repeated several times in the course of the evening. We had no trouble in enlisting co-operators, the rage for quadrilles spread, the dancing-master was in every house and every other style discarded. Room being required for the display, much smaller parties were invited. Two, or at most three, instruments sufficed for band, refreshments suited better than suppers, an economy that enabled the inviters to give three or four of these sociable little dances at less cost than one ball; it was every way an improvement. My mother gave several of these small parties so well suited to the accommodation of our house, and at no cost to my father, uncle Edward having sent her for the purpose of being spent in any way she liked upon her daughter, a hundred pounds.

The most important social occasion of Edinburgh in the Age of Scott was the visit of George IV in 1822, flamboyantly stage-managed by Scott himself. This was preceded by another piece of showmanship in which Scott played the leading part – the discovery at a public ceremony of the lost regalia of Scotland – the crown, sceptre and sword of state – which had not been seen since the Union of 1707. Scott persuaded the Government to set up a commission to search for the regalia, which were eventually found in a locked box in a room in Edinburgh Castle on 4 February 1818. Lockhart, in his biography of his father-in-law, tells of Scott's emotion:

His daughter tells me that her father's conversation had worked her feelings up to such a pitch, that when the lid was again removed, she nearly fainted, and drew back from the circle. As she was retiring, she was startled by his voice exclaiming, in a tone of the deepest emotion, 'something between anger and despair,' as she expresses it, – "By G— No!" One of the Commissioners, not quite entering into the solemnity with which Scott regarded this business, had, it seems, made a sort of motion to put the crown on the head of one of the young ladies near him, but the voice and aspect of the Poet were more than sufficient to make the worthy gentleman understand his error; and respecting the enthusiasm with which he had not been taught to sympathise, he laid down the ancient diadem with an air of painful embarrassment. Scot whispered 'pray, forgive me;' and turning round at the moment, observed his daughter deadly pale, and leaning by the door. He immediately drew her out of the room, and when the air had somewhat recovered her, walked with her across the Mound to Castle Street. 'He never spoke all the way home,' she says, 'but every now and then, I felt his arm tremble; and from that time I fancied he began to treat me more like a woman than a child.'

Two years later, with Scott's approval, William Mackenzie of Inverness and Colonel David Stewart of Garth founded the Celtic Society. Scott later wrote: 'I like this Society and willingly give myself to be excited by the sight of young men with plaids and claymores and all the alertness and spirit of Highlanders in their native garb.' It was this romantic image of picturesque Highland garb that inspired Scott to arrange for the visit of George IV to Edinburgh – the first visit to Scotland of a reigning monarch since the youth of Charles II – in a context of Highland panoply.

The King landed at Leith on 15 August 1822, and from there was escorted to Holyrood by a procession organized by Scott. At the head of the procession were three trumpeters from the Midlothian Yeomanry Cavalry, a squadron of the Midlothian Yeomanry, two Highland pipers, 'Captain Campbell and Tail [retinue of followers] of Breadalbane', a squadron of the Scots Greys, two more Highland pipers, Colonel Stewart of Garth and the Celtic Club, Sir Ewan McGregor on horseback and his 'Tail', heralds, more Highlanders, the Sheriff on horseback and the Sheriff's officers, 'Deputy Lieutenants in green coats, mounted,' two more pipers, General Graham Stirling and 'Tail', the chief Law Officers of Scotland followed by the Lords of Justiciary and Session, other dignitaries and more Highland chiefs in full panoply, four herald trumpeters, White Rod with equerries, the Lord Lyon Depute, the Earl of Erroll, Lord High Constable (all these 'mounted') two mounted heralds, a squadron of the Scots Greys – and then the royal carriage and six with the King accompanied by officials of the royal household. There were 'three Clans of Highlanders and banners' in the rear, followed by two squadrons of Midlothian Yeomanry and representatives of other Scottish regiments. King George himself only wore the kilt once, at the Levee held at Holyrood on 17 August. He wore the Royal Stewart tartan, directed by Colonel Stewart of Garth. He wore flesh-coloured tights underneath, and tartan stockings going a little way up the leg. 'As he is to be here for so short a time, the more we see of him the better,' remarked Lady Hamilton with reference to the shortness of the kilt.

The whole thing was a remarkable attempt to claim the House of Hanover for the Highlands and the Highlands for the House of Hanover. Lockhart thought that the whole tartan business was overdone, and indeed Scott knew very well that Highland dress and customs had little if anything to do with the culture of Lowland Scotland. But he wanted to bring the whole area of feeling associated with the long lost cause of Jacobitism into association with the Crown as it now was. In doing so, he gave Edinburgh a tartan atmosphere which is in some ways quite unhistorical: it is perpetuated today in the tartans flaunted in Princes Street shops and in kilted junketings in Princes Street Gardens.

Just over ten years later Scott was dead, one year after his admired friend Henry Mackenzie. 1832, the year of Scott's death, was also the year of the Scottish Reform Act. Things were changing in Edinburgh and throughout Scotland.

CHAPTER 11

The Athens of the North

The first record we have of any comparison between Edinburgh and Athens is in 1762, when James Stuart, in the preface to his *Antiquities of Athens*, remarked on the similarity between the two cities. But the term 'The Modern Athens' only began to be applied to Edinburgh, Cockburn tells us, from about 1815. The book of views of Edinburgh, from Thomas Shepherd's drawings, published in 1829 with descriptive accounts by John Britton, was entitled *Modern Athens: Displayed in a Series of Views of Edinburgh in the Nineteenth Century*. This name for the city reflected a shift from planning elegant and symmetrical residential areas to civic architecture. Of course the building of the second New Town with its streets of houses continued to proceed, but there was also now a heightened interest in what could be done to dignify the city with public buildings that would adorn its natural features as Athens had adorned itself in the Age of Pericles. 'It was the return of peace that first excited our attention, and tended to open our eyes,' wrote Cockburn. 'Europe was immediately covered with travellers, not one of whom, whether from taste, or conceit, or mere chattering, failed to contrast the littleness of almost all that the people of Edinburgh had yet done, with the general picturesque grandeur and unrivalled site of their city.' Cockburn singled out for praise William Playfair, 'to whom Edinburgh had been more indebted since, than to the taste of all the other modern architects it has produced'. Playfair not only laid out Royal Terrace and Regent Terrace, among the other streets of the New Town: he also (as we have seen) designed the Royal Institution as well as the College of Surgeons, St Stephen's Church, the Free Church College, Donaldson's Hospital and other buildings. 'There were more schemes, pamphlets, discussions, and anxiety about the improvement of our edifices within the ten years after the war, than throughout the whole of the preceding one hundred and fifty years.'

Shepherd's drawing of 'Waterloo Place, the National and Nelson's Monuments, Calton Hill, &c.' shows precisely the kind of ambitious classical townscape that now came to be desired. Waterloo Place was built in 1815, one of the earliest products of this new mood. 'A direct challange (as Colin McWilliam has put it) to Nash's London equivalent, its twin porticos frame the prospect of the Calton Hill, Edinburgh's acropolis.' In his description of Shepherd's picture John Britton vividly expresses what contemporaries were looking for and most admired:

There is no portion of the New Town of Edinburgh more worthy of graphic illustration than that represented in the annexed Engraving. Public buildings, private houses, and national memorials, of varied design and styles of architecture, are here placed in juxtaposition, and altogether form a scene at once imposing and interesting. Nelson's Monument, a lofty castellated tower, in the New Town, as the castle in the Old, is one of the most prominent features; and in this view forms a pleasing termination of the street, although the proximity of the neighbouring building, called the National Monument, certainly detracts from its character and consequence. They are like two pictures in one frame, of different compositions, different subjects, and different effects: and apparently challenging rival admiration. From the eastern end of Waterloo-place, a flight of broad steps leads to the foot-path which winds round the *Calton Hill*. In traversing this, the spectator views in succession, the endless range of streets which compose the New Town, bounded by the Corstorphine Hills; – the Firth of Forth, with the distant mountains; – the Town and Harbour of Leith; – Musselburgh Bay, terminated by North Berwick Law, – Arthur's Seat, and Salisbury Crags, with Holy-Rood House in the plain beneath; – and lastly, the darkened and irregular masses of the Old Town, skirted and guarded on one side by the ancient Citadel.

The houses of Waterloo Place are built upon several small arches, and one of larger dimensions, which bear the name of the *Regent Bridge*. This crosses the low Calton, and connects the Hill with the ridge upon which the New Town is chiefly built. The Act of Parliament authorizing the erection of this bridge, and the formation of the road from Princes Street to the Calton, which may be deemed one of the most important of the recent improvements of Edinburgh, was passed in 1814.

The modern observer shares John Britton's enthusiasm. Between the porticos of Waterloo Place, Colin McWilliam has noted, 'and over the Regent Bridge (Robert Adam's conception now realized), then between sombre Doric screen walls dividing the Calton cemetery, the road sweeps round a shelf blasted from the side of the hill by Robert Stevenson, till it finally gains an open view of the old town to the right and Thomas Hamilton's High School of 1825 piled up on the slope to the left; this, with its romantic deployment of classical elements, set the seal of Edinburgh as one of the main centres of the international Greek revival'.

The foundation stone of the new High School was laid on 28 July 1825 by Viscount Glenorchy, Grand Master of the Masons in Scotland, 'in the presence of an immense multitude'. A building in Doric style with a central portico flanked by low colonnaded wings terminating in a pilastered pavilion at each end, it stands impressively on the hillside, not visible from the New Town but (as Shepherd's engraving makes clear) magnificently visible from the Canongate churchyard. Sir John Summerson has called it 'the noblest monument of the Scottish Greek Revival'. As so often with Edinburgh public buildings, there was trouble with money, the original contractor running out of money and then dying, but the school was eventually finished by the spring of 1829 at a cost to the Town Council of £24,200.

Meanwhile there had been agitation in Edinburgh for another school, 'separate from and altogether independent of the High School of the City', in the words of the Town Council Minutes of 3 July 1822. Originally the Town Council were to build this school, but after they had decided instead to rebuild the existing High School on a new site (many sites were discussed before the Calton Hill site was agreed on) the advocates of the new school went ahead to raise the necessary money for it by private subscription. The original proponents of the new school had been Cockburn and the Edinburgh merchant Leonard Horner, brother of the brilliant advocate and economist Francis Horner. Walter Scott was also active in planning for it. Whig and Tory were thus joined in a venture that was very much what in the jargon of today would be called 'élitist'. It was to be a private school ('public' in the English sense except that it was not to be a boarding school), with shareholders, and much higher fees than those charged at the High School. And, according to a statement by its Directors issued in December 1823, it would be a classical school, with more emphasis on Greek than in the High School, and there would be 'a Master for English, who shall have a pure English accent: the mere circumstance of his being born within the boundary of England, not to be considered indispensable. The object of this appointment is to endeavour to remedy a defect in the education of boys in Edinburgh, who are suffered to neglect the cultivation of their native language and literature, during the whole time that they attend the Grammar Schools, and in most cases to a later period'. This was in many respects the ideal of the Scottish Enlightenment as it emerged in the second half of the eighteenth century – a classically oriented Scottish culture using standard English as its medium.

The Edinburgh Academy, as the school was called (the word 'Academy' having certain overtones of social superiority over mere 'School'), designed by William Burn, was opened in October 1824. It is in Henderson Row, north of St Stephen's Church, near the Water of Leith, on land feued by the directors from the governors of Heriot's Hospital (the Heriot Trust owned a considerable amount of the land on which the New Town was built). It did not satisfy the classical ambitions of some enthusiasts as much as the new High School did. It has a splendid assembly hall, but its exterior, as James Grant put it, 'is ... somewhat low and plainlooking ..., in the Grecian style, with a pillared portico, ... constructed with reference more to internal accommodation than to external display'. Yet Grant conceded that nevertheless it 'is not unsuited to the architecturally opulent district in the neighbourhood'. He added: 'Though similar in scope to the High School, it was at first more aristocratic in its plan or principles, which for a time rendered it less accessible to the children of the middle classes.' Even before the Town Council abandoned its sponsorship of the school, the proposal to raise money for it by charging a two guinea entrance fee was attacked as calculated to exclude poorer children and confine them to the High School. Merchant Councillor Blackwood objected to this proposal, as the Town Council Minutes for 26 February 1823 record, on the grounds that 'the effect would evidently be to create a separation between the different classes of the Community, thereby destroying what has heretofore been one of the proudest Characteristics of the Scottish system of education, and attended with consequences of the most beneficial kind, both to persons of all ranks individually, and to the general character of the Nation'.

Though Whig and Tory had collaborated in promoting the Edinburgh Academy, a difference of opinion soon arose over the appointment of the Rector. Scott, who was one of the Directors, strongly supported the Tory candidate, the Reverend Charles Williams, who had taught his younger son Charles at Lampeter, while Williams was opposed by Cockburn and his fellow Whigs. In the end Williams was selected. Cockburn accepted his defeat with a good grace – the conflict between the two parties on this issue was not really one of principle – and in his *Memorials* recorded with pride the opening of the school on 1 October 1824 'amidst a great assemblage of proprietors, pupils, and the public'. Scott and the seventy-nine-year-old Henry Mackenzie made speeches, the latter's address being especially animated, 'exulting in the rise of a new school upon a reformed system'. The 'reform' was not in the modern sense 'progressive': its aim was to assimilate the education it gave to that of the English public schools in order to enable Scots boys to compete with English public-schoolboys in securing worthwhile positions in the Empire.

The class element in the argument about schools reflected a new kind of class consciousness that emerged in nineteenth-century Edinburgh. As Colin McWilliam has pointed out, the Heriot Trust, in allowing land of which they were feudal superiors to be built on in the development of the second New Town, 'developed the idea of a hierarchy of parallel streets providing different classes of accommodation'. The difference is visible today: if one walks north from the corner of Heriot Row and Dundas Street one can compare the formal elegance of the houses in Heriot Row itself and those in Great King Street with the somewhat less imposing houses in Northumberland Street and, at a third level, the artisan tenements of Cumberland Street. Or one could compare Gloucester Place with St Stephen Street. Jamaica Street, like Rose Street and Thistle Street earlier, was planned for 'the better class of artisans'.

The New Town was at first regarded as a purely residential area, apart from its public buildings. Only in Rose Street and Thistle Street was there some provision for shops. These streets, running between the great residential thoroughfares of Princes Street and Queen Street, were meant to house those who serviced the big houses, but shops developed in their ground-floor flats. At the beginning of the century New Town shoppers still went to the markets in the Old Town, but eventually the practice grew of putting ground-floor shops in flats or tenements in the New Town: when houses were so converted, the upper floors were often made into offices. In the later development of the New Town we find the distinctive Edinburgh (and Glasgow) feature of a row of shops forming 'a sort of flat colonnade with a continuous fascia and cornice overhead' (McWilliam), with painted lettering on the fascia and often on the pilasters. (They can still be seen, in, for example, Deanhaugh Street,

Stockbridge.) The take-over of Princes Street by shops was a less well planned development, as was the modern conversion of many of the larger New Town houses into offices.

Social developments in Edinburgh, as elsewhere in Scotland, ran ahead of the political. But the reform both of parliamentary representation and municipal government could not be put off indefinitely, and in the fifteen years after the end of the Napoleonic wars pressure for such reform mounted rapidly. In a population of about 2,360,000 there were only about 3,000 parliamentary electors. County votes were confined to the freeholders, often mere 'parchment barons' without property who had been given the nominal freehold of land by the great county families in order that they might have the right to vote (in the proper way!). Parliamentary representatives of the burghs were chosen by their self-elected Town Councils: Edinburgh with its population of 17,000 in 1829, had a single Member of Parliament, chosen by the thirty-six members of the Town Council.

By the middle 1820s there were at least three groups in Scotland agitating for reform, who have been neatly classified by Professor Smout: 'there were the radicals, partly working class people, working towards a democracy; there were the middle-class reformers who wanted a constitution in the burghs and in Parliament that made the county safe for property of all kinds and representative of all honest men of means; lastly, there were a number of aristocratic Whigs, ... who were both impatient of municipal corruption, and wanted a county franchise in Scotland that would represent landed property and power as accurately as the county franchise did in England'. Cockburn and Jeffrey represented the second group, with in Cockburn's case some sympathy with the third.

Edinburgh was much involved (though not so much as Glasgow) in the excitement about reform. When the first English Reform Bill passed its second reading on 22 March 1831 there was great rejoicing in Edinburgh and a demand was made that the city should be illuminated: the Town Council objected, but the magistrates were forced to yield to public opinion. The subsequent defeat of the Bill in committee and the resignation of the Government brought about a General Election in which for the first time in forty years there was a real contest between rival candidates for the representation of Edinburgh. Previously the Town Council had automatically voted in the Dundas interest, but now there were two Tories, the Lord Provost and Robert Adam Dundas, and the Whig reformer Francis Jeffrey. Dundas received seventeen votes, Jeffrey fourteen, and the Lord Provost two. On the declaration of the vote a riot broke out, the Lord Provost was mobbed, and the military had to be called in. (It was at this General Election that the failing Walter Scott was howled down for opposing reform at Jedburgh.) But in the country as a whole the election brought a great majority for the Whig Government and for Reform, and the Reform Bill passed the Commons in September, only to be rejected by the Lords in October. When the Bill was rejected by the Lords in May 1832 the Government again resigned, but Wellington was unable to form a Government for the Tories and on 15 May Lord Grey was back in office and, with William IV exerting his influence on the peers, the Bill became law on 4 June. Three weeks later, on 27 June 1832, the Scottish Reform Bill was read a third time, receiving the royal assent on 17 July.

The Scottish Reform Bill was drafted by Cockburn and Thomas Kennedy of Dunure, the Whig member for Ayr Burghs. It increased the number of burgh constituencies from 15 to 23 and gave the franchise to every householder whose property was valued as at least £10 per annum. The function of Town Councils as parliamentary electors was abolished, and direct franchise was introduced. Edinburgh was granted two members instead of the former one. In the counties, the Bill was in some degree vitiated by what William Fergusson has called 'muddled thinking and bad drafting': its effect in the cities was to give the vote to the propertied classes. Scotland as a whole increased its number of seats from forty-five to fifty-three.

Edinburgh celebrated the passing of the Scottish Reform Bill with a 'Reform Jubilee' organized by the Council of the Trades' Union, which had been founded the previous May. Fifteen thousand men assembled on Bruntsfield Links, organized according to their respective trades and crafts whose banners and symbols they bore: they marched into the Old Town through an arch on which was inscribed the motto 'A United People makes Tyrants Tremble'. Addresses expressing loyalty and gratitude were sent to the King and the Government, and, significantly, a black placard recorded the names of the earlier martyrs for reform – Thomas Muir, the Dundee Unitarian minister T. F. Palmer who had suffered a fate similar to Muir's, and Joseph Gerrard, an English leader of the radical movement, who had also been arrested and transported. But the aims of these radical leaders were not achieved by the Scottish Reform Act. As Cockburn realized, its passing meant the turning of the

Whigs into the defenders of the status quo. 'The regeneration of Scotland is now secured!' he noted triumphantly in his Journal in August 1832. 'Our Reform Bill has become law ... Nobody who did not see it could believe the orderly joy with which the people have received their emancipation, or the judgment with which they seem inclined to use it.' He added, however: 'In the few years the Whigs will be the Tories and the Radicals the Whigs'.

Burgh reform followed soon after national electoral reform. Agitation for burgh reform had been begun in 1784, when delegates from Scottish burghs met in Edinburgh to consider appropriate measures, but the French Revolution stopped further developments. The matter was not brought up again until 1818, and in 1819 Lord Archibald Hamilton, member for Lanarkshire, managed to obtain a committee of inquiry into the condition of the Scottish burghs. Its report in 1822 showed the existence of many abuses. The basic abuse was the self-election of magistrates, but Tory governments consistently refused to do anything about this. Finally, in March 1833 Francis Jeffrey, now Lord Advocate, introduced into the Reform Parliament proposals for Scottish burgh reform and on 28 August Parliament voted a complex measure, making different provisions for burghs with different constitutions, but in general granting to the burgesses the right to elect their own Town Councils. All those who had a vote in a parliamentary election in royal burghs were given also a municipal vote. Edinburgh was divided into five wards, each returning six members, except for the fourth ward which had seven. In the first election after the passing of the Burgh Reform Act there were fifty candidates for thirty-one seats, and not a single Tory was returned. Twenty-four Whigs and seven Radicals were elected. The first Lord Provost elected by popular franchise was James Spittal.

Edinburgh celebrated the triumph of both parliamentary and burgh reform by according a triumphal welcome to Lord Grey when he visited the city in September 1834. This was seen as a deliberate rival to the welcome accorded to George IV on his visit in 1822, and contemporary accounts make it clear that it exceeded the royal welcome in demonstrativeness. Fifty horsemen rode out to meet Lord Grey as he arrived from Dalkeith (where, as at Pathhead, he had been welcomed with demonstrations). He was awarded the freedom of the city in a gold box, and was entertained to a magnificent banquet in the evening in a gas-lit pavilion of wood and canvas erected on Calton Hill in the High School Yards. Such was the enthusiasm of the citizens that they changed the name of Wellington Street (by Tollcross) to Earl Grey Street. Cockburn recorded in his Journal his delight in the proceedings:

> It was like one of the creations of the Arabian Nights. The whole was lighted by gas, chiefly from a splendid lustre taken from the theatre. Including about 240 ladies, there were nearly 2800 persons in this pavilion, as it was called. All got in by sections of thirty ranged in the area, and moving off by ballot without any tumult, and all were well accommodated. There could not have been a more inspiring spectacle. It was the homage of Scotland to its greatest public friend ...
>
> This meeting will do much practical good. It is an honour to the country. It shows the force of Liberal opinion, and the peaceful intensity of the people in the public cause. This one evening is perfectly conclusive as to the condition of the public mind. No public man, least of all one retired from power, had ever such homage paid to him in Scotland.

But Liberal was not Radical. Cockburn also recorded how the Radical leaders tried in vain to prevent the magistrates and the trades from welcoming Earl Grey at Newington 'in all the glory of banners and music'. The welcome to Lord Grey could in retrospect be seen to be chiefly a welcome from that respectable and comfortably-off Edinburgh that was to become so essentially the Victorian city that Robert Louis Stevenson so deeply loved yet against whose social and moral stuffiness he so fiercely rebelled.

Respectability and piety did not always co-exist with self-interest, as the Disruption of 1843 clearly showed. The eighteenth century literati had for the most part been leading members of the Moderate Party of the Church of Scotland, opposed to the rigours of Calvinism yet without any very precisely defined theology of their own: they tended towards a sort of genial Deism. As the century came to an end the Moderates became more and more associated with power, respectability and worldliness. They ceased to represent, in the eyes of an increasing number of people, any genuinely religious or for that matter any genuinely Scottish feeling at all. An evangelical revival at the beginning of the nineteenth century brought the old question of patronage (appointment of parish ministers by the landowner) to the fore again. In 1837 the Court of Session ruled that the presentation of a candidate who had been rejected by the Presbytery of Auchterarder, on the grounds that a majority of the responsible parishioners objected, was nevertheless valid, and the House of Lords upheld the decision in 1839. Further cases of the same kind followed, and the General Assembly came into direct conflict with the government on the whole issue of patronage. The crash – as Cockburn called it – came in the General Assembly in June 1843. The Moderates were for the Government, the Evangelicals against. Dr Welsh, the previous year's Moderator for the General Assembly, opened the proceedings with a protest, and then walked out with more than a third of the ministers and elders, to form the Free Church of Scotland under the leadership of Thomas Chalmers. Cockburn recorded the scene:

They all withdrew slowly and regularly amidst perfect silence, till that side of the house was left nearly empty. They were joined outside by a large body of adherents, among whom were about 300 clergymen. As soon as Welsh, who wore his Moderator's dress, appeared on the street, and people saw that principle had really triumphed over interest, he and his followers were received with the loudest acclamations. They walked in procession down Hanover Street to Canonmills, where they had secured an excellent hall, through an unbroken mass of cheering people, and beneath innumerable handkerchiefs waving from the windows. But amidst this exultation there was much sadness and many a tear, many a grave face and fearful thought; for no one could doubt that it was with sore hearts that these ministers left the Church, and no thinking man could look on the unexampled scene and behold that the temple was rent, without pain and sad forebodings. No spectacle since the Revolution reminded one so forcibly of the Covenanters . . .

For the present the battle is over. But the peculiar event that had brought it to a close is as extraordinary, and in its consequences will probably prove as permanent, as any single transaction in the history of Scotland, the Union alone excepted. The fact of above 450 clerical members of an Establishment, being above a third of its total complement, casting it off, is sufficient to startle any one who considers the general adhesiveness of Churchmen to their sect and their endowments. But when this is done under no bodily persecution, with no accession of power, from no political motive, but purely from dictates of conscience, the sincerity of which is attested by the sacrifice not merely of professional station and emoluments but of all worldly interests, it is one of the rarest occurrences in moral history. I know no parallel to it. There have been individuals in all ages who have defied and even courted martyrdom in its most appalling forms, but neither the necessity of such a fate nor its glory have been within the view of any one in modern times, and we must appreciate recent sacrifices in reference to the security of the age for which these clergymen were trained. Such a domestic catastrophe never entered into their calculations of the vicissitudes of life. Whatever, therefore, may be thought of their cause, there can be no doubt or coldness in the admiration with which all candid men must applaud their heroism. They have abandoned that public station which was the ambition of their lives, and have descended from certainty to precariousness, and most of them from comfort to destitution, solely for their principles ... What similar sacrifice has ever been made in the British empire? Among what other class, either in Scotland or in England, could such a proceeding have occurred? The doctors? the lawyers? Oxford? the English Church? the Scotch lairds? It is the most honourable fact for Scotland that its whole history supplies. The common sneers at the venality of our country, never just, are now absurd.

Thomas Chalmers, who had worked in Glasgow on what he called (in the title of a treatise he wrote) 'the problem of poverty' resulting from the industrial revolution, pleasing some people and infuriating others by his view that the poor should be supported by active Christian charity and not on compulsory poor rates, was appointed Professor of Moral Philosophy at Edinburgh University in 1828, and in 1832, in which year he published his *Political Economy*, he was Moderator of the General Assembly. After the Disruption he became the first Moderator of the General Assembly of the Free Church of Scotland and the first Principal of its College.

William Ferguson has called the Disruption 'the most momentous single event [for Scotland] of the nineteenth century', and its effects were felt in Edinburgh as elsewhere. Among the areas affected were poor-law administration and education, with both of which the Church was deeply involved. Four hundred teachers in parish schools, which were controlled by the Established Church, joined the seceders in the Disruption, and the problems that resulted hastened the application of the principle of state aid to education. In 1845 the Governor of Edinburgh prison proposed to set up an

industrial school for poor children at risk of being led into crimi-
nality (as, he revealed, 740 under fourteen including 245 under ten
had been in the previous three years). The cause of 'ragged schools'
was enthusiastically taken up by Thomas Guthrie, a Church of
Scotland minister (of Old Greyfriars 1840, of St John's 1840–43)
who joined the seceders and formed the Free St John's Church on
Castlehill. His *Plea for Ragged Schools*, published in 1847, made a
great impression, and his work as an organizer of non-sectarian
schools for poor children brought him world-wide fame. His experience of drunkenness among the poor led him to become a
total abstainer and to fight for the control of liquor supply: he
was one of those responsible for the passing of the Forbes-Mackenzie
Act of 1853, which curtailed the hours of public houses and closed
them completely on Sundays. This was to have considerable effect
on the social life of Victorian and modern Edinburgh.

CHAPTER 12

'A Sort of Three Distinct Cities'

Few places, if any, offer a more barbaric display of contrasts to the eye. In the very midst stands one of the most satisfactory crags in nature – a Bass Rock upon dry land rooted in a garden, shaken by passing trains, carrying a crown of battlements and turrets, and describing its warlike shadow over the liveliest and brightest thoroughfare of the new town. From their smoky behives, ten stories high, the unwashed look down upon the open squares and gardens of the wealthy; and gay people sunning themselves along Princes Street, with its mile of commercial palaces all beflagged upon some great occasion, see, across a gardened valley set with statues, where the washings of the old town flutter in the breeze at its high windows. And then, upon all sides, what a clashing of architecture! In this one valley, where the life of the town goes most busily forward, there may be seen, shown one above and behind another by the accidents of the ground, buildings in almost every style upon the globe. Egyptian and Greek temples, Venetian palaces and Gothic spires, are huddled one over another in a most admired disorder; while, above all, the brute mass of the Castle and the summit of Arthur's Seat look down upon these imitations with a becoming dignity, as the works of Nature may look down upon the monuments of Art. But Nature is a more indiscriminate patroness than we imagine, and in no way frightened of a strong effect. The birds roost as willingly among the Corinthian capitals as in the crannies of the crag; the same atmosphere and daylight clothe the eternal rock and yesterday's imitation portico; and as the soft northern sunshine throws out everything into a glorified distinctness – or easterly mists, coming up with the blue evening, fuse all these incongruous features into one, and the lamps begin to glitter along the street, and faint lights to burn in the high windows across the valley – the feeling grows upon you that this also is a piece of nature in the most intimate sense; and this profusion of eccentricities, this dream in masonry and living rock is not a drop-scene in a theatre, but a city in the world of everyday reality, connected by railway and telegraph-wire with all the capitals of

Europe, and inhabited by citizens of the familiar type, who keep
ledgers, and attend church, and have sold their immortal portion
to a daily paper.

R. L. Stevenson's evocation of Edinburgh was written in 1878, the
heyday of the Victorian city. Though her citizens were still proud
of the romantic associations of the Old Town, where Stevenson
noted washing fluttering from high windows, this was a period
during which a great number of its ancient buildings were destroyed.
In 1908 an Edinburgh local historian recorded with sorrow that
'since 1860, two-thirds of the ancient buildings of the Old Town
of Edinburgh have been demolished'. A map accompanying his
article showed the surviving old houses in the High Street and
Canongate, and though many had been demolished there were considerably more than there are today, notably on the site of the
present Lothian Region Building, then still occupied by old houses.

Though still the intriguing blend of old and new that so fascinated
Stevenson, Edinburgh was changing. The City Improvement Acts
of 1867 and 1871 marked the beginning of a number of significant
new developments, notably the clearing away of North College
Square, Brown Square, Argyle Square and Adam Square to make
way for the seventy-foot wide thousand-foot long Chambers Street
(called after the Lord Provost Sir William Chambers who promoted
the scheme) linking the South Bridge and George IV Bridge. Chambers Street was paved with wooden blocks – 322,000 of them – in
1876. With the north front of the University on its south-eastern
corner and the new Renaissance Venetian Museum of Science and
Industry (now the Royal Scottish Museum), begun in 1861 and
considerably extended in 1871–4, next to it, soon to be connected
with the University across West College Street with a glass bridge,
Chambers Street could now be considered Edinburgh's street of
learning, known to students, professors and scientists. Also in Chambers Street (from 1874) was the Watt Institute and School of Arts.
Originally founded in 1821 as a School of Arts and Mechanics'
Institute to provide evening classes in basic science for young
artisans, and housed first in Niddry Street and then in a rented
building in Adam Square, it was re-named the Watt Institution and
School of Arts as a memorial to James Watt. When Adam Square
was demolished the school was transferred to its present site in
Chambers Street. In 1885 it became the Heriot-Watt College, as a
result of the amalgamation of its endowments with that of George

Heriot's Hospital. In 1965 it became the Heriot-Watt University.

The Elliots of Minto had their town house in Argyle Square (built by a tailor called Campbell in the 1720s and for some decades vying with George Square as a challenge to the New Town for fashionable residents). It continued to be called Minto House long after they ceased to live in it: in 1811 it was fitted out as a surgical hospital for street accidents and other cases. When Argyle Square was demolished to make way for Chambers Street a 'New Medical School of Minto House' was built in the new street. Minto House it remained, adding to the academic flavour of Chambers Street when in the 1920s and 1930s it housed the English and some other departments of the University.

Other changes had been going on further south. In January 1859 'the new drive through the Meadows' was formally opened, called Melville Drive after Sir John Melville, Lord Provost from 1854 to 1859. There had been significant residential development in the Newington area from 1806, but from mid-century development of the whole South Side as largely a residential area proceeded apace. Between the old road from Liberton (coming north from present Kirk Brae and Mayfield Road into the present Causewayside) and the present Morningside Road – an area which, as we have seen, included much of the old Grange of St Giles – grew up an Edinburgh with an atmosphere that differed equally from that of the Old Town and of the New Town. East of the road from Liberton ran Dalkeith Road, one of the oldest roadways in the country, which branched into two on nearing the city, one branch continuing along the present Crosscauseway, Bristo Street and Candlemaker Row to the West Bow to form the main entrance to Edinburgh from the south, through Bristo Port, while the other went along the Pleasance and St Mary's Wynd to join what Edgar's map of 1765 called 'the Western Road to Leith'. Dalkeith Road and Morningside Road were joined by Mayfield Loan, known in the sixteenth and seventeenth centuries as Cant's Loaning (after John Cant who bought the estate of Grange from the Wardlaws in 1526), and the present Grange Loan and Newbattle Terrace. The filling in of the area between these two roads was one of the most important developments of middle and late nineteenth century Edinburgh.

Tenements as well as villas were built in this area. The comfortable middle class tenements round Bruntsfield Links to the west of the Meadows speak of solidity and dignity, in spite of the uniformity of the window sizes (unlike Georgian buildings, where the windows grow smaller towards the top) with their effect overall of 'remorse-less verticality indefinitely prolonged, whether on the flat, up-hill or down dale' (Colin McWilliam). 'These,' says McWilliam, 'are the fortresses, comfortable within but anonymous without, into which the mass of Edinburgh's middle class abdicated from partici-pation in the city's townscape.' They were, as they were planned to be, more dignified and better built than the tenements designed for artisans in the northern and western approaches to the city (Easter Road, Leith Walk, Dalry Road, Fountainbridge), many built by James Steel in the 1870s. Steel also built middle class tenements in Comely Bank on land acquired from the Learmonth family. Comely Bank estate was earlier the property of Sir William Fettes, who died in 1836 leaving in his will provision for the endowment of Fettes College which, designed by David Bryce, was opened in 1870, a building, as James Grant admiringly noted, 'remarkable for the almost endless diversity and elegance of its details'.

The Warrenders of Lochend, a prosperous family of Edinburgh merchants already well established when George Warrender was created a baronet in 1715, owned the 'Lands of Bruntisfield' south and east of Bruntsfield Links and it was on the Warrender or Brunts-field estate that much of the solid middle-class housing already described was built. Bruntsfield Links, the last unfeued portion of the old Burgh Muir to remain in possession of the city, was for long used for quarrying sandstone. It early became a favourite spot for playing golf (with the mound of débris resulting from quarrying occupying the place of the more usual bunkers), and it was this use that helped to keep it an open space. As early as 1717 there is a reference to 'the house on the Bruntsfield Links built in the current year by James Brownhill called Golfhall': this is the earliest tavern on Bruntsfield Links on record, and it became the headquarters of a number of Edinburgh golfing societies. The present Golf Tavern still stands on its site.

The villas and terraced houses on the South Side expressed with considerable precision the class and social status of their inhabitants. The tenements of flats, with their back greens, have a different social flavour from the houses with their neat front gardens. Immediately south of the Meadows, for example, one finds Livingstone Place (called after David Livingstone, who was made an honorary burgess of Edinburgh in 1857), where there are flats for artisans, and the street immediately adjacent to it on the west, Millerfield Place (called after the owner of the property on which the street was built, one

Mr Miller, father of William Miller the engraver) was a full notch up in the social scale, with individual terraced houses each with its own small back garden and even smaller front garden. (The present writer, who grew up in Millerfield Place, was very conscious as a child of the social difference between this street and the adjacent Livingstone Place.) The nearer one gets to Blackford Hill the leafier the streets, and the larger the houses, many of which stand in substantial walled gardens. Blackford Hill itself was acquired by the city as a public park in April 1884, the same year that saw the opening of the Suburban Railway which, running just north of the Hill, in the course of its circuit of the city, was a significant factor in speeding up the development of high quality housing in the area, so that almost all the South Side right up to Blackford Hill became residential before the end of the century.

Railways were well established in Edinburgh by mid-century. The Edinburgh and Glasgow Railway Company was formed in 1838 and the 46-mile railway was completed at the beginning of 1842. Its formal opening took place, with great ceremonial rejoicing in both cities, on 18 February 1842. The North British Railway Company issued its prospectus in 1842 and was incorporated in 1844 after the granting of parliamentary approval of a line from Edinburgh to Berwick, with a branch from Longniddry to Haddington, making a total of 62 miles. This railway not only connected the rich agricultural districts of Haddington with Edinburgh but also formed a link in the chain of railway communications to England. Its opening on 18 June 1846 was marked by two trains, one with twelve carriages and four engines and the other with twenty-six carriages and five engines, taking a company of seven hundred people along the line, with a lunch at Dunbar. In September of the same year the line from Berwick to Newcastle was completed, thus uniting Edinburgh and London by rail. Railways also moved northwards. The Edinburgh and Northern Railway received approval in 1845 for a line from Burntisland to Ladybank and from there to Newburgh and Perth and to Cupar and Ferryport-on-Craig (the present Tayport). This line was opened in 1848, making possible a reasonably direct rail route from Edinburgh to Dundee, both the Forth and the Tay being crossed by train ferries, the first of their kind in the world. The Caledonian Railway Company was formed in 1845 after parliamentary authorization of a line from Carlisle to Edinburgh: the section from Beattock to Edinburgh was opened on 15 February 1848. In 1869 the Caledonian Railway opened the

Cleland Mid-Calder line, thus giving it a shorter route (46 miles) between Edinburgh than the 56-mile route via Carstairs they had previously used. From June 1862 a train has left Waverley Station, Edinburgh at 10 o'clock for King's Cross Station, London, simultaneously with the departure of a train from King's Cross for Waverley. Exactly when this train became known as the 'Flying Scotsman' cannot be determined, but the name has been known since at least the early years of the present century. The opening of the Forth Bridge on 4 March 1890 ended the train ferries across the Forth and thus speeded up rail communications northwards from Edinburgh.

Before railways came canals. As early as 1817 an Act of Parliament had authorized a joint stock company to cut a canal from Edinburgh to the Forth and Clyde Canal, which had been completed in 1790. This was the Union Canal, completed in 1822. Its original function was to convey both heavy goods and passengers between Edinburgh and Glasgow, but it was chiefly for the former purpose that it was successfully employed. Its Edinburgh terminus at Fountainbridge was called Port Hopetoun, and this occasioned the rapid building up of an area where previously there had been only a few scattered houses in the midst of fields and groves of trees. Long after the canal was largely put out of business by the railway the canal basin on the western side of Lothian Road remained, until in the years just before the Second World War it was massively built over to accommodate shops, offices and a cinema. Lothian Road itself was made in 1787, going south from what we now call the West End, as an elegant wide street which, however, went only as far as Earl Grey Street (formerly Wellington Street), where as a consequence there developed a bottle-neck. Into this from the west comes Riego Street, apparently so-called in honour of Major James Weir who served through the Peninsular War. It was on Weir's property of Tollcross that the street was built. This complex corner of what once was the south-west edge of the city, where Lauriston Place comes in from the east, Brougham Place (opened in 1859 when Melville Drive was opened, as a continuation of it going north-west, and called after Lord Henry Brougham, who received a complimentary banquet in Edinburgh in that year) from the south-east and Home Street from the south, is still known as Tollcross. The name is very old – it has been found as early as 1458, long before the days of tolls – and there is no certainty about its origin, except that it has nothing to do with a toll.

In the years after the middle of the nineteenth century the area between Tollcross and the West End – essentially, Lothian Road – contained public houses frequented by prostitutes where the rebellious youth of Edinburgh showed their contempt for the puritan proprieties of their elders. Among them was young Robert Louis Stevenson, who in later years looked nostalgically back to the days when he and Charles Baxter acted out there their bohemian role. 'Your remarks about your business forcibly recalled the early days of your connection,' he wrote to Baxter from Davos in November 1881, 'and the two pence that we once mustered between us in the ever radiant Lothian Road.'

'O sweet Lothian Road ...
O dear Lothian Road ...'

It was in Lothian Road that the ill-tempered Thomas Brash, 'that immortal Brash' as Stevenson called him, kept his public house. 'A little Edinburgh gossip, in heaven's name,' pleaded Stevenson in another letter to Baxter the following December. 'O for ten Edinburgh minutes, sixpence between us, and the ever glorious Lothian Road, or dear mysterious Leith Walk!'

For all Stevenson's nostalgia for his native city, in the days when he lived there there were moments when he could barely endure the stiffness of its official morality or the chill of its winds, and he would 'lean over the great bridge which joins the New Town with the Old – that windiest spot, or high altar, in this northern temple of winds – and watch the trains smoking out from under them and vanishing into the tunnel on a voyage to brighter skies'. The 'great bridge' was the North Bridge before its rebuilding in 1896–7. He would have got a better view of the trains from Waverley Bridge, but this was not completed until 1873, the very year in which Stevenson went to the south of France for his health. Waverley Bridge joins Princes Street with Market Street and Cockburn Street, thus also joining the New Town with the Old, and it gives access to Waverley Station, the North British Railway's Edinburgh terminus built in 1848, partly on the site of the old Church of the Holy Trinity.

The disruption of Edinburgh's townscape wrought by the railways and their stations brought a new concern for the face of the city. The running of the line through the valley just north of the Castle aroused many fears that it would destroy the whole prospect of the Castle from the north, but even though many continued to object to it after it was laid – 'a railway pollutes the valley' Cockburn drily noted – it was in fact ingeniously concealed as it ran in a deep cutting under the foot of the Castle Rock from Waverley Station until it disappeared into a tunnel as it approached the West End. At the West End was the terminus of the Caledonian Railway, whose new Caledonian Station was reconstructed in 1895–99. At the turn of the century each station produced its adjoining massive hotel, the North British at the east ('standing at the hinge of Old and New Towns, it is coarse and obstructive at once,' Colin McWilliam has observed, but it has long been so familiar a part of the Edinburgh townscape that, like the Scott Monument of 1840–46, it is accepted almost as a natural feature). At the West End the Caledonian Hotel, in red sandstone, is less aggressive in appearance.

The Edinburgh Railway Station Access Act of 1853 reflected the concern brought by the completion of the first phase of the railway routes into and out of Edinburgh. It laid down precise regulations for preserving the character of those parts of the Old Town which gave access to Waverley Station, and the result is the steep and dignified yet lively Cockburn Street (1860), which brought back the Scottish baronial style as something between the vernacular vigour of the Old Town and the international elegance and regularity of the New. Already in the 1830s and 1840s there had been conscious efforts to see that new approaches to the Old Town were in keeping with the dignity of the city. Thomas Hamilton's Victoria Street (1840), running on to George IV Bridge from the West Bow, George Smith's north side of Victoria Street and George IV Bridge itself, by Henry Hardy (finished after financial and other difficulties in 1836), as well as Hardy's Melbourne Place, involved the destruction of Mauchine's Close, Liberton's Wynd and other old alleys around the Lawnmarket, but the results, a considered combination of conservation and dignified innovation, made on the whole a pleasing transition from the old to the new.

Yet Edinburgh remained in some degree 'a sort of three distinct cities', as Robert Forsyth had described it in 1805. While the approaches to the Old Town from both north and south were being improved, development continued in the New Town. Telford's Dean Bridge, opened for traffic at the end of 1831, was largely financed by Lord Provost Learmonth who had bought the estate of Dean north of the Water of Leith and wanted to have easy access to it in order to develop it for housing. It was in fact some decades before new streets appeared north of the Water of Leith adjoining Queensferry Road. In the early fifties the first houses of Clarendon Crescent were built. Writing nearly thirty years later James Grant noted that 'now all the site of the [Dean] village and farms, and the land between them and the Dean Bridge, is covered by noble streets, such as Buckingham Terrace and Belgrave Crescent, the position of which is truly grand'. Grant also recorded:

In 1876 a movement was set on foot by the proprietors of this crescent [Belgrave], led by Sir James Falshaw, Bart., then Lord Provost, which resulted in the purchase of the ground between it and the Dean village, at a cost of about £5,000. In that year it was nearly all covered by kitchen gardens, ruinous buildings and broken-down fences. These and the irregularities of the place have been removed, while the natural undulations, which add such beauty to the modern gardens, have been preserved, and the plantations and walks are laid out with artistic effect.

This development was part of Victorian Edinburgh, clearly distinguishable architecturally from Georgian Edinburgh, notably by its bay windows, yet contiguous with it and retaining something of its atmosphere. Very different was an interesting development to the north-east, between Stockbridge and Canonmills and between the Water of Leith and Glenogle Road. This consists of the area now known as the 'Colonies', eleven parallel blocks of simple two-storey houses built by the Co-operative Building Society in 1861. They were intended for working-class owner-occupiers and were originally sold for between £130 and £250, but they very soon fell into the hands of investors and have ever since been regarded as desirable middle-class houses with their unpretentious charm and their suggestion, as has been said, of 'the vernacular of the Georgian fishertown'.

An expanding city needed expanding public transport, and the development of tramways in the late nineteenth and early twentieth centuries is an important part of Edinburgh's history. Horse-drawn trams first appeared in November 1871, when the Edinburgh Street Tramways Company opened their route from Bernard Street, Leith, up Leith Walk to the East End of Princes Street and then westward along Princes Street to Haymarket. By 1874 the Company had thirty-seven tramcars and three hundred horses, and ten years later, with a total length of track of eighteen miles, there were ninety tramcars and a few horse-drawn buses for use in country districts. With the steady growth of the tramways system Edinburgh Corporation (the name now given to the Lord Provost, Magistrates and

Councillors) decided to take it over and on 9 December 1893 they acquired all of the system within the city boundaries and leased it to the Edinburgh and District Tramways Company Ltd. Meanwhile the Northern Tramways Company, formed in 1884, saw the advantage of cable traction for the steep northward ascents of Hanover Street and Frederick Street, and on 28 January 1888 opened the first cable line, from Hanover Street to Goldenacre, followed soon afterwards by another cable line from Frederick Street to Comely Bank. The Corporation acquired the Edinburgh Northern Tramways Company's system in July 1897 and began running cable cars on other routes. On 26 October 1899 a cable-car route, replacing a horse-tram route, began to run from the boundary of Leith at Pilrig along Princes Street via Tollcross to Morningside, and then further to the new Braid Hills Road terminus. After this cable-cars progressively took over from horse-trams until all the routes were cable, and at the same time existing routes were extended.

Meanwhile, the Edinburgh Street Tramways Company continued to operate horse-drawn cars in Leith, but in October 1904 Leith Corporation bought the system from the Company and proceeded to electrify it by the overhead system. Edinburgh Corporation had their own electric line from June 1910, on the short route from Ardmillan Terrace to Slateford, but continued to run cable-cars on their other routes for more than two further decades. The Edinburgh and District Tramway Company's lease expired in June 1919, and the Corporation then took over the cable system and began to convert it to electric trams. Leith was brought into Edinburgh's boundaries by the Act of 1920, with the result that the first electric tramcars in Edinburgh ran from Leith up Leith Street to the Bridges and south to Nether Liberton, and west to Churchill via Grange Road. There was considerable anxiety lest the putting up of overhead wires would spoil the appearance of Princes Street, but they were skilfully and not wholly disagreeably placed along central pillars in a remarkable one-night operation on 21 to 22 October 1922. Cable cars ceased to function in Edinburgh on 23 June 1923, and for nearly two decades after that the system of electric tramways kept extending until the decision to change those buses in the early 1950s brought a final end to the city's tramways on 16 November 1956.

Though never so picturesque or warmly loved as Glasgow's tramcars, Edinburgh's were an essential part of the city scene for eighty-five years and are still recalled by many with nostalgic affection. The old cable cars, well remembered by the present writer, had a romance all their own, and the regular breaking of the cable, which left groups of cars stranded on the tracks like beached whales until a repair could be effected, added to the sense of adventure. The advent of electric trams caused great excitement. Constantly improved models made them increasingly comfortable and efficient, and there are many who think (like the present writer) that, in spite of the advantages to the appearance of streets brought by the removal of tram-lines and wires, their replacement by buses was a mistake if not a disaster. Edinburgh's public transport has never been so good as it was in the years immediately preceding the Second World War, when the city was served not only by the multiple routes of the Corporation's electric tramcars but also by a suburban railway with both an inner and an outer line, the inner line running from Waverley to Haymarket, Gorgie, Morningside, Blackford, Newington, Duddingston, Portobello and so back to Waverley.

Edinburgh grew in size as in area during the nineteenth century. Its population (i.e., the population of the area now included in the city boundaries) was 90,768 in 1801, 150,674 in 1821, 179,897 in 1841, 222,015 in 1861, 320,549 in 1881 and 413,008 in 1901. The most rapid increase was in the first two decades of the century and between 1860 and 1880. In 1896 an Act of Parliament brought the popular seaside town of Portobello, on the Forth east of Edinburgh, into the city limits. An attempt was made at the same time to bring in Leith, but Leith successfully opposed this and as a result of pressure brought by the opposition Parliament threw out the part of the Bill applying to Leith.

Increase in population brought its own problems, and though these were never as great as those of Glasgow they were serious enough. The city's notorious carelessness in the matter of sanitation was at last largely remedied in the Victorian period, thanks partly to the taking over of the city's water supply by a public trust in 1869 and to the laying of sewers on the lines of all the streets, a task completed by the mid-1860s. The Public Health Act of 1867 gave important powers to local authorities in dealing with matters relevant to public health and required the appointment of Medical Officers of Health. Edinburgh was fortunate in its first M.O.H., Dr H. D. Littlejohn, who had already published his *Report on the Sanitary Conditions of the City of Edinburgh*. This report showed up the squalor that had developed in the Royal Mile by the middle of the century. In the words of Lesley Scott-Moncrieff writing in the Edinburgh volume of *The Third Statistical Account of Scotland* (1966): 'Like the Canongate, and for the same reasons, the scene in the High Street, Lawnmarket and adjoining West Bow in the last half of the 19th century was one not only of dirt, near-starvation and chronic poverty, but almost incredible overcrowding. Thus in 1865 there were 646 people to the acre in the Tron area of the High Street.' Dr Littlejohn said in his Report that it was thought 'that with the possible exception of some districts of Liverpool, in no part of the world does there exist greater over-crowding of population'. During the reconstruction of Bible Land in the Canongate in 1954 a description of the state of affairs in the parish written by one Adam Profit at the beginning of the present century was discovered lodged behind a wall. It gave a fearful picture of drunkenness, poverty, prostitution, neglected children whom he described as 'rickety, ill-bred brats, growing up to fill their mothers' places and act like them', the mothers being 'sly drinkers, taking on debt, depressed by instalments, deceiving their husbands' while the husbands were demoralized, debt-ridden and dissolute.

What had happened was that a quarter once inhabited by the aristocracy of the city, having been progressively deserted by all with any claims to means and respectability first for the new Squares to the south and then for the New Town, was left to decay into a festering slum. This situation lasted well into the present century, although Dr Littlejohn did his best to turn the tide by his sensible recommendations. These included the regular inspection of cow byres in the city (of which there were still many, in most unsanitary condition, in courts and closes), the weekly (instead of fortnightly) lifting of manure, and the compulsory introduction of water closets into the houses of the poor. He made other recommendations about the supply of water and gas lighting, the cleaning of common stairs, the limitation of the number of persons living in each flat, and the destruction of ruinous tenements. The appointment of sanitary inspectors following on Dr Littlejohn's report did have a significant effect on the improvement of health, especially the control of infectious diseases, though this did not prevent an outbreak of smallpox in the city in the summer months of 1894 during which seventy-six cases occurred in the week ending 23 June.

Victorian Edinburgh, like so many Victorian cities, was a city of contrasts. No one was more aware of this than Robert Louis Stevenson, as he roamed the city at night as a young man in the late 1860s and early 1870s. We can fittingly end this chapter, as we began it, with his testimony :

It is true that the over-population was at least as dense in the epoch of lords and ladies, and that nowadays some customs which made Edinburgh notorious of yore have been fortunately pretermitted. But an aggregation of comfort is not distasteful like an aggregation of the reverse. Nobody cares how many lords and ladies, and divines and lawyers, may have been crowded into these houses in the past – perhaps the more the merrier. The glasses clink around the china punchbowl, some one touches the virginals, there are peacocks' feathers on the chimney, and the tapers burn clear and pale in the red fire-light. That is not an ugly picture in itself, nor will it become ugly in repetition. All the better if the like were going on in every second room; the *land* [tall tenement] would only look the more inviting. Times are changed. In one house, perhaps, two score families herd together; and, perhaps, not one of them is wholly out of the reach of want. The great hotel is given over to discomfort from the foundation to chimney-tops; everywhere a pinching, narrow habit, scanty meals, and an air of sluttishness and dirt. In the first room there is a birth, in another a death, in a third a sordid drinking-bout, and the detective and the Bible-reader cross upon the stairs. High words are audible from dwelling to dwelling, and children have a strange experience from the first; only a robust soul, you would think, could grow up in such conditions without hurt. And even if God tempers his dispensations to the young, and all the ill does not arise that our apprehensions may forecast, the sight of such a way of living is disquieting to people who are more happily circumstanced. Social inequality is nowhere more ostentatious than at Edinburgh. I have mentioned already how, to the stroller along Princes Street, the High Street callously exhibits its back garrets. It is true there is a garden between. And although nothing could be more glaring by way of contrast, sometimes the opposition is more immediate; sometimes the thing lies in a nutshell, and there is not so much as a blade of grass between the rich and the poor. To look over the South Bridge and see the Cowgate below full of crying hawkers, is to view one rank of society from another in the twinkling of an eye.

One night I went along the Cowgate after every one was abed

but the policeman, and stopped by hazard before a tall *land*. The moon touched upon its chimneys and shone blankly on the upper windows; there was no light anywhere in the great bulk of building; but as I stood there it seemed to me that I could hear quite a body of quiet sounds from the interior; doubtless there were many clocks ticking, and people snoring on their backs. And thus, as I fancied, the dense life within made itself audible in my ears, family after family contributing its quota to the general hum, and the whole pile beating in tune to its timepieces, like a great disordered heart. Perhaps it was little more than a fancy altogether, but it was strangely impressive at the time, and gave me an imaginative measure of the disproportion between the quantity of living flesh and the trifling walls that separated and contained it.

CHAPTER 13

The Changing Scene

Modern Edinburgh is a city of nearly half a million inhabitants extending from the Firth of Forth in the north to the Pentland Hills in the south. On 16 May 1975, in terms of the Local Government (Scotland) Act of 1973, it ceased to be the 'County of the City of Edinburgh' and became that District of the Lothian Region known as the City of Edinburgh. This newly defined City of Edinburgh included not only the existing County of the City of Edinburgh but also the burgh of Queensferry, the district of Kirkliston and Winchburgh (with some small exceptions) in the existing County of West Lothian and the district of Currie and the parish of Cramond in the existing County of Midlothian. This added over fifty square miles of country to the west, though only increasing the population by about five per cent.

This is the latest in the series of extensions of the city which began with the Act of 1767 extending the Ancient Royalty. An extension northward from the Water of Leith took place in 1809; in 1856 there were further extensions both to the north and to the south; in 1896 Portobello was included; 1901 saw the inclusion of the area between Portobello and Arthur's Seat (including Duddingston); in 1920 there was a massive extension not only southward and westward to take in Corstorphine, Juniper Green, Colinton, Swanston, Liberton and Gilmerton, but also northward to the Forth to include (at last) Leith as well as Newhaven and Granton. The Edinburgh Boundaries Extension Act of 1920 defined the area of the city that most adults who grew up in it know today – an area of 53 square miles as contrasted with the one-quarter square mile of the Ancient Royalty.

If Robert Forsyth in 1805 had discerned three distinct cities in Edinburgh, after 1920 one could discern four. In addition to the Old Town and its southward extension towards the Meadows, the New Town together with its northward Victorian extension, and the later nineteenth century developments in the south and west – both the terraces of tenements in Morningside, Warrender Park and adjacent areas and the more socially ambitious houses in the Churchill, Grange and Mayfield areas, with a variety of terraced houses and villas in between – there was the new suburban Edinburgh which developed after the First World War and grew with especial rapidity after 1951. Sometimes two stages of growth can be easily distinguished, as in Liberton, where there was a gradual and limited development of private building followed by an outburst of public building by Edinburgh Corporation. The first phase, in the words of Liberton's local historian Campbell Ferenbach, 'was confined mainly within the Liberton Brae, Alnwickhill Road, Little Road, Lasswade Road and Kirk Brae boundaries plus a slightly detached colony at Captains Road'. This called for 'a few extra shops in Liberton Brae and Lasswade' but did not seriously change the rhythm of life of the existing community. The rapid development of public housing in the 1950s and 1960s brought social strains of a new kind. 'The vast new communities in the Inch, Gracemount, Southhouse, Hyvot's Bank, Gilmerton Dykes, Moredun, had a hundred and one focal points – elsewhere. The fact that established communities already existed at Liberton, Gilmerton and Greenend, was at first, more a handicap than an advantage as the problem of the incomer arose, both for the old residents moulded into a way of life they were reluctant to lose, and for the new, whose self-awareness often erected barriers.' Time, a new generation, the deliberate efforts of clubs and community movements, helped to develop new kinds of community identity and loyalty: in the case of Liberton this was later helped by the 'Liberton Festival', founded in 1972 and appealing strongly to a sense of local loyalty.

More spectacular, and in some ways more disturbing, was the growth of Corstorphine and Colinton and the area southward from Morningside to Fairmilehead, where between the wars a rash of speculative builders' houses arose, such as those advertised in 1938 on hoardings at Fairmilehead as 'Paterson's real homes combining old-world charm with modern elegance and dignity'. The approaches to Edinburgh from the south and south-west were more and more built up in a style of house easily adaptable to ribbon development on a national scale but often out of harmony with any of the city's existing architectural moods.

Corstorphine was still an agricultural village in the earlier part of the present century, and when the Zoological Society in Scotland, founded in Edinburgh in 1909, opened its Zoological Park in Corstorphine Hill House and its grounds in 1913, this was still separated from Edinburgh by open country. Even in the decade after the absorption of Corstorphine into Edinburgh in 1920, going to the

Zoo (as the present writer well remembers) was quite an expedition. The old cable car route was extended as far as Murrayfield, and from the terminus there one either walked to Corstorphine or took a tiny bus, with the passengers sitting in two rows facing each other, that ran from the tram terminus to the Zoo. In 1923 the electric tram-cars ran past the Zoo to their Corstorphine terminus, and the line was further extended in 1937 to what had become the edge of the city's built-up area. Before 1920 the principal means of public transport to Corstorphine was the railway, by a branch line opened in 1902 – the journey from Waverley to Corstorphine took eleven minutes – and then in 1906 the Scottish Motor Traction Company began its motor bus services there. Corstorphine is now a solid middle-class suburb of Edinburgh. There is still a green area between Murrayfield and Corstorphine, partly because the mass of Corstorphine Hill prevented development to the east of the original village and partly because isolated eighteenth-century mansions and the nineteenth-century Convalescent Home of the Royal Infirmary provided obstacles: as you drive westward along Corstorphine Road you will find on your right a stretch of almost continuous green extending for over a mile from just west of Belmont Crescent until just beyond the Zoo at Kaimes Road.

Colinton, too, was a separate village before its absorption into Edinburgh in 1920, with mills operating on the Water of Leith from an early period. Some at least of the mills survived until the 1960s, a century after Robert Louis Stevenson stayed with his maternal grandfather at Colinton Manse in the late 1850s:

> It was a place in that time like no other: the garden cut into provinces by a great hedge of beech, and overlooked by the church and the terrace of the churchyard, where the tombstones were thick, and after nightfall 'spunkies' might be seen to dance, at least by children; flower-pots lying warm in sunshine; laurels and the great yew making elsewhere a pleasing horror of shade; the smell of water rising from all round, and an added tang of papermills; the sound of water everywhere, and the sound of mills – the wheel and the dam singing their alternate strain; the birds of every bush and from every corner of the overhanging woods pealing out their notes until the air throbbed with them; and in the midst of this, the manse.

An idealized, nostalgic memory, perhaps. But some trace of the atmosphere of the village of Colinton evoked by Stevenson still lingers on in the modern Edinburgh suburb (though nothing like to the degree it does in his beloved Swanston, further south at the foot of the Pentlands, which has not been encroached on by building development and is still the hillside village it was in Stevenson's day). The coming of the railway to Colinton in 1875 enabled people to live in the village and commute to work in Edinburgh, and some substantial houses were built for what Colonel Trotter, the last laird of Colinton House, called 'the new-rich from Edinburgh'. Later development was intermittent, and consisted of smaller houses. Colinton has retained its own green belt and, though no longer considered a holiday resort by Edinburgh families as it was something over a century ago, it remains an attractive Edinburgh suburb with a life of its own.

These are some of the developments of what might be called southern Edinburgh suburbia, a phenomenon of the present century that is quite distinct from the older South Edinburgh between the Meadows and Blackford Hill and between Dalkeith Road and Morningside. Then there are the ports on the Forth that were absorbed into Edinburgh in 1920, Leith, Granton, Newhaven. Leith has a long and rich history of its own, for centuries the great Scottish port for traders with the Low Countries, Scandinavia and Europe in general. Long before Glasgow and the Clyde came to the fore, as a result of the opening of trade with the West Indies and America and the deepening of the Clyde to make it navigable up to Glasgow, Leith was the outstanding Scottish port. Much of the old town has been cleared away, and, like Clydeside, it has had to face problems in coming to terms with the modern world. But, close as the association between Leith and Edinburgh has been since the beginning of the recorded history of both, Leith has never been as integral to Edinburgh as the Clyde has been to Glasgow, and it would be disproportionate – and unfair to Leith – to try and fit an account of its history into an account of Edinburgh: it deserves a book to itself. As for Newhaven, once famous for its picturesque fish-wives with their characteristic costume and their baskets of fresh fish carried through the Edinburgh streets to be sold, there are still many memories of its past life and colour, but there is little sign today of the ship-building and smuggling that once went on there, although the influence of Flemish architecture can still be seen in some older parts. There is still fishing there, and a famous fish market, as there are still trawlers (though now outnumbered by yachts and other pleasure craft) in Granton harbour. Granton's enormous gas holder is visible from north-facing windows of most New Town houses, but this represents only one of its many industries. While Newhaven's harbour goes back to the late fifteenth century – it was the new haven of James IV – Granton's only goes back to 1835, when the fifth Duke of Buccleuch began its construction. A steam ferry from Granton to Burntisland was the regular means of transport between Edinburgh and Fife before the building of the Forth Bridge. There was also the old ferry route from South Queensferry that remained in constant use until the opening of the Forth Road Bridge in 1964. East of the Forth Bridge at the mouth of the River Almond the old village of Cramond, whose long history of continuous human settlement goes back at least to Roman times, has been restored by the Town Council as a picturesque community of gleaming white-washed cottages.

A few miles east of Leith along the Forth coast is the resort of Portobello, so called after the capture of the Spanish town of Puerto Bello in Panama by Admiral Vernon in 1739 and the settling near the Figgate Burn, in a house he had built for himself, of a retired sailor who had taken part in the campaign. Portobello first established itself as a centre for ceramics and brick-making, but as sea-bathing became fashionable in the early nineteenth century it became increasingly popular as a sea-side resort, with its fine stretch of sandy beach. It acquired all the amenities of such resorts in Britain, with a promenade, a pier, a bathing station, donkey rides, and steamer trips across the river to Fife. Its heyday was the decades before the First World War (its pier was demolished in 1917), when, as was said by one who knew it at the end of the last century, it 'had an animation and gaiety superior to those of any other sea-bathing station in Scotland'. Today, when most of its inhabitants probably commute to work in Edinburgh proper, it still attracts visitors who come to its parks, nine-hole golf course, beach, two-mile long promenade, indoor and open-air swimming pools, and other facilities for recreation. It is also an important shopping centre for a large surrounding area.

Between Portobello and Arthur's Seat lies the old village of Duddingston, with its Norman kirk and its Sheep Heid Inn where the ancient skittle-alley has been in continuous use for centuries and where a variety of convivial societies met (and some still meet) for refreshment and mutual entertainment: the Trotters Club is probably the best-known of these. Protected by Duddingston Loch and Arthur's Seat, Duddingston is effectively cut off on the west and south from the built-up city and retains an air of village peace in spite of the traffic eastward along Duddingston Road to Portobello. It has had a colourful history that goes back to the twelfth century when Herbert, first Abbot of Kelso, granted the lands of Eastern and Western Duddingston to Reginald de Bosco for an annual rent of ten merks. Bonnie Prince Charlie spent the night in Duddingston before the Battle of Prestonpans. Walter Scott was an elder in Duddingston Kirk. The charm which in some degree it still possesses was enthusiastically evoked by a writer in 1851 :

> Overhung by the green slopes and grey rocks of Arthur's Seat, and shut out by its mountainous mass from every view of the crowded city at its further base in Duddingston, a spectator feels himself sequestered from the busy scenes which he knows to be in his immediate vicinity, as he hears their distant hum on the passing breezes by the Willow Brae on the east, or the gorge of the Windy Goule on the south; and he looks southward and west over a glorious panorama of beautiful villas, towering castles, rich coppice, hill and valley, magnificent in semi-tint, in light and shadow, till the Pentlands, or the lonely Lammermuir ranges, close the distance.

The Corporation's development of the Meadowfield site on the eastern side of Arthur's Seat north of Duddingston Road did not spoil the southern view from the village here so lyrically described, but it did cause considerable outrage among Edinburgh citizens, for the 700 new houses built on the site threatened to engulf Duddingston, already threatened by a ribbon development of bungalows built in the later 1930s along the north side of Duddingston Road. Out of the controversy emerged in 1959 the Society for the Preservation of Duddingston Village, one of many such societies Edinburgh has produced in order to combat vandalism acting in the name of improvement.

Expansion or conservation, homes for the people or 'amenity', relief from traffic congestion by building motor roads through the city or perennial problems of bottlenecks and lack of parking space – these controversial choices and the agonizing dilemmas involved in trying to come to a decision have troubled Edinburgh as they have troubled other cities. But Edinburgh, with its historic Old Town, its elegant and orderly New Town, and that older New Town just north of the Meadows, has felt the dilemmas in a particularly acute form. On the outskirts of the city first the private speculative builder and then the Corporation erected respectively their small suburban houses then their great housing estates each in their own way departing from the Scottish vernacular. Houses and tenements of solid stone gave way first to brick faced with harling and then to the concrete of the modern high-rise flats. There was a national problem here, and progress towards its solution was guided by national Housing Acts. The maintenance of the special characteristics of Edinburgh's first three towns was a quite separate problem. What has happened, briefly, is that much of the surviving Old Town has been cleaned up and restored; the New Town has been zealously watched over and declining parts of it to the north of Heriot Row have been refurbished and restored to gentility; what was historically the second Edinburgh – that first New Town, built in a genuinely vernacular classical style – has been for the most part deliberately destroyed.

The problems of planning in Edinburgh were explained by William Kininmonth, the distinguished Edinburgh architect, in 1966:

> The arrival of motor transport and the shift of emphasis to the New Town, where a geometric and self-contained road system is superimposed on the organic radial roads, lie at the root of Edinburgh's traffic and central redevelopment problems, but the issue is further confused by the natural and wholly laudable desire of the community to preserve the architectural spaciousness of the Georgian New Town with its romantic counterpart, the Old Town on the Castle Ridge. Hence the many and violent controversies which break out with monotonous regularity to bedevil the city and which in recent years have been highlighted by acrimonious disputes over Princes Street Gardens, George Square, Randolph Crescent and Charlotte Square.

The New Town could bring more wealth and influence to bear on the final decisions – which were taken by the Secretary of State for Scotland – and so on the whole the New Town won its battles. The Old Town was not involved in these controversies and has been well treated by the Corporation. The real loser was South Central Edinburgh, the older New Town just north of the Meadows, and the most conspicuous victim was George Square. As Colin McWilliam has tartly expressed it: 'In Edinburgh the Secretary of State's advisers decided in 1959 that the sacrifice of George Square was permissible because it was of inferior quality to Charlotte

Square.' The vigorously vernacular second Edinburgh was sacrificed for the sake of the third Edinburgh, the New Town.

The villain of the piece was Edinburgh University, led by its Principal Sir Edward Appleton. In the late 1950s and early 1960s the University bought up a large variety of shops, houses, flats, workshops and other buildings in South Central Edinburgh (i.e., what we have called the second Edinburgh, immediately north of the Meadows). This was to be in preparation for a grandiose new scheme which would involve what Sir Edward Appleton called a vast new 'University in the City and ... City in the University'. This area included not only George Square but also much property between the Potterrow – Chapel Street – Buccleuch Street line on the east and Lauriston Place as far as Keir Street on the west. The objective was an ambitious new development, commercial and residential as well as academic, which involved not only the University but also Edinburgh Corporation and the Murrayfield Real Estate Company (who were later to develop that hurtful blot on the Edinburgh townscape, the St James' Centre, replacing Craig's decayed St James's Square in the angle between Leith Street and York Place). The University went ahead with putting massive new tall buildings on the south and west sides of George Square, and watched approvingly while the Corporation pulled down pretty well everything between George Square and the Old Quadrangle except for the University Union and the McEwan Hall (built in 1899 and 1897 respectively). But other aspects of the grand plan for rebuilding the whole area were postponed and some abandoned, so that planning blight extended over the whole district from Buccleuch Street to the block bounded by Lauriston Place, Keir Street and Heriot Place. Other uncertainties, notably the controversy over a plan to solve Edinburgh's traffic and transport problems by building a major road through the centre of the city, extended the blight to Tollcross and Fountainbridge and elsewhere, so that by the 1970s the whole of South Central Edinburgh seemed to be in decay, with intermittent new tall 'filing-cabinet' buildings rising over selected demolished older buildings.

The residents of the threatened and blighted area, taking their cue from the efficient activities of the New Town organizations, founded their own South Central Road Action Protest Group and eventually were able to force their views on a reluctant Lothian Regional Council (which under the Local Government (Scotland) Act of 1973 became in 1975 the unit of local government taking in the redefined 'Districts' of West Lothian, Midlothian, East Lothian and the City of Edinburgh). In September 1976, after what was described as 'one of the most successful public participation exercises ever carried out by a local authority' but which in reality was highly successful pressure by the public on the authority, the chairman of the Transport Committee of Lothian Regional Council announced that, though it was contrary to the advice of officials, the Council were acting in accordance with the wishes of the public in finally abandoning proposals for major road development in the centre of the city. The decision to abandon what was known as the Bridges Relief Road and the central area 'loop' was welcomed with rejoicing by the South Central Road Action Protest Group, who saw it resulting in the end of planning blight and clearing the way for the renovation of South Central Edinburgh. 'The decision in favour of a complete outer-Edinburgh city by-pass and against the Bridges Relief Road will be seen as a historic turning point in transport and environment planning in Edinburgh,' declared Dr Gavin Strang, Labour Member of Parliament for Edinburgh East.

Meanwhile, one of the most historic and architecturally interesting parts of eighteenth century Edinburgh had been deliberately swept away. What happened, wrote David Black in his contribution to an indignant study entitled *The Unmaking of Edinburgh* brought out in 1976 by the Edinburgh University Student Publications Board, was 'a rampage of wholesale destruction which Edinburgh had scarcely known since the sacking of the city in the sixteenth century. Not only was the entire community of Bristo evicted from a district which had been thriving since the time of Burns, Hume and Scott ... but every trace of occupation was so absolutely obliterated that even the medieval Bristo street line has now been lost. Where once there flourished a locality of numerous shops and small businesses, a dozen pubs, several public halls and hundreds of ordinary people, there exists now nothing but furrowed wasteland, a patchy asphalted car park, and the Edinburgh University student health centre and refectory, one of the most barbaric of Edinburgh's concrete edifices ...'

This is strong language, but anyone who knew that corner of Edinburgh – Potterrow, where Burns's Clarinda lived, Bristo Place and Bristo Street, where the old road to Edinburgh from the south came in, and the whole area between George Square and Nicolson Square – must mourn the disappearance of something deeply and intimately associated with the city and full of Edinburgh atmosphere.

Of course old buildings cannot last for ever; periodic demolition and re-building are necessary in any healthy town; and Edinburgh University certainly needed to provide new accommodation for expanding numbers of students and academic and other staff. But must it have been done so as to replace a living community and many sound and fascinating buildings (like the turreted inner court-yard of Parkers triangle) by a wasteland? And surely university accommodation could have been built in George Square – as was indeed proposed – without totally destroying its character and contributing to the change in the Edinburgh skyline that is one of the most disastrous effects of so much new building in the city?

Distinguished architects were involved in the University expansion, and some of the individual buildings are in themselves interestingly and even imaginatively designed (which cannot be said for the Lothian Region buildings at the corner of the Lawnmarket and George IV Bridge, which Colin McWilliam has rightly called 'an example of anti-townscape' and which literally hurts the eyes of at least one observer). But they do not belong where they are. They kill what remains of George Square (thus adding to the arguments in favour of its total destruction) and destroy that special Edinburgh atmosphere that used to be refreshingly and indeed movingly encountered by anybody who, like the present writer, for years daily crossed the Meadows from the south to approach the University through George Square.

It is all the sadder that this should have happened in Edinburgh, the city (though he was not a native) of the great modern master of townscape, Sir Patrick Geddes, whose contributions to the genuinely thoughtful, as distinct from the merely nostalgic and sentimental, conservation of old Edinburgh were so significant in the last decades of the nineteenth century and the early years of the present. It was under the influence of the Geddes tradition that in 1937 the fourth Marquis of Bute preserved and restored Acheson House in the Canongate, to the plans of that perceptive restoring architect Robert Hurd, and restored to their original state four houses in Charlotte Square thus leading the way to the whole Square's coming under a protective City of Edinburgh Order in 1937. But, as we have seen, Georgian Edinburgh, the New Town, was from the beginning in a favoured position where conservation was concerned. And the Old Town has been served well in recent years. It is the first New Town, in South Central Edinburgh, that has suffered most conspicuously. Not that the New Town has escaped altogether:

Princes Street, which Moray McLaren in 1960 described as 'one of the most chaotically tasteless streets in the United Kingdom', is saved only by its position, facing the open gardens and the towering Castle. Its north side, the only side built on, is a jumble of ill-assorted styles. It has changed quite a bit since 1960, and familiar buildings have been replaced by modern designs such as the British Home Stores at no. 64, but it remains a chaos saved by its southern outlook.

It would be unfair to leave the University of Edinburgh with words of damnation for what it has done to the Edinburgh town-scape. The Universities (Scotland) Act of 1858, though George Davie has seen it as the beginning of the movement away from progress 'on independent and Continental lines' in the face of anglophile forces, gave the University for the first time its complete independence and provided a constitution which, modified by the further Acts of 1889 and 1922, and by recent elements of democratization, is still working. If Davie sees these Acts as threats to 'the democratic intellect' and as the abandonment by the Scots of 'the attempt to regulate the higher education of their country according to their own ideals', they nevertheless set Edinburgh University on a course which attracted increasing numbers of distinguished scholars as teachers in a wide range of subjects. The old Faculties of Divinity, Law, Medicine and Arts were supplemented by the Faculty of Science in 1893, the year in which Science had become a separate Faculty though scientific subjects had long been taught in the Faculty of Arts, the Faculty of Music in the same year, and the Faculty of Social Sciences, which was not established as a separate Faculty until 1963. New subjects, new diploma courses, new research centres, have shown Edinburgh's University's ability to keep up with new knowledge and interests without succumbing to mere fashion. With the establishment of the now flourishing School of Scottish Studies Edinburgh University has broken away in some sense from the tradition of the eighteenth century literati to assert itself as, among other things, a centre for the study of virtually everything that can be considered a manifestation of a distinctively Scottish culture. But its wide-ranging scholarly interests and international reputation have not diminished.

Changing emphases, changing degree patterns, more varied methods of teaching than the large lecture course traditional in the Scottish universities, have all contributed to modern developments in Edinburgh University as elsewhere. There have also been important changes in primary and secondary education. The Education (Scotland) Act of 1872 set up the Scotch (late Scottish) Education Department which in turn was responsible for the development of popularly elected School Boards who took the administration of public education away from the Church and developed a number of new secondary schools, such as Boroughmuir (1904) and Broughton (1909). The Act of 1918 created Education Authorities specially elected for this function and laid on them a statutory obligation to provide enough free places in their secondary schools to fulfil the needs of their areas. The 1929 Act provided that while the Town Council was the Education Authority, education should actually be administered by statutory Education Committees, so that henceforth educational affairs in Edinburgh were controlled by a committee of twenty elected members from the Town Council and nine members representing other interests, including the University and the various Churches. After the reorganization of local government in 1975 the Regional Council became responsible for education and the Council had the obligation to appoint an Education Committee half of whom were not members of the Council and should include representatives of the Churches and of 'teachers employed in educational establishments'. Edinburgh independent schools, with their proud traditions, have inevitably become involved in the modern debate about secondary education and have had to face the special problem of coming to terms with the withdrawal of Government grants from schools which refuse to accept the new national policy of non-selective entry.

Among other educational institutions of modern Edinburgh is the College of Art, founded in 1907, with its five schools of Architecture, Town and Country Planning, Drawing and Painting, Design and Crafts, and Sculpture. The National Galleries of Scotland were, by an Act of 1906, given both a grant and an annual sum for the purchase of works of art and maintenance provided in the Parliamentary Estimates. These galleries are the National Gallery of Scotland, greatly enriched since the early years of the present century; the Scottish National Portrait Gallery in Queen Street, opened in 1889; and the Scottish National Gallery of Modern Art, still only a hope and a promise as a separate building but since 1960 housed temporarily in Inverleith House in the Royal Botanic Garden, which was specially adapted for the purpose. A tremendous stimulus to art exhibitions in Edinburgh was given by the Edinburgh International Festival, originally conceived by Harry Harvey

Wood when he was Director of the British Council in Scotland, enthusiastically supported by Rudolf Bing after Harvey Wood had put his plan to him in late 1944, taken up with equal enthusiasm by Lord Provost Sir John Falconer in 1945, and launched in late August 1947 during a spell of positively Mediterranean weather.

The story of the Edinburgh Festival, which has made Edinburgh one of the great international centres of the performing arts, needs (as it has indeed received) a book to itself. Though in spite of much agitation and many promises it has not yet brought Edinburgh its much needed opera house, which at the time of writing remains literally a hole in the ground and seems destined to remain so indefinitely, so that Edinburgh has had to cede the palm to Glasgow in this respect, every conceivable theatre and hall is pressed into use during Festival time not only for major performances of opera, orchestral concerts, plays and chamber music but also for 'fringe' events which have sometimes been exciting pioneering performances that have later made their mark elsewhere. There has been some criticism of the whole concept of the Festival, on the grounds that to fill the city with a surfeit of artistic events during a few weeks in the year, in order to attract visitors, was less important than to provide continuous artistic nourishment for Edinburgh citizens throughout the year. But the two aims are not mutually incompatible, and if Edinburgh's theatres and concert halls are not as exciting or as full as they might be throughout the year that is not the fault of the Festival.

The theatre in Edinburgh, as in other British cities, changed significantly in the present century. Robust 'variety', though never as strong in Edinburgh as in Glasgow, flourished especially in the Empire Theatre until it changed over to bingo in the early 1960s. The Gaiety Theatre in Leith was specially known for its panto-mimes, although the tradition of Christmas pantomimes was long maintained also at Edinburgh's two main theatres, the King's and the Lyceum. The Theatre Royal shared with the Gaiety a reputation for pantomime, but it was burned down in 1946. For the most part, twentieth century standard Edinburgh theatre fare has been light entertainment, although visiting repertory companies bringing Shakespeare or Shaw or Greek tragedy were favourites at the Lyceum between the two World Wars. Social habits have changed. The theatre where the stalls and dress circle were filled with ladies and gentlemen in evening dresses and dinner jackets has given way (except in Festival time) to a theatre filled with casually dressed

spectators who have managed to tear themselves away from tele-
vision. This means that the serious theatre has been left more and
more to the dedicated experimentalists working in small and often
makeshift theatres while the commercial theatre has gone its own
way. The Gateway Theatre in Leith Walk, sponsored by the Church
of Scotland, was opened in the 1950s to concentrate on Scottish
plays, and the consequent establishment of the Edinburgh Gateway
Company brought Scottish dramatists and actors into prominence,
among the former Robert Kemp being the most notable. Tyrone
Guthrie, whose splendid production of Sir David Lyndsay's *Satire
of the Thrie Estatis* made theatrical history at the 1948 Festival,
also had several plays of his own put on at the Gateway. The
Gateway Company survived until 1965. The most experimental of
modern Edinburgh theatres has been the Traverse Theatre Club,
set up in the Lawnmarket in 1962 to produce in an intimate and
informal atmosphere plays deliberately designed to probe the limits
of theatrical possibility. The Traverse has in its own way won an
international reputation.

Sir George Mackenzie established the Advocates' Library in
Edinburgh in 1689 and Allan Ramsay set up in the city what is
said to have been the first circulating library in Britain in the
1720s. Edinburgh has thus a long tradition of pioneering in libraries,
and the tradition has been maintained in the present century.
Though the Advocates' Library soon developed in fact if not in
name into a national library it was not until 1925 that it became
the National Library of Scotland, the Faculty of Advocates handing
over its remarkable collection of about 750,000 books and invaluable
manuscripts, retaining only, in a continuing Advocates' Library,
about 45,000 legal books. A new National Library building was
opened in 1956 on the site of the old Sheriff Court House, and it is
now one of the most comfortable and efficiently serviced research
libraries in the country. Among the other learned libraries of
Edinburgh the most distinguished is the University Library, which
originated in 1580 in a bequest by Mr Clement Little (or Litel),
advocate, who left his 300 books to the city 'and the Kirk of God'
in order to found 'ane commoun librarie' for the use of men training
for the ministry. The books were kept in the manse of St Giles until
the completion of the original old college buildings, to which it was
removed in 1583. Later benefactors included Drummond of Hawthornden, who left his entire library to the University. The original
library building survived the completion of the first stage of the

Adam-Playfair building begun in 1789, but was eventually pulled down in 1827 and the library nobly accommodated on the southern side of the new quadrangle that was later known to generations of students as the 'Old Quad' and is now officially the Old College. In 1967 the library was moved to the new building in George Square designed by Sir Basil Spence, Glover and Ferguson.

Edinburgh's public library system dates back to Andrew Carnegie's original gift to Edinburgh of £25,000 – later raised to £50,000 – for the building of a public library in the city. This was part of Carnegie's massive programme of financing the building of public libraries both in the United States (where he had gone with his father from his native Dunfermline in 1848) and in Britain on the condition that the local authority provided site and maintenance. The result was the 'Carnegie Library' (as it was known to several generations) in George IV Bridge, now known as the Central Public Library with a massive collection of books both for reference and for lending, its Scottish and Edinburgh Rooms, with their specialist collections of local history and topography, its Fine Art Library and its Music Library. Branch libraries followed in different parts of the city.

Edinburgh has had, at least since the late eighteenth century, a tradition of supplementing what might be called its formal sources of culture – now consisting of its University, schools, libraries, art galleries and museums – with the activities of printers, publishers and booksellers. We have seen the importance of the publisher Constable and of the *Edinburgh Review* and *Blackwood's Magazine* in the Age of Scott. Before this, in 1771, the year of Scott's birth, the first, three-volume edition of the *Encyclopedia Britannica* was produced 'by a society of gentlemen in Scotland, printed in Edinburgh for A. Bell and C. Macfarquhar and sold by Colin Macfarquhar at his printing office in Nicolson Street'. Its editor and principal author was the printer William Smellie, the same man who printed the Edinburgh edition of Burns's poems and who sang bawdy songs with the poet at meetings of the Crochallan Fencibles, the club which he founded. Smellie was a remarkable man. Educated at Duddingston Parish Church and the High School of Edinburgh, he read voraciously and made himself master of a wide range of literature and science. He knew all the important writers and thinkers of the Edinburgh of his day, and had a genuinely encyclopedic mind. His career was not dissimilar to that of Robert Chambers (1802–71), who began as a small boy in Peebles by storing his mind with the books in the town's small circulating library and the articles in the *Encyclopedia Britannica* his father had bought and set up as a bookseller in Edinburgh in 1818, branching out soon afterwards as an author. He joined with his older brother William to form the publishing firm of W. & R. Chambers, became joint-editor of the weekly *Chambers's Edinburgh Journal* (later *Chambers's Journal of Literature, Science and the Arts*) and amassed enormous quantities of information which he poured out, in vivid and lively prose, in encyclopedias, dictionaries and other works of reference. His *Cyclopedia of English Literature* (1844) remained a standard work until well into the present century; his *Vestiges of Creation* (2 volumes, 1843–46) published anonymously, created a sensation by developing arguments from geology for something like a Darwinian view of the development of the earth and its inhabitants; his *Traditions of Edinburgh* (2 volumes, 1824) remains an invaluable work for any historian of the city. These works are only a fraction of his large output.

David Brewster's *Edinburgh Encyclopedia* (1808–30) provided work for young Thomas Carlyle when he lived in humble quarters in Bristo Street trying to make a living by writing. After Carlyle married Jane Welsh in 1825 the couple set up house at 21 Comely Bank, where, having made the acquaintance of Francis Jeffrey, he started contributing to the *Edinburgh Review*. De Quincey's connection with *Blackwood's* brought him to Edinburgh in 1828 and he remained there for twelve years, moving from lodging to lodging as he found himself unable to pay his landladies (he once took refuge from his creditors in the Sanctuary of Holyrood) and contributing to *Blackwood's*, the *Edinburgh Literary Gazette* and *Tait's Edinburgh Magazine*, founded by the Edinburgh bookseller and publisher William Tait in 1832.

Browsing in bookshops was an old Edinburgh pastime. It was while rummaging among the shelves of James Sibbald's bookshop in Parliament Square that the young Walter Scott 'had a distant view of some literary characters' and 'saw at a distance the boast of Scotland, Robert Burns'. (Sibbald founded the *Edinburgh Magazine* in 1783.) After Archibald Constable moved his bookshop from the Old Town to 10 Princes Street in 1822 his new commodious premises were much frequented by writers and those who wanted to see writers; this was true, too, of the offices of William Blackwood at 45 George Street. Later generations would browse uninterrupted among the well-stocked shelves of the bookseller James Thin, opposite the University, or among the second-hand bargains at John Grant's in George IV Bridge or among the books in Robert Grant's in Princes Street.

Edinburgh was still a great city for bookshop browsing in the years between the two World Wars. Besides Thin's and the two Grants, there was Baxendine's (competing with Thin's in the supply of school and university text-books), McNiven and Wallace in Princes Street, Douglas and Foulis in Castle Street, William Brown's in George Street, and several others. Robert Grant's and Brown's later merged to form the Edinburgh Bookshop. Thin's have expanded and remain one of the great bookshops in the country. The Princes Street and Castle Street bookshops have gone, and have been replaced by a branch of the ubiquitous John Menzies. Bauermeister, who sold foreign books in Bank Street, later opened a large general bookshop in George IV Bridge, beside where John Grant's second-hand department used to be. John Grant and James Thin used jointly to own the old established Edinburgh publishers Oliver and Boyd, with their picturesque old offices in Tweeddale Court off the eastern end of the High Street, but, like so many British publishers, the firm is now a subsidiary of a multiple parent company based elsewhere. But the tradition of Edinburgh publishing begun by Constable and Blackwood survives: and the names of Blackwood, Chambers, Nelson (whose conspicuous premises at the corner of Parkside Terrace were swept away in the slaughter of South Central Edinburgh) and others, including several specialist publishers of law, medicine, theology and cartography, are still seen. And there are a number of new small publishers interested in Scottish literature.

There cannot be said to be a class in modern Edinburgh that plays the role of the old literati, in spite of the numerous professors, men of law, men of letters and assorted scholars in the city. Poets can still be seen imbibing in those of the city's numerous pubs which specially attract them: of these the splendidly Edwardian Abbotsford in Rose Street and Milne's Bar in Hanover Street have long been popular, and in the 1950s and 1960s the veteran Chris Grieve (Hugh MacDiarmid), Norman McCaig and Sydney Goodsir Smith among others could regularly be seen taking refreshment there. The Café Royal, tucked away behind the East End of Princes Street, is a Victorian pub of considerable elegance, a haunt of professional and business men rather than poets. Advocates and solicitors frequent Valentine's in the High Street, conveniently near the Law Courts, and they are sometimes to be found as well in several bars of the private hotels into which quite a number of houses and groups of houses in the New Town have been turned in the last few decades. There is still a lot of hard drinking going on in Edinburgh, among its still dominant legal class as well as among its bohemian poets. Yet it retains the reputation of being more formal and aloof than its rival city Glasgow. It is perhaps a more class-conscious city than Glasgow, and profession rather than wealth tends to determine one's status in it. When H. J. C. Grierson came to Edinburgh from Aberdeen in 1915 to succeed George Saintsbury in the Chair of English there, he found it, as he later used to recall, 'East Windy and West Endy', with the region of the city where a man lived determining the degree of social respect paid to him. R. L. Stevenson remarked on the same phenomenon, and there can be little doubt that in spite of rapid social change in Edinburgh as elsewhere, something of this survives.

Before the restructuring of local government in Scotland that took effect in May 1975 Edinburgh was a County of a City governed by a Town Council of 71, of whom 69 were elected by the citizens, the other two being the Dean of Guild (president of the Dean of Guild Court which has statutory power to regulate building in the city) and the Deacon Convener or Convener of Trades. There were eleven magistrates, of whom the chief was the Lord Provost and the other ten were Bailies. The new Act did not abolish the long established title of Lord Provost, but provided that that title 'shall attach to the chairman of each of the district councils of the cities of Aberdeen, Dundee, Edinburgh and Glasgow'. Edinburgh being now a District of the Lothian Region, its Town Council became a District Council. The Act defined the respective functions of the District Council and the Regional Council, making, for example, the former the Education Authority and giving the latter responsibility for housing. The decision of the Lothian Regional Council in September 1976 to abandon proposals for major road development in the centre of the city was hailed by some as proof that the new system of 'regionalization' was working well. But it remains to be seen what this new stage in the richly varied history of Edinburgh will bring in the long run.

Epilogue

On 5 October 1785 the Italian balloonist Vincenzo Lunardi ascended in a balloon from the garden of George Heriot's Hospital and after crossing the Forth descended the same evening, as he wrote to a friend, 'at a place called Ceres [in Fife], ... after a most delightful and glorious voyage of 46 miles, 36 over the water and 10 over land, and was received with the most affecting demonstrations of joy'. The send off at Edinburgh was enthusiastic. 'The beauty and grandeur of the spectacle,' reported *The Scots Magazine*, 'could only be exceeded by the cool, intrepid manner in which the adventurer conducted himself; and indeed he seemed infinitely more at ease than the greater part of his spectators.'

The most disastrous fire in Edinburgh's history broke out on the night of Monday 15 November 1824 in a large seven-storey house at the head of the Old Assembly Close, and, except for one tenement left standing opposite the Cross, all the buildings on the south side of the High Street from the head of the Old Assembly Close to the Exchequer buildings in Parliament Square were destroyed, with much of the property behind, towards the Cowgate. On the Tuesday, when the fire seemed to have burned itself out, it was discovered that the steeple of the Tron Kirk was on fire; after burning for three-quarters of an hour the steeple (which was of wood cased in lead) fell with a mighty crash, but firemen managed to save the rest of the church. Fire broke out again on the west side of Parliament Square and spread to the east side, doing much further damage. Nearly four hundred families were made homeless; damage amounted to £200,000; and the whole city spent the subsequent week in mourning.

In 1827 William Burke and William Hare together committed between sixteen and thirty murders in Edinburgh in order to make money by supplying corpses for dissection by the distinguished anatomist Dr Knox. The whole gruesome story of the 'resurrectionists' and their supply of badly needed corpses for dissection, the replacement of grave-robbing by murder in order to make the business more profitable to the suppliers, the lack of questions asked by Dr Knox and others of the medical profession about where the corpses came from, the final recognition of a recently murdered victim and the subsequent conviction and hanging of Burke after Hare had turned King's evidence, and the hysteria of the citizens, constitute one of the most violent and picturesque episodes in the violent and picturesque story of Edinburgh, and it has attracted more than one writer.

> Burke an' Hare
> Fell doon the stair
> Wi' a leddy in a box
> Gaun tae Doctor Knox.

The popular rhyme long preserved the popular feeling.

None of these three events will be found recorded in the body of this book. Nor will innumerable other picturesque details nor much information about buildings, projects, developments, public services and other matters. Edinburgh is too rich and too daunting a subject to allow the writer of a single volume about it to indulge himself in all the fascinating facts about its civic progress. James Grant's *Old and New Edinburgh*, published in 1883, runs to three massive volumes and far from exhausts the subject. And there are over thirty volumes of *The Book of the Old Edinburgh Club*. The bibliography of Edinburgh, of which only a small selection follows, is enormous. One must be selective, even impressionist, and shift the scale from time to time, if one wants to tell the truth in reasonable space.

So this is, inevitably, one man's history of Edinburgh. It is not written in the first person anecdotal style of the excellent books about the city written by Moray McLaren and Eric Linklater, partly because I (if 'the present writer' may now move from the third person to the first) have already written personally about the city and partly because the book represents a conscious attempt to stand back a bit from a subject in which my mind and heart are both deeply involved.

When Robert Louis Stevenson offended some Edinburgh citizens by some rather critical remarks about their respectability and materialism, he noted that the offence given in his native town was balanced by 'a proportionable pleasure to our rivals of Glasgow'. He added: 'To the Glasgow people I would say only one word, but that is of gold: *I have not yet written a book about Glasgow*.'

I can make no such protestation, for I *have* written a book about Glasgow, an Edinburgh man's sympathetic but inevitably outside view. It proved in fact easier for me to do this than to write about Edinburgh. It is a hard city to capture in its entirety. But, though I have tried not to let this appear openly in my narrative, this is an account by one who can never feel neutral about the subject.

Appendix: College or University?

When did the town's college, to which James VI gave the official title of 'King James's College' (*Academia Jacobi Sexti*) in 1617, become known as the University of Edinburgh? It seems that for a long time the terms 'college' and 'university' were used interchangeably with reference to this institution. The Latin term was for long *academia* rather than *universitas*. The earliest extant code of Edinburgh University is found in the *Register of the Universitie of Edinburgh*, 1644 (note the term 'Universitie' at this early date), and that code is designated *Disciplina Academiae Edinburgenae*. A revised version of the section of the *Disciplina* dealing with the conduct of students, entitled *Leges Discipulorum*, dating from 1701, also calls the institution *Academia Edinburgena*, but the Town Council, in approving it on 24 January 1701, refers to the institution as 'the Colledge of Edinburgh'.

Throughout the sixteenth century the Town Council minutes refer to the 'Townis Colledge'. In the seventeenth century it is sometimes 'the Colledge of Edinburgh'. On 8 January 1640 the Council passed 'Laws for the Conduct and Act creating a Rector for the Colledge'. On 10 November 1665 it was minuted that 'The Counsell agrees that the Provost of Edinburgh present and to come be allwayes the Rector and Governor of the Colledge of this burgh in all tyme comeing'. Defoe, in his *Tour Thro' the whole Island of Great Britain* (1726), discusses the High School ('Humanity School') and University:

> The Humanity School is kept in the same Park, which is reckon'd as a Part of the University, as being employ'd in the finishing Youth for the College. West of these is the College itself, they call it the University. But as it consists of but one College, I call it no more. However, here are all the usual methods of Academick Learning in their full Perfection.

The Town Council minutes continue to refer to the 'Colledge of Edinburgh' in the early decades of the eighteenth century. But on 1 December 1742 we find the following:

Upon a representation from the Principall and Professors of this city's University, setting furth that they were informed an attempt was made to set up a Stage in this place without Warrant of Law, that they could not but be apprehensive that idleness and corruption of manners among the youth was likely to flow from a licentious acting of Stage plays ... Praying therefore the Honble Council on these accounts to take proper measures for suppressing the same.

On 27 June 1760 it is noted that Hugh Blair is appointed 'Professor of Rhetorick In this Citys University', but in September 1763 there is a reference to 'Dr William Robertson, Principal of the College of Edinburgh'. In an address to the Lord Provost of 10 November 1825 the Town Council refers to 'the Principal and Professors of the College of Edinburgh' but in the 1830s we find the term 'university' used about as frequently as 'college'. Thus in 1832 we find a reference to 'the Professors of the College'; in 1835 'the Secretary of the University' is mentioned; in 1839 we find a reference to 'the Principal and Professors of the University'. In a minute of 27 September 1842 we find in the same paragraph a reference to 'the usefulness of the University' and 'the eminence of the College of Edinburgh', the two terms being used quite interchangeably. (Hugo Arnot, in his *History of Edinburgh*, 1779, refers indifferently to 'the University of Edinburgh' and 'the College of Edinburgh'.) The 'Statutes of the University of Edinburgh relative to the degree of M.D.', promulgated in 1845, refer consistently to the University. But even in the 1850s the institution is still sometimes called the College: in April 1852 there is a reference to 'next Session of College'. After the passing of the Universities (Scotland) Act of 1858 (which the Town Council opposed and the University supported), 'university' becomes the usual as well as the legal title.

The University's internal documents show a similar history in the use of the two words. The *Laws of the Bibliothec*, 1668, refer to 'the Colledge'. In 1691 we find the institution referred to as 'the Colledge of Edinburgh', but on 14 June 1699 we find a regulation that those graduating Master of Arts should subscribe an obligation 'never to take any inferior degree than Master of Arts in any other University or Colledge'.

In the eighteenth century internal university documents refer much more frequently to the 'university' than to the 'college', differing in this respect from the Town Council minutes. Sometimes it is clear that the term 'college' refers to the actual building (as it still does, in such a present day usage as the 'Old College') while 'university' refers to the institution: 'none but students in some class or other of the University are to enter the College gates' (January 1736). The phase 'the Principal and Professors of the University of Edinburgh' is now common, indeed standard, but there are still references to 'the College Laws' (1738), 'the Session of the College' (1741), 'the College Library' (1760), 'the Principal of the College' (1763), though such references are greatly outnumbered by references to the 'University'.

In the 1820s the University and the Town Council were at loggerheads on the Town Council's supervisory and regulatory role with respect to the University. The documents in this struggle make clear that, although the term 'university' was now common, and indeed virtually standard in the University itself, the legal designation was still 'the College of King James'. Thus on 13 November 1827 we find the interlocutor of Lord Mackenzie in the action at the instance of the Magistrates of Edinburgh against the Senatus Academicus of the University of Edinburgh stating:

The Lord Ordinary ... Finds that the Pursuers have right of making Regulations or Statutes for the College of King James ... the Principal and Professors of the said College have not right to make Regulations or Statutes or Laws for the College in contradiction to the Pursuers ...

But from now on internal university documents consistently use the term 'university'. On 8 May 1858 the Senatus resolved to express approval of the objects contemplated by the new Universities (Scotland) Bill, and when this Bill became law on 2 August 1858 the title 'University of Edinburgh' was established not only by common usage but by the law of the land.

Bibliography

Arnot, Hugo, *The History of Edinburgh*, Edinburgh, 1779.

Boog Watson, Charles B., *Notes on the Names of the Closes and Wynds of Edinburgh*, Edinburgh, 1923.

The Book of the Old Edinburgh Club, Vols. I–XXXIII, Edinburgh, 1908–1969.

Britton, John, *Modern Athens, Displayed in a Series of Views of Edinburgh in the Nineteenth Century … from Original Drawings by Mr Thomas Shepherd*, London, 1929.

Brown, P. Hume, *Scotland Before 1700 from Contemporary Documents*, Edinburgh, 1893.

Burt, Edward, *Letters from a Gentleman in the North of Scotland to his Friend in London*, Vol. I, London, 1754.

Carlyle, Dr Alexander, of Inveresk, *Autobiography*, ed. J. Hill Burton, London and Edinburgh, 1910.

Catford, E. F., *Edinburgh, the Story of a City*, London, 1975.

Charters and Other Documents relating to the City of Edinburgh A.D. 1143–1540, Edinburgh, 1871.

Cockburn, Lord, *Memorials of His Time*, ed. W. Forbes Gray, Edinburgh, 1946.

Cockburn, Lord, *Journey of Henry Cockburn*, 2 vols., Edinburgh, 1874.

Cockburn, Lord, *Life of Lord Jeffrey*, 2 vols., Edinburgh, 1852.

Defoe, Daniel, *A Tour Thro' the Whole Island of Great Britain*, Vol. II, London, 1927.

Dibdin, J. C., *The Annals of the Edinburgh Stage*, Edinburgh, 1888.

Drummond, William, of Hawthornden, *Poems and Prose*, ed. Robert H. MacDonald, Edinburgh, 1976.

Dunbar, William, *The Poems of William Dunbar*, ed. W. Mackay Mackenzie, Edinburgh, 1932.

Extracts from the Records of the Burgh of Edinburgh 1403–1528, Edinburgh, 1869.

Extracts from the Records of the Burgh of Edinburgh 1558–1571, Edinburgh, 1875.

Extracts from the Records of the Burgh of Edinburgh 1573–1589, Edinburgh, 1882.

Ferenbach, Campbell, *Annals of Liberton*, Edinburgh, 1975.

Fergusson, Robert, *Poems*, ed. M. McDiarmid, 2 vols., Edinburgh, 1954–56.

Forsyth, Robert, *Beauties of Scotland, containing a Clear and Full Account ... of the Population, Cities, Towns, Villages, etc. of Each County*, Edinburgh, 1805.

Fraser, Duncan, *Edinburgh in Olden Times*, Montrose, 1976.

Graham, Henry Grey, *The Social Life of Scotland in the Eighteenth Century*, 2 vols., London, 1899.

Grant, Sir Alexander, *The Story of the University of Edinburgh during its First Three Hundred Years*, 2 vols., London, 1884.

Grant, Elizabeth, of Rothiemurchus, *Memoirs of a Highland Lady*, London, 1950.

Grant, James, *Old and New Edinburgh*, 3 vols., London, 1883.

Gray, W. Forbes, *A Short History of Edinburgh Castle*, Edinburgh, 1968.

History and Romance of Edinburgh Street Names, Edinburgh Corporation City Engineers' Department, Edinburgh, 1975.

Kay's Edinburgh Portraits, London and Glasgow, 2 vols., 1885.

Keir, David (Ed.), *The City of Edinburgh* (Third Statistical Account of Scotland), Glasgow, 1966.

Linklater, Eric, *Edinburgh*, London, 1960.

Lindsay, Ian G., *Georgian Edinburgh*, Edinburgh, 1948.

Lockhart, J. G., *Memoirs of the Life of Sir Walter Scott Bart.*, 7 vols., Edinburgh, 1837–38.

The Lord Provosts of Edinburgh 1296–1932, Edinburgh, 1932.

Mackay, John, *The Burgh of Canongate*, Edinburgh, 1886.

McLaren, Moray, *The Capital of Scotland*, Edinburgh, 1950.

McWilliam, Colin, *Scottish Townscape*, London, 1975.

Mair, William, *Historic Morningside*, Edinburgh, 1947.

Maitland, William, *The History of Edinburgh from its Foundations to the Present Time*, Edinburgh, 1753.

Martin, Burns, *Allan Ramsay*, Cambridge, Mass., 1931.

Marwick, Sir James D., *Edinburgh Guilds and Crafts*, Edinburgh, 1909.

Menzies, G. (Ed.), *Who are the Scots?*, Edinburgh, 1971.

Miller, Karl, *Cockburn's Millenium*, London, 1975.

Morgan, A., *University of Edinburgh Charters, Statutes and Acts of the Town Council and the Senatus 1583–1858*, Edinburgh, 1937.

Pagan, Theodore, *The Convention of the Royal Burghs of Scotland*, Glasgow, 1926.

Scott-Moncrieff, G., *Edinburgh*, London, 1947.

Sinclair, Sir John, (Ed.), *The Statistical Account of Scotland*, vol., VI, Edinburgh, 1793.

Sitwell, Sacheverell and Bamford, Francis, *Edinburgh*, London, 1938.

Stevenson, Robert Louis, *Edinburgh: Picturesque Notes*, London, 1879.

Stevenson, Robert Louis, *Memories and Portraits*, London, 1887.

Stuart, Marie W., *Old Edinburgh Taverns*, Edinburgh, 1952.

Topham, Captain Edward, *Letters from Edinburgh Written in the Years 1774 and 1775*, London, 1776.

Turner, A. Logan (Ed.), *History of the University of Edinburgh, 1883–1933*, Edinburgh, 1933.

Watt, Francis, *The Book of Edinburgh Anecdote*, London and Edinburgh, 1913.

Wright, Ronald Selby, *The Kirk in the Canongate*, 2nd ed., Edinburgh, 1958.

Wilson, Sir Daniel, *Memorials of Edinburgh in the Olden Time*, Edinburgh and London, 1891.

Youngson, A. J., *The Making of Classical Edinburgh 1750–1840*, Edinburgh, 1966.

Index